HIGH WYCOMBE

A Pictorial History

Certificate from the High Wycombe Chairmakers' Protection Society.

HIGH WYCOMBE

A Pictorial History

Ivan G. Sparkes

Phillimore

1990

Published by
PHILLIMORE & CO. LTD.
Shopwyke Hall, Chichester, Sussex

ISBN 0 85033 751 8

Printed and bound in Great Britain by
BIDDLES LTD.
Guildford, Surrey

List of Illustrations

Frontispiece: High Wycombe Chairmaker's Protection Society certificate

1. Charter portrait of Elizabeth I, 1598
2. Coat of arms of the former Borough
3. Carved Borough arms in the Guildhall
4. The 'Great Mace'
5. Procession to the Mayor's Parlour, c.1909
6. The Cornmarket area
7. The Guildhall
8. The Shelburne Room, the Guildhall, in the 1920s
9. Opening of the town hall, 1904
10. The town hall
11. The 'weighing-in' ceremony, 1907
12. 'Weighing-in' in 1924
13. Municipal offices
14. Chepping Wycombe Borough Council, 1934
15. Police outside Litte Market House
16. Newlands police station
17. The police station, Queen Victoria Road
18. Hospital of St John the Baptist
19. Wycombe Union House
20. Queen Elizabeth's Almshouses
21. The fire brigade on The Rye, c.1890
22. The fire station and engine
23. Fire at Crendon Street, 1906
24. The post office, Easton Street
25. The Cottage Hospital
26. The High Wycombe and District War Memorial Hospital
27. Castle Hill House
28. The Royal Grammar School
29. The new Royal Grammar School building
30. The Grammar School, Amersham Hill
31. Priory Road School
32. The National School
33. The Science and Art School, Frogmore
34. Class I, Wycombe Marsh Infant School, 1936
35. Interior of Wycombe High School for Girls
36. All Saints' church, 1920
37. Painting of the interior of All Saints' church, 1848
38. The Watch House
39. Castle Street
40. Crendon Street in 1922
41. St Augustine's church
42. White Hart Street chapel
43. Trinity Congregational chapel, Easton Street
44. The Union Baptist chapel, Easton Street
45. St John's church, Desborough
46. Hull, Loosely and Pearce, undertakers of Oxford Road
47. Preacher and caravan mission, c.1895
48. Wycombe Abbey
49. Portrait of Lord Shelburne by Joshua Reynolds
50. The Rupert Gates
51. Lord Carrington in 1888
52. Poster announcing Lord Carrington's return, 1878
53. Stained glass portrait of Disraeli from the town hall
54. Queen Victoria at High Wycombe railway station, 1877
55. Triumphal arch celebrating the Queen's visit, 1877
56. The Great Chair Arch, 1880
57. Children in High Street, 1880
58. Diamond Jubilee bonfire, 1897
59. The band and carnival floats in High Street
60. Cart carrying 600 chairs in a parade
61. Launching the lifeboat, 1907
62. Procession passing the Liberal Headquarters
63. The *Red Lion*
64. Satirical political poster
65. C. H. Berry's shop
66. Portrait of General Le Marchant
67. Royal Bucks Hussars, c.1890
68. Celebrating the Relief of Mafeking
69. Return of troops from the Boer War, 1902
70. The Bucks Militia in 1902
71. The Bucks Militia on parade, 1908
72. Women in the Gomme factory during the First World War
73. The *Railway Hotel*, Castle Street
74. Armistice service, All Saints' church, 1918
75. The Wycombe Excelsior Cyclists Club
76. The Wycombe Alexandra Cricket Club, 1920
77. Wycombe Trinity Football Club, 1910

78. Wycombe Rovers, 1917
79. Westbourne Street billiards team, 1922
80. The Dyke
81. Diploma from the National Fisheries Exhibition, 1895
82. Trout fishing from a punt in The Dyke
83. Desborough Recreation Ground
84. The Palace Cinema
85. The Grand Cinema, Desborough Road
86. The Majestic, Castle Street
87. The *Red Lion*
88. The carved red lion
89. The Wellington Room of the *Red Lion*
90. Wheeler's Brewery, Easton Street
91. Wheeler's Brewery vaults beneath the High Street
92. The *Falcon Hotel*, High Street, in 1901
93. Paul's Row
94. The *Black Boy*
95. The *Red Cross Knight*, Temple End
96. The *Three Tuns*, High Street, c.1900
97. The *White Horse*, Crendon Street, 1895
98. The *Old King of Prussia*, London Road
99. Advertisement for Brakspear's Brewery, 1894
100. John Leadbetter's spirit merchant's, High Street
101. The Oxford-London coach at the *Falcon*, 1901
102. Horse-bus at Little Market House, 1900
103. Worley & Sons transporting chairs
104. Glenister's waggon
105. Keen's steam waggon, 1904
106. Loading timber into the first steam engine
107. Excavating the Saunderton cutting, 1905
108. The railway station in 1854
109. Moving the down line, 1904
110. Train on the direct line to London
111. Davenport's Garage, High Street
112. Bowdery Lane Mill, 1895
113. Bassetsbury Mill
114. Map showing mills on the Wye
115. View across The Rye at Marsh Green
116. Cows in High Street
117. Bowerdean Farm, 1905
118. The Rope Walk, Wycombe Rope Factory, in the 1940s
119. Thomas Towerton's sawmill
120. Band saw at Plumridge's, Denmark Street
121. Mrs. Betsy Ray making lace, c.1910
122. Chair-seat caning
123. Darvill's mill
124. Workers at R. H. Hulls, Easton Street
125. Preparing chair-legs, 1905
126. A turner
127. Pit-sawing
128. Chair factory and waggon
129. Glenister's factory, 1902
130. 'Bottoming' chair seats
131. The polishing shop
132. The workforce of Henry Goodearl, 1886
133. Workers at Ercol Furniture Ltd. in 1925
134. Advertisement for Edwin Skull, c.1865
135. Certificate from the High Wycombe Chairmaker's Protection Society
136. Jack Goodchild completing a chair
137. 1920s humorous song celebrating High Wycombe's chairs
138. The Little Market House, 1880
139. A. Timms' butchery, 1891
140. The 'hiring fair'
141. Sale of a wife at the cattle market, 1824
142. High Street market
143. McIlroys and Stevens in Church Street
144. Christmas display at Aldridges, 1931
145. John R. Dring, draper and outfitter, Church Street
146. Navarino House
147. Corporation Street
148. Chas. H. Berry, jeweller
149. Frank Cross's hand-delivery cart
150. Goodman's Corner
151. St Mary Street
152. Archway to Lily's Walk
153. Newland
154. Houses in Oxford Road on the Wye
155. Desborough Road
156. Fountain at Frogmore
157. Painting of High Street in the 1840s
158. High Street in the 1930s
159. The *Greyhound*, Easton Street
160. London Road and the Wye, 1910
161. The Wye towards Wycombe Marsh
162. Amersham Hill
163. Terriers

Acknowledgements

I would like to take this opportunity to thank those who, over the years, have supplied me with information or advice, or given me access to illustrations and photographs relating to the history of High Wycombe and its neighbourhood. In particular I would like to thank Ken Fordham, Ronald Goodearl and David Youens for their help in copying some photographs and granting permission to reproduce others. I am also grateful to Mr. R. Kin for the many slides he has produced for me, from which it has been possible to obtain prints when required, and to the many authors of books and pamphlets written over the past 150 years about High Wycombe's history which have given me much valued information. Grateful thanks go also to Ian Horwood and to the staff of the High Wycombe Reference Library, who have willingly answered many questions for me.

Introduction

High Wycombe now forms the administrative centre of the Wycombe District Council which was created in 1974. The town itself has a population of 61,514. The ancient borough can be traced back to Norman times, and a series of charters, ledger books and other documents records its progress from the medieval period.

The town lies in a long narrow valley, and traces of prehistoric, Bronze Age and Iron Age as well as Roman occupation have been found here over the years. One feature of High Wycombe is the open space to the east of the town, known as 'The Rye', which was the site of a 2nd-century Roman Villa. This had a remarkable bath house, a building which contained four heated rooms and a cold plunge bath. The site had been excavated several times since the 18th century, but it was finally brought to light when the present open-air swimming pool was built in 1957.

The position of High Wycombe, on one of the main roads out of London, has been an important influence on its development over the years. As early as 1351, Walter Neel left a bequest in his will for the repair of the road from Newgate to Wycombe. Over the years many attempts were made to ensure that this highway remained serviceable before the toll-road took over that responsibility in 1724 for the Oxford-London Road, and for the Hatfield-Reading toll road via Hazlemere in the years after 1768. With the arrival of the railway in 1854, the use of horse-drawn coaches declined dramatically. The original branch line from Maidenhead was extended to Thame in 1862, and to Oxford in 1864. In 1906 a new track, which involved moving the up-line platform of the station, was opened to Marylebone station. In time the street omnibus arrived, first as a horse bus running from West Wycombe to Loudwater in 1882 and then a motor bus in 1908.

The original London Road leading out of the Borough was the old Windsor Road, which ran in front of Wycombe Abbey along the line of the waterway known as 'The Dyke' on The Rye, under which, it is said, the original road still lies. The traffic on the London Road almost touches the ancient arches of the medieval hospital of St John the Baptist in Easton Street. The arches and remaining piers formed part of the Hospital Hall, approximately 60ft. by 20ft. It was the function of the medieval hospital to provide shelter for pilgrims and other travellers on the road, and it also had a small chantry chapel for the devotions of the passers-by.

This building formed part of the original Grammar School established in 1549 which was granted a Royal Charter by Queen Elizabeth I in 1562. Now the Royal Grammar School, it was almost the only educational establishment in the town until the late 19th century. The British School was opened by the Nonconformists in Church Street in 1830 and the National School, organised by the Church of England, was opened in White Hart Street in 1855, and only after the passing of the Education Act in 1870 did state schools appear in the town. The first were the Priory Road Schools which opened in 1874 under the management of a Joint Schools Board, followed in 1893 by the first technical school, the Science and Art School in Frogmore. The High School for Girls opened in Frogmore in 1901, and during this period many primary and elementary schools were built in the

Borough and surrounding villages. Many of these have since been closed, others demolished or their use changed, but the Royal Grammar School still exists and the School of Science and Art was the forerunner of the present Bucks. College of Higher Education in Queen Alexandra Road.

Opposite the ruins of the hospital, on the edge of The Rye, stands a small timbered building and the waterwheel of Pann Mill, demolished in 1973. The mill was probably one of the six listed in the Domesday survey of 1086, and was known as Pinel's Mill in 1185. Its site, where the lands of the mill and the hospital met, was the end of the original medieval Borough, and here in Easton Street, sometimes called Eastowne or Estends Street, the road from the town petered out. Domesday also recorded 17 watermills which indicates industrial usage, as one or two mills could have supplied domestic needs. Much grain was milled in the early years, and in 1245 Henry III sent an order for £10 of bread at four loaves to the penny (i.e. 9,600 loaves) for consumption at the Palace of Westminster on the Feast of St Edward. Later, cloth-weaving was introduced and the mills played their part in the fulling of cloth. Lace-making developed from a 17th-century domestic craft into an 18th-century industry, and by 1717 a report to the House of Commons mentions it as a trade 'whereby thousands of poor persons and those of tender years are able to get their livings'. Papermaking was evident by the beginning of the 17th century, also using the watermills. Discarded rags were hand-sorted by local workers and then soaked in water and hammered to separate their fibres and turn them into paper-pulp. Every time an industry declined another took its place, and following the mechanisation of papermaking in the 1930s, many workers turned to the chairmaking industry for jobs.

It has been suggested that the furniture industry in Wycombe stemmed from a local farmer who made use of his workmen during the quieter winter months by setting them turning chairlegs in the woods. Whatever the origin, it is certain that the mid-18th-century cottage craft had grown to factory proportions by the 1790s and by the 1860s was a full-scale mass-production industry. An estimated 4,700 chairs were produced daily in factories sometimes employing over 60 men. The industry dominated the community, with whole streets, such as St Mary Street in 1875, almost totally inhabited by benchmen, caners, sawyers, backmakers, polishers and other furniture factory employees. It also invaded local government, and the chapels relied on the wealthy chairmasters for financial aid and rebuilding programmes. After the 1930s the town's industries began to diversify, but there is still a backbone of furniture workers supporting the many other industries in the area.

High Wycombe, like other towns on a main highway, was well supplied with coaching houses, inns and breweries. Easton Street alone boasted six inns within a short distance, and at one time there was one licensed premises for every 120 persons. These establishments played a large part in the life of the community, and were used in elections and for the changing and shoeing horses as well as for food, drink and accommodation. Several innkeepers were involved in the chair industry, and the landlord of the *Cow and Hare* in Easton Street employed 60 men and young people in the trade in 1871. At certain times inns were called upon to accommodate army personnel, as recorded in the census of 1861 when 12 public houses provided lodging for 90 men of the Bucks Militia, while in 1898 the 4th Squadron of the Royal Bucks Hussars gave a voluntary class in sword exercise and the theory of musketry at the *Nags Head* in London Road.

The two main breweries in the town were Wheeler's Wycombe Brewery and Frogmore Brewery, although several others traded at different times, while outside breweries at

Marlow, Henley and Amersham had tied houses in the town. Ale was sent out to farm workers in the fields by the gallon, and the chair makers waited at the public house at weekends to be paid. On market day, or during the annual fairs, the public houses were the centre of both business and social activity.

Wycombe Abbey, always the most important house in the town and now the home of the famous Wycombe Girls' School, stands in extensive grounds. A continual rivalry existed between 'The Abbey' and 'The Borough'. The Abbey had the upper hand in the social realm, but politically they were more evenly matched, and within the Borough Council the chairmasters created a hierarchy of their own: the names of the mayors, aldermen and councillors echo the lists of furniture-makers in the local trade directories. Formerly the home of the Archdale family, the Abbey passed in time to the Petty family, of whom the most notable was Lord Shelburne (Prime Minister 1782-3), and to the Carrington family in the 19th and 20th centuries. The Abbey was largely rebuilt by James Wyatt in 1795 of grey squared stone and mortar mixed with pieces of flint. It is large and picturesque, castellated and turretted. The school was founded in 1896 and two of the houses along Marlow Hill were designed by Caroe and erected in 1898-1902. The Abbey was the Headquarters of the U.S. 8th Army-Air Force during the Second World War, and the Freedom of the Borough was granted to Lieut. General Ira. C. Eaker, 1st Commander of the 8th U.S. Air Force, to mark this event.

Behind the Abbey grounds is Daws Hill, which became the home of Lord Carrington after he sold the Abbey. This in turn became part of the growing Abbey School. In the grounds behind is a U.S.A.F. Base with the London Central High School, established for the children of U.S. Forces in the area. Lord Shelburne was responsible for altering the route of the old road to Windsor, and he also moved the entrance gates of Wycombe Abbey closer to the High Street where the traffic lights stand, with his carriageway running along what is now Queen Victoria Road. Following the death of Queen Victoria in 1901, the road and bridge crossing the Wye near the police station were built by Carrington, and donated to the town, the road being dedicated to the erection of public buildings. The first to be erected was the town hall, built in 1904 to the designs of J. J. Bateman and C. E. & A. Hale. Later buildings were the municipal offices in 1931, the public library in 1932, the post office in 1934 and the police station in 1935.

Civic building in High Wycombe reached its zenith in the 1930s and it was not until the 1950s that a new wave of building commenced. This started with the College of Technology and Art, built on the junction of Queen Alexandra Road and Abbey Way in 1955. More recently, a large hospital has replaced the earlier War Memorial Hospital of the 1920s, and the new law courts, opened in 1974, have been erected opposite the medieval ruins of St John the Baptist in Easton Street. The law courts are of modern design, built in red brick and red/brown roofing tiles, but do, however, reproduce something of the Georgian grace of the 1930s buildings.

The High Street is a wide road with the earlier civic buildings, the church, the Guildhall and the Market House, clustered around its western end. It is a typically Georgian street and above the modern shop fronts many of the early 17th- and 18th-century buildings appear clearly. Quite impressive is the long brick façade of the former *Red Lion* with the figure of the lion standing boldly on the portico. The *Red Lion* has had an eventful past. It was here that Benjamin Disraeli stood when he campaigned, unsuccessfully, to become M.P. of Wycombe in the 1832 election. From the same spot, just over one hundred years later, Sir Winston Churchill rallied support in the post-war election of 1946.

Adjacent to the *Red Lion* was the *Antelope*, which between 1799 and 1813 was the home of the Wycombe Military Academy, an organisation of some importance which was later transferred to Sandhurst, where it has achieved much in the training of junior officers. Further along the High Street, standing in front of the church, is the Market House. It is an octagonal structure, rebuilt in 1761 to the designs of Robert Adam – it replaces the earlier Shambles built in 1604 on the site of the Hog Market. The lantern and leaded roof of the present Market House were added in about 1900.

The right to hold markets and fairs was formally granted to the burgesses of the Borough by Alan Bassett in 1237. However, people 'farmed' the Borough and its privileges in the 1160s for £4 a year, so this right had probably been in existence for many years. The market place was bounded by White Hart Street, Church Street and Queen Square, and contained the medieval market stalls and the Guildhall. In time the stalls were turned outwards and built in a more solid form, and before long became permanent shops, the moveable market being transferred to the High Street. Besides the weekly cattle and produce markets, special fairs were held by both the Borough and the Hospital of St John the Baptist in Easton Street which drew crowds into the town. Craftsmen working in the Borough would sell their wares, but if those from outside the boundaries wished to trade in Wycombe, they had to pay fees for permission to do so. The market was open when the 'Cryer's bell was rung at ten o'clock in the forenoon ... and if any person shall sell before the said bell shall ring ... shall forfeit the value of the goods'.

The Guildhall stands opposite Market House and is one of a sequence of buildings, references to which go back to 1380 when the gallery of the Guildhall was leased to John Deye for 3s. 4d. per annum. The present building was designed by Henry Keene and was the gift of the Earl of Shelburne to the town in 1757. It is built of brick and supported by an arcade of stone columns. It was renovated by Sir G. H. Dashwood in 1859, and again by the Wycombe District Council in 1982-3.

The medieval borough of Chepping Wycombe was quite small, its boundaries stretching from Pann Mill in the east to the Bird-in-Hand in the west, from the railway station in the north, to the Abbey roundabout in the south. All those who lived outside these boundaries, even if they lived in the parish of Chepping Wycombe, were considered foreigners. The Wycombe traders who worked from the High Street or the market did their best to prevent foreign traders from taking up residence in the town or selling their goods. In 1564 shoemakers paid the bailiff 20s. annually to stop others selling their shoes in the town, and in 1610 the tailors paid 10s. to keep out other tailors. However, over the centuries this policy changed as the town's boundaries were extended. First Newland was incorporated, followed by Marsh, Terriers, Totteridge, West Wycombe and Cressex, until the area of the Borough in the years before its demise had increased out of all recognition from its medieval beginnings.

High Wycombe celebrated 700 years of its Mayoralty in 1985, while 1987 saw the 750th anniversary of the first charter of the Borough, an agreement dated 1237. Before this date, in the 1160s, the burgesses had gained control of Borough activities through a lease from Alan Bassett which enabled the growth of the commercial and industrial life of the town in the medieval period. Over the years the area and nature of the town's government has changed, but in 1974 the ancient Borough was absorbed into the new Wycombe District Council, created under local government reorganisation. Now the district councillors who represent the wards of the old Borough are formed into a group of charter trustees who elect the town's mayor, continuing the traditions and dignities of the former age.

The Guildhall is the scene of one of the town's annual customs known as the 'weighing in' ceremony. This takes place on Mayor-making Day, usually in May, after the new mayor has donned his robes of office. The charter trustees leave the upper room of the Guildhall and proceed to the yard in front of the *Falcon Hotel*, where the weighing machine is set up. Here, one by one, starting with the mayor, all the trustees and officers are weighed. As their weight is recorded, the mace-bearer, resplendent in his uniform, shouts out the weight, adding the words 'and some more' if the mayor or charter trustees have gained weight over the year. He shouts 'and no more' if the weight is the same or less. The spectators stand by waiting for the call, and if the words 'and some more' are heard, jeer at the person being weighed in, for it is traditionally believed that he has grown fat at the expense of the ratepayers. If, however, the cry 'and no more' is heard, cheers accompany the trustee to his place. This ceremony is believed to date from medieval times, but it was dropped in the early 19th century until reintroduced in 1892. The heaviest weights recorded were 18st. 4lb. in 1921, and 20st. 5lb. in 1960. The Borough has retained the historic regalia, including the silver and gilt Great Mace dating from 1694.

The parish church of All Saints, which lies in the centre of the town, was founded in Norman times and was consecrated by Wulfstan, Bishop of Winchester (1062-95). A landmark which can be seen from all directions, it has been much altered, enlarged and restored. The original building was considerably extended in 1275. It had a central tower which was removed in 1505-10 and replaced at the west end by the west tower in about 1520. In 1755 the pinnacles on the tower were added by the Earl of Shelburne to designs by Henry Keene, and the Victorian restoration of the exterior took place in 1887-89 under the guidance of Oldrid Scott. Monuments in the church include the large tomb of Henry Petty, erected in 1754 and sculpted by Peter Scheemaker. In the south chapel is a memorial to Sophia, Lady Shelburne, the first wife of William Petty, Marquis of Lansdowne.

High Wycombe also has a strong Nonconformist heritage, including connections with William Penn and the Quakers, and John Wesley and the Methodists. The Baptists and Congregationalists also built chapels. The motto attributed to High Wycombe in the Victorian period was 'Chapels, children and chairs'. The Roman Catholic church was built in Castle Street in 1900, only to be rebuilt in Amersham Hill in 1955-7. More Anglican churches were erected as the town grew, including St John's in Desborough Road in 1882 (which was replaced by a permanent building in 1903), St Francis' at Terriers in 1903, St Mary and St George's in Dashwood Avenue in 1938, St Anne's at Wycombe Marsh in 1858 and St James' at Downley in 1938, the last having been rebuilt since as a joint church. In more recent years other religious groups have opened or taken over disused chapels, and in Desborough the minaret of the mosque is a familiar sight.

The town has always centred around Easton Street, the High Street and Frogmore, a triangular area leading to the bridge at Temple End on the road to Hughenden. Much of this area of the old town remains as it was 100 years ago, with only the shop fronts modernised. but in 1987-8 the new Chiltern Shopping Centre was built, which involved demolishing the old Palace Cinema and other adjacent shops, but the modern building is attractive and fits in remarkably well with its surroundings. A much more drastic treatment was given to Newlands and also to the area beyond the Royal British Legion Hall, once St Mary Street, where the bridge led over the River Wye and on to Wycombe Abbey and Marlow. Here were the traditional working-class areas of the 19th century, with rows of small houses, open drains and communal wells. Here too lived almost half of the chair makers of the Borough during the early years of the growth of the furniture industry.

In the 18th century 'all inhabitants of the Borough have liberty at all times to walk, and use sports and pastimes such as running, leaping, wrestling, riding, backswords and other plays at their pleasure' on The Rye, which obviously acted as the contemporary 'sports centre' of the area. The first recorded cricket match took place there in 1774, and on Tuesday 15 February 1803 the St Mary Street Theatre were performing 'Blue Beard: Or, the Punishment of Female Curiosity' with an 'oriental procession of Janizaries, Guards, Attendants and Banner Bearers'. Wycombe's first cinema, the Palace at Frogmore, opened in 1909, and a swimming pool was opened by Aleck Stacey at the Dovecote in 1910 on the site of the old Wycombe Steam Saw Mills. Football was always a favourite, and a number of teams existed in the town and surrounding villages. The 'Wycombe Wanderers' were formed in 1884, first using The Rye and then moving to Spring Gardens before acquiring the Loakes Park ground in 1895. The Dyke on the Rye was a good place for a quiet row or an illegal swim, and real fish, Wycombe trout, could be caught in the river Wye until about 1901.

Among the casualties of the Central Development Plan was the Wye itself, which now runs for almost a mile under the new developments of the Octagon and the Oxford Road area until it rises once again near Queen Victoria Bridge next to the police station. From this point the river runs along the open space of The Rye, bordered on one side by the London Road and on the other by The Dyke and the trees of The Rye and Wycombe Abbey. It originally formed part of the lands belonging to the Hospital of St John, but at some point became common meadow owned by the Corporation of Chepping Wycombe. Burgesses had the right to pasture two cows and a heifer on The Rye, and in 1642 a Civil War battle took place here in which, according to contemporary accounts, over 1,200 soldiers were killed. Since this time, Wycombe has been connected with the armed forces. The Royal Military College was based here from 1799-1813, and army units were stationed during the 19th and early 20th centuries. During the First World War a military hospital commandeered the Girls' High School in Benjamin Road, and during both wars the furniture industry turned its attention to munitions and aircraft production and repair. The stained glass window on the stairway of the Guildhall records the many units of the armed forces in which personnel from High Wycombe served in the Great War, while a plaque in the church records the exploits of 2nd Lieut. Frederick Youens, who was awarded the Victoria Cross in 1917.

Seven centuries link Roger Outred, the town's first recorded mayor, with the present mayor, and residents of the town are indeed fortunate that many of its traditions and customs, together with some of its architectural heritage, have survived the ravages of time. Nonetheless, it is imperative that, in the light of the many changes which have taken place over the last 40 years, every effort be made to ensure that this heritage remains intact for the benefit of future generations.

The Plates

The Ancient Borough

1. The Borough was empowered to govern the community by royal charters which date from 1237. Only those from Mary I to Charles II have survived in the Borough archives, and this contemporary portrait of Queen Elizabeth I comes from the charter granted in 1598.

2. The coat of arms of the former Borough was taken from the badge of the de Bohun family, who owned estates in Buckinghamshire which included Wycombe. It was probably used from medieval times as a seal, and was confirmed by the Clarenceux Herald at his 'Visitation' of 1566.

3. This carved version of the arms of the Borough is shown in the hands of an angel, and came from the Guildhall which stood in Church Street, now demolished. It depicts the swan with open wings, a variation on the accepted version of the arms, and was originally the end of a corbel which supported the roof beams.

4. High Wycombe is justly proud of its historic regalia, which includes the magnificent silver-gilt 'Great Mace' dating from 1694. This was presented to the town by Thomas Lewes and Charles Godrey, who were Members of Parliament at the time. It bears their personal coats of arms, those of the Borough, and the royal arms of William and Mary.

5. On special days the mayor goes to church and back to the Mayor's Parlour in procession. This photograph shows the procession in about 1909. The event was described *c.*1700: 'First goes the Beadle with his staff, then the Sergeant-at-Mace in a cloak carrying a large silver mace, gilt with gold, then goes the Mayor in his gown, always walking with a silver staff, then the recorder, then the Aldermen in their gowns two and two, close the procession'.

6. A view of the Cornmarket area at the end of High Street, showing the earlier Market House or Guildhall which was built c.1604. The 'Old Guildhall', built c.1480, survived until the 1930s opposite the present entrance of the Chiltern Shopping Centre in Chapel Street. The common prison was in the dungeons underneath, and was probably used until the Newland police station was built in 1817.

7. The present Guildhall started life as 'The Great Market House', and was erected in 1757 to designs by Henry Keene as a gift to the town by the Earl of Shelburne who resided at Wycombe Abbey. It is built of brick supported on a stone arcaded colonnade, and was renovated in 1859 and again in the early 1980s. It is used for the Heritage Exhibition in the summer months, and also for the annual general meeting of the charter trustees and the traditional 'weighing-in' ceremony which is unique to High Wycombe.

8. In the upper section of the Guildhall are two rooms, used in the 19th century as committee and council rooms when it was designated the 'Town Hall'. This photograph shows portraits in the Shelburne Room in the 1920s before the new municipal offices were built in 1931. The large Mayor's Chair is on the left of the lower table.

9. The new town hall was opened on 12 October 1904. It was built to designs by J. J. Bateman and C. E. & A. Hale, and was the first building to be erected in the newly-created civic road which ran along the line of the drive to Wycombe Abbey and was called Queen Victoria Road.

10. Talk of a new town hall began at the time of Queen Victoria's Diamond Jubilee, when Lord Carrington offered a site in Castle Street for this purpose. However, it was after the queen's death in 1901 that negotiations were completed for the present site in the new Queen Victoria Road, built after the Abbey had been sold and had become the Wycombe Abbey School. It contained a main hall to seat 1,100, including a stage, dressing-rooms and an organ installed in 1905. Above the entrance is the Oak Room which contained five stained glass windows by Arthur J. Dix. The building adjoining to the right is the public library, opened in 1932.

11. The ceremony of 'weighing-in'. Robert S. Wood, elected mayor in November 1907, is being weighed on the former coal scales, with the mace-bearer standing by to call out the weight.

12. For some time after the old scales were discarded, new brass scales were hired each year from their owners who used them at local fairs and fêtes, weighing people for a half-penny. Here we see Councillor Walter J. Butler, J.P., being weighed-in in November 1924.

13.   The new municipal offices were opened with great ceremony in 1932. They were built to designs by
R. G. Brocklehurst & Cowles Voysey in neo-Georgian style and consisted of 11 bays and a five-bay entrance. It was
a style to which other buildings in Queen Victoria Road and Crendon Street conformed, and the design was granted
an award by R.I.B.A.

14.   The official photograph of the Chepping Wycombe Borough Council taken on 16 October 1934 in the new
council chamber. Councillor W. S. Toms is mayor and sits flanked on each side by the mace-bearer and beadle. A
new set of oak furniture was designed for this chamber, most of which is now in the Mayor's Parlour in the recently
remodelled council offices.

15. Police on duty outside the Little Market House. This illustrates another function of the Chepping Wycombe Borough, for the mayor was magistrate and he was responsible for the police and night constables who patrolled the town from 11 p.m. until 6 a.m. The beadle and town crier was appointed superintendent of police in 1839, a position he held for 40 years.

16. Newlands police station was built at a time when this district contained rows of small terraced houses in which many of the furniture workmen lived. There was a public house or ale house on almost every corner. This police station served Newlands until it was replaced by the new building in Queen Victoria Road which was opened in 1935.

17. The new police station was designed to fit in with the civic buildings in Queen Victoria Road. Its matching neo-Georgian architecture was designed by E. A. L. Martyn. The building was constructed in 1935 and served the Borough Council until it was transfered to Bucks County Constabulary in 1947.

18. After *c.*1175 the poor of the town could be housed in the Norman Hospital of St John the Baptist which contained a form of hall of residence with a chapel attached for a number of elderly persons. It remained in use at the extreme eastern edge of the medieval Borough boundaries until the Dissolution by Henry VIII. In 1549 the mayor and burgesses of Wycombe had the building and its land conveyed to them on payment of £30, for use as a grammar school.

19.   By the 1830s new legislation encouraged several parishes to group together to build large workhouses for their poor. Wycombe Union House was built at Saunderton in 1843 of brick and flint, with accommodation for 450 inmates. This is the architect's drawing. A workhouse school was built at Bledlow for 106 poor children.

20.   Various buildings over the years were used as almshouses for the poor. In 1856 this row in brick and stone in mock-Tudor style was built and became known as Queen Elizabeth's Almshouses, standing opposite the Grammar School where the law courts have since been built. They were demolished in the 1960s.

21. A furniture town like High Wycombe needed an efficient fire service. A voluntary brigade was founded in 1868, its engine and equipment purchased with funds supplied by public subscription. Later the Borough took over these costs and built a fire station at the end of Frogmore to house the fire engine which had been in the church porch until then. This photograph shows the brigade on The Rye c.1890. The horses were provided by Mr. L. Weston, job and post master, whose stables were close to the railway station.

22. The new fire station opened in Priory Road in 1899, and is seen here with the new engine bought in 1887. The charge for calling out both fire engines was seven guineas, five guineas if only one engine was used, although the cost of horse and driver was added. In 1903 W. H. Butler was the Chief Officer, in charge of 19 men, and in 1938 G. T. Miles was awarded a certificate for 52 years' service. The fire brigade remained in existence as such until 1941.

FIRE AT CRENDON ST. WYCOMBE, MAY 28. 1906.

23. It was all hands to the pump when fire broke out at Crendon Street on 28 May 1906. The crisis over, six firemen pose on the ladder, the officer stands proudly by, and a rescued child is wrapped in an eiderdown.

24. The old post office in Easton Street has 1901 carved in the brickwork over its imposing doorway. This was the date it was transferred from High Street although it was to have been located in the newly opened Coronation Street which linked High Street to Castle Street. Later, in 1934, it was closed when the post office moved to join the other civic buildings in Queen Victoria Road. The counter service was moved again in the early 1980s, this time to The Octagon.

25. For the sick or infirm there was a Cottage Hospital, founded in 1875 in premises at Shrubbery Road. A new wing was opened in December 1891 by Coningsby Disraeli, called the Disraeli Wing, and the building was renamed the High Wycombe and Earl of Beaconsfield Memorial Cottage Hospital.

26.   The High Wycombe and District War Memorial Hospital was opened on Marlow Hill in 1923 to replace the Cottage Hospital. The site was given by the Marquis of Lincolnshire and the hospital acted as a memorial to the 500 men of the Borough and surrounding district killed in the First World War. It originally provided for 35 patients but, like its predecessor, was demolished to make way for the new regional hospital, a multi-storey building erected during the 1970s and 1980s.

27.   Castle Hill House, just beyond the station, houses the Wycombe Chair Museum and the main part of the building dates back to the late 17th century. The flint façade was added c.1800 and another bay on the right-hand side was built c.1900. The house stands on the site of a defensive motte and bailey castle built during the Stephen and Maud conflict of the 12th century, and the museum exhibits were transferred from the present central library in about 1965.

Education

28. The old Royal Grammar School building was originally the Hospital of St John the Baptist, built in about 1175. In 1549, following the Dissolution of the Monasteries, it was transferred to the Borough for £30 to become the town's Grammar School. In 1562 it received a royal charter and the school continued in its Norman building for just over 300 years.

29. As the town expanded, the Royal Grammar School outgrew its ancient accommodation, and in 1883 it was replaced by this typically Victorian building of red and white brick, designed by Arthur Vernon, at a cost of £5,000. It was the temporary home of the Girls' High School from 1914-19, after which it housed the Technical College until c.1988.

30. In Edwardian times new premises were again needed, and the site chosen was at the top of Amersham Hill, where the Grammar School was rebuilt at a cost of £20,000 in 1915 to designs by A. S. Vernon in a stately neo-Georgian style with projecting wings and a turret clock. More recently, an extension has been built in front of the main structure which includes the Queen Elizabeth Hall, opened by Elizabeth II in 1962 during celebrations for the 400th anniversary of the school's charter.

31. Priory Road School was opened in 1873 at a cost of £8,071 and was run by the Borough and parish through a joint school board. It catered for 380 boys, 380 girls and 200 infants and was designed by Arthur Vernon in early Gothic style. It originally had a pyramid spire, but this disappeared sometime between the wars, and the original name of Cemetery Road Schools was wisely dropped before 1888.

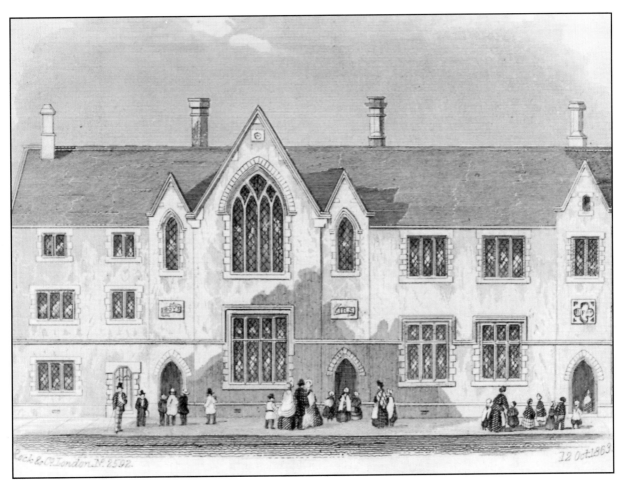

32. The National School in White Hart Street was established by the Church of England and erected in 1855 in Gothic style to designs by Mr. Bond. It accommodated 470 children and remained in use until the new Church of England School was erected. It was eventually converted into Nutt's Auction Rooms and was finally incorporated into Murray's Store when major rebuilding took place.

33. The Science and Art School in Frogmore was erected at a total cost of £2,200 and opened by Lord Carrington in 1893. It contained classrooms, a lecture hall, laboratories, an art room and a life room. When the old Royal Grammar School became vacant in 1919, most of the departments moved there. In 1929 this building was converted into swimming baths, and in 1946 became the town's Repertory Theatre. When this failed, it remained unused and derelict until 1983 when it was renovated and became an office block called The Clock-House.

34. A school group photograph of class I of Wycombe Marsh Infant School in 1936.

35. This is an interior view of the Wycombe High School for Girls in its building in Benjamin Road. The school started in Frogmore in 1901 and moved to Benjamin Road in 1906. It stayed there until 1914 when the buildings were turned into a War Hospital. The girls moved to the old Royal Grammar School, returning to their former school in 1919. Modern premises were erected at the top of Marlow Hill, and the Girls' High School moved there in 1956.

Church and Chapel

36. This photograph of the parish church of All Saints in 1920 shows clearly the majestic tower which replaced the earlier central tower in the 1520s and the additional north and south chapels built in the 13th century. The south chapel, on the left of the picture, was the corporation or guild chapel and so was maintained by the Borough. The church was built in the 11th century and has been altered, enlarged and restored at intervals ever since. It is large, light and roomy and provides an ideal venue for the many musical and religious events which take place in the town.

37. The interior of All Saints' church from a painting by E. J. Niemann of 1848. It shows the view from the west end through the chancel arch with the heavy and elaborate wooden pew of the Shelburne family. This was removed in 1858 and is now in Wycombe Abbey School. The box pews which were removed in 1865 gave it a somewhat crowded appearance, while the wooden pulpit with its sounding board was replaced in the late 19th-century restoration.

38. Near the south porch was the Watch House, a Tudor building used by the Watch or constabulary in earlier days. Soldiers could be quartered here in an emergency, but this building and the row of overhanging cottages which linked it to the *Black Boy* in Church Street were demolished in a road widening scheme in the 1930s.

39. Across from the north side of the parish church is Castle Street, formerly All Hallows Lane, where 18th-century buildings stand on the site of earlier premises which housed the chantry priests connected with altar duties. The tall building is still called Chantry House, and further up was the Vicarage and Vicarage Farm, with a narrow path or lane through to Crendon Lane.

40. Crendon Street in 1922 is still the narrow lane which caused so many problems for traffic using the railway station. Halfway up can be seen the tower and spire of Christ Church on the right-hand side. This church was built to designs by Arthur Vernon for the breakaway parish of Christ Church in 1889, and was demolished in the second phase of rebuilding Crendon Street in the 1950s. The Sunday School stood across the High Street in Queen Victoria Road, between the present post office yard and the municipal buildings.

41. The Catholic church of St Augustine was built in 1900 in Gothic style in brick and stone, and could seat 120 persons. It stood in Castle Street on the site now occupied by the row of modern shops opposite the bookshop, and remained in use until the new church was erected in Amersham Hill to designs by J. Sebastian Cooper in 1955-7.

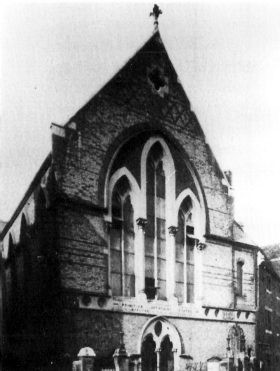

42. White Hart Street chapel, built for the Primitive Methodists in 1875 to designs by Arthur Vernon. It was partly demolished when incorporated into the extensions to Murray's Store. The hidden sections were for a brief time exposed during the rebuilding in the 1980s.

43. Trinity Congregational chapel, now United Reformed, in Easton Street, was originally founded in 1807 and moved to the present building in 1851. It was designed in Romanesque style with a nave and two aisles, flanked by two distinctive towers. Opposite was The Rye and Pann Mill with the wide stretch of the mill pond shown here which is now reduced to a narrow river. Pann Mill disappeared in the 1970s, along with the *Coach and Horses* and the small community which lived behind it adjacent to Trinity chapel in Railway Place, which is now a large car park serving the east side of town.

44. The Union Baptist chapel in Easton Street was built to designs by Octavius Jordon in 1845. As shown here, it was a fairly monumental looking stone building with a classical air which almost seems foreign to Wycombe. The chapel burnt down in a spectacular fire in 1908 but was quickly rebuilt to designs by Thomas Thurlow with an Italianate façade.

45. St John's church, Desborough, was designed by W. D. Caroe, built in 1901-2 and consecrated in 1903, and is of red brick with stone facings in the Decorated style. It consists of a nave and chancel, and was erected at a cost of £7,000. It replaced an earlier iron building erected in 1882, which can also be seen in this postcard.

46. Hull, Loosely and Pearce, undertakers of Oxford Road. The glazed hearse, drawn by two black horses and covered in floral tributes, must have been an impressive sight at funerals.

47.   Tent missions and travelling evangelists were all part of 19th-century Nonconformist chapel life, and fine Sundays were often spent in powerful sermons, lengthy prayers and lusty hymn-singing. This photograph, *c.*1895, shows a preacher on the right with his caravan mission which toured the villages of the High Wycombe area. This particular photograph was taken at Bledlow.

CHRIST DIED

FOR OUR S

People, Politics and Local Events

48. Wycombe Abbey stands on the site of the old manor house, called Loakes. The estate, which passed to Henry Petty in 1700, was the home of the Earl of Shelburne and was sold to the Carrington family in 1798. The earlier building was enlarged and remodelled by James Wyatt in 1795 when it was given its present castellated appearance. The house and part of the grounds, excluding the entrance drive, were purchased by the Girls' Education Company Ltd., and opened as the Wycombe Abbey School in 1896. During the Second World War, Wycombe Abbey became the headquarters of the U.S. 8th Army Air Force and, during one of his tours of Britain, Glenn Miller played at the Abbey.

49. This portrait of Lord Shelburne is one of several painted by Joshua Reynolds and his school. In his time Wycombe Abbey became an important political centre and many famous people such as Dr. Johnson, Edmund Burke and Benjamin Franklin were visitors there. The Earl of Shelburne held several important offices of State under successive Prime Ministers, and became Premier himself in 1783 for a short period. He was also responsible for building the new Guildhall to the designs of Henry Keene in 1757.

50. The Rupert Gates, now rebuilt halfway up Marlow Hill, were the entrance to Wycombe Abbey and stood in front of what is now the Museum Gardens which adjoin the library. The gates were removed about the time the Abbey was sold. They were rebuilt as the entrance to Daws Hill House, Lord Carrington's new abode.

51. A portrait photograph of Lord Carrington, taken in Sydney in 1888 when he was Governor of New South Wales. He had a close relationship with H.R.H. the Prince of Wales, whom he served as Aide-de-Camp during his state visit to India. This was the reason for several royal visits to the town, and in 1884 the Prince and Princess were each presented with a chair by the Borough.

HIGH WYCOMBE.

Arrangements for

RECEPTION

OF

LORD & LADY CARINGTON

JULY 31st, 1878.

THE COMMITTEE have endeavoured to ascertain the views and wishes of Lord Carington, and with his Lordship's concurrence have made the following arrangements, which it is hoped the public will assist in carrying out.

His Lordship is expected to arrive by the train which reaches High Wycombe at 2.33 p.m. The public bodies and tenantry will meet His Lordship at the Railway Station and form a procession, preceded by the Band, to a space reserved for the purpose in front of the Red Lion Hotel, High Street, where the several Addresses will be presented to LORD AND LADY CARINGTON, After which the Procession will proceed to the Abbey.

It is expected that the Horses will be taken from the Carriage **after the Addresses have been presented and received,** and the Carriage will be drawn to the Abbey by Ropes.

Fireworks in the Rye at 9.15 p.m.

BUTLER, PRINTER, WYCOMBE.

52. This poster was printed to ensure that the whole town knew of the arrangements planned for the reception of the newly-wedded Lord and Lady Carrington on their return to Wycombe Abbey on 31 July 1878.

53. Benjamin Disraeli did not have the advantages of Lord Shelburne or Lord Carrington when starting his political career. In the 1830s he had failed three times to win a parliamentary seat at Chepping Wycombe, so it must have given him great satisfaction to take up residence at Hughenden Manor as Prime Minister and order his cigars from the town. This portrait is from the series of stained glass windows in the Oak Room of the town hall, depicting famous people of the area.

54. Disraeli was Queen Victoria's favourite Prime Minister and, as a special honour, she visited him at Hughenden in 1877. She is seen here at High Wycombe railway station.

55. To honour the Queen's visit in 1877 the town built a triumphal arch across the road near the Guildhall. Flags and banners were displayed, and Victoria was led to a carriage as the school children sang 'God Save the Queen'. To the accompaniment of church bells, the procession wound slowly through the town on its way to Hughenden.

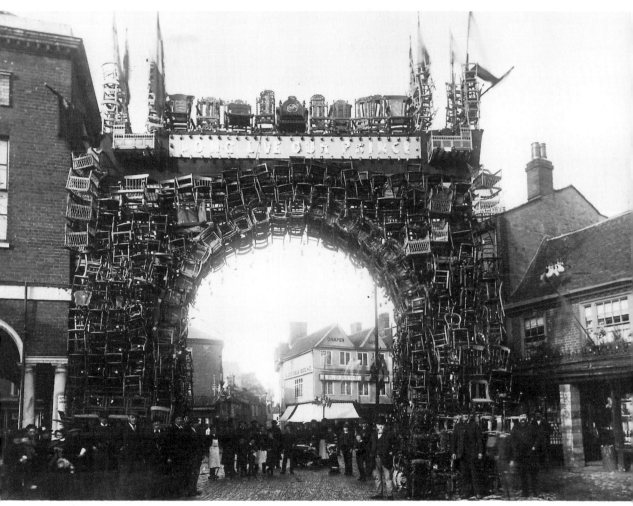

56.   The Great Chair Arch was erected across the road at the Guildhall to celebrate Prince Edward's visit to Wycombe in 1880 on his way to Hughenden. Gone was the slight elegance of the Victoria arch, and here almost 400 chairs were built into the structure to cover completely the framework with furniture. On top of the arch was the ceremonial Mayor's Chair, representing the town's allegiance to the throne.

57. In High Street school children are getting into place for the ceremony in the afternoon, where some 4,600 children gathered to celebrate Queen Victoria's Diamond Jubilee in 1897. At the signal from a bugle, they all burst into the Doxology and then the National Anthem. Led by the band, the children then began to march through the Rupert Gates into the park for their celebration tea.

58. Lord Carrington gave 1,000 faggots and other employers gave many loads of spare wood and shavings for a bonfire after the Diamond Jubilee tea. The bonfire was lit by the mayor at 9.55 p.m. and soon there was a magnificent blaze on Tom Burt's Hill. The National Anthem could be heard in The Rye and in London Road that night.

59. The band, followed by carnival floats including a group of children in white around the maypole, processing along High Street towards the entrance gates of Wycombe Abbey. The ladies looking over the balcony to the right are standing at what is now the window of Abbey National, while the Central Hall sign at the extreme left marks the present position of the entrance of Corporation Street.

60. The furniture industry features prominently in all High Wycombe parades. Here a horse-drawn cart is carrying 600 chairs, almost twice the normal load. Behind rides the lifeboat crew.

61. The launching of the lifeboat brought from Southend-on-Sea was the highlight of the gala day on
Saturday 21 September 1907, in support of the funds of the Royal National Lifeboat Institution. The launching took place o
The Rye, with the lifeboat drawn up near to the river bank, and the crew took up their positions accompanied by
the mayor, Alderman Vernon, and the vicar.

62. Many of the processions passed the Liberal Headquarters in High Street, as well as the Conservative Rooms on the opposite side of the road. While peace reigned on these festive occasions, politics itself was often far from peaceful.

63. The *Red Lion* was an important political symbol in High Wycombe for it was here that Disraeli stood to plead for the townsfolk's votes in the 1830s. Here, during the post-war election of 1946, Winston Churchill is standing on the portico of the *Red Lion* in High Street, encouraging the community to support the Tory candidate.

LOST!

The following articles are supposed to have been lost in certain parts of the Borough on the Evening of Monday, November 2nd, 1874, or early on the following Tuesday morning :—

1.—Two unfinished Councillors' Gowns, one without the sleeves, and the other without skirts, marked in tailor's chalk J.W. and R.S.

2.—Ward's "majority," a somewhat slippery article, and resembling in character a "Will o' the wisp," but with the slight difference that it is visible only in the morning and usually disappears about four o'clock.

3.—Spicer's ditto, (a similar article).

4.—Wootton's ditto, a very minute particle, resembling in size a homoeopathic globule, but black as a "Smith." (A doubt has been expressed as to the actual existence of this article, so that too close a search need not be made for it.)

5.—The Brass Band, used at great political victories; supposed to have been overcome by excitement in a preliminary rehearsal of the "Conquering Hero."

6.—A quantity of torches, marked *G. M. Young, maker, Wycombe*, intended to have been used in a triumphal procession, headed by Messrs. Westrup, Phillips, Cockram, Briden, Darvill, &c., &c., but which, from unavoidable circumstances, was indefinitely postponed.

7.—A "Globe," with a face of brass, and marked L. Rolls about with a great noise, but is known to be hollow, and only dangerous to people of weak intellect.

8.—A Councillor's Gown, re-made and entirely re-lined in November, 1873, but since much stained and otherwise damaged, marked W.V.B., Loakes.

9.—A rusty Key of the Municipal Borough, labelled "Wycombe Abbey," dropped in front of the Town Hall about four o'clock on Monday afternoon.

Any person bringing either of the above articles to the Crier will be rewarded out of the funds generously placed at his disposal for charitable purposes by Messrs. Ward and Spicer, the future Aldermen of the Borough.

P.S. No. 9 was picked up by Mr. Justice Wheeler when in company with Councillors Thurlow and Raffety, and taken at once to the Mayor, who, in thanking them, expressed his decided opinion that no person was entitled to have such a Key in his possession; that the *proper* Key was held by him in trust for the people, and he hoped that the Burgesses would take great care not to send anybody to the Council Board who was likely to take a wax impression, either for the Abbey or Loakes. The Borough would not tolerate any tampering with its Independence.

November 3rd, 1874,

64.   This poster is one of many which poked fun at political opponents, illustrating the issues on which the two rival factions of town and Abbey candidates disagreed.

Wycombe at War

65. The former shop of C. H. Berry, just along from Lloyd's Bank, was the *Antelope Inn* during the 18th and early 19th centuries, and for some years it had been connected with the military life of the town. In 1799 it was converted into the headquarters of the Wycombe Military College, with a junior branch at Marlow. In 1813 the Wycombe section moved to Farnham and the Marlow branch to Sandhurst.

66.   The key figure in the Wycombe Military College was General le Marchant. He lived at The Priory on the corner of Castle Street and was Lieut. Governor. He was promoted to Major General in 1811 and embarked for service in the Peninsular War, dying from his wounds following the Battle of Salamanca in 1812.

67. An impressive line-up of Royal Bucks Hussars in
their frogged uniforms, photographed *c*.1890. With
them is Lieut. Coningsby Disraeli, nephew of
Benjamin, who succeeded to Hughenden Manor and
its estates on the death of his uncle in 1881.

68. Wild scenes took place in the streets of High
Wycombe when the news of the Relief of Mafeking,
after a siege of 217 days by the Boers, was announced
on 18 May 1900.

69.   The Boer War ended in 1902 and there was great rejoicing in the town on the return of local troops. A decorated arch was built at the top of Crendon Street to greet the men as they left the railway station. Here, outside the *Red Lion* at the end of St Mary Street, another arch and patriotic flags can be seen.

70.   Members of the Bucks Militia at ease during a parade following their return to High Wycombe from the Boer War. As a military town, High Wycombe was a reception centre for troops, as well as having a Military Hospital in Benjamin Road in the premises of the Wycombe Girls' High School between 1914 and 1919.

71. The Bucks Militia (3rd Battalion Oxford and Bucks Light Infantry) on parade in 1908.

72. The First World War brought women into a more active role in the factories, helping to produce munitions in particular. Here, working in wing assembly, are ladies from the Gomme factory.

73. Opposite the station, on the corner of Castle Street, was the *Railway Hotel*, with 'John's Hotel Restaurant' attached. During the First World War it was frequented by troops stationed in the town or moving from Wycombe to another military base. Morale had to be kept up, so details of the current programme at the Grand Cinema in Desborough Road were prominently displayed.

74. In a mood of both sorrow and rejoicing the Armistice service, marking the end of hostilities, took place in the church of All Saints, High Wycombe, in 1918. The church is full, with many military personnel present, and the banner of the Carrington family hangs on the left over the chancel.

Sports and Pastimes

75.   The Wycombe Excelsior Cyclists Club was formed in High Wycombe in 1882, to which both bicyclists and tricyclists were admitted. Here a group of cyclists on a variety of vehicles pose in the grounds of Wycombe Abbey.

76.   The earliest recorded cricket match in Wycombe was played on The Rye in July 1774 when the trophy was a silver cup worth five guineas. This photograph shows the runners-up in the Wycombe and District Cricket League, Division 1, for the 1920 season, the Wycombe Alexandra Cricket Club, with captain A. Crook.

77.   Many of the Nonconformist chapels encouraged their members to play team games such as football, cricket and tennis, as well as expecting them to make an appearance at church or choir practice. Here, the Wycombe Trinity Football Club celebrates its 1909-10 victory in the Berks and Bucks Junior Cup and the Maidenhead Norfolkian Charity Cup. Left to right, *back row*: J. Tibbles, W. Youers, Mr. M. J. S. Dent (President), F. Blatchford (Captain), W. Tibbles, A. Bryant, F. G. Oxlade (Hon. Sec.), A. Parsons; *middle row*: A. Walker, A. Rogers, A. Bass, A. Dean, T. Moore (Vice-Capt.), A. Ball, J. Smith; *front row*: F. Free, F. Weedon, H. Morris, A. Crook, W. Harris, F. Bird, O. Crook.

78.   Team photograph of the Wycombe Rovers, 1917. Left to right, *back row*: W. Parker (Trainer), B. Newell, S. G. Fryer (Vice-Capt.), C. F. Styles, E. Wingrove (Assnt. Trainer); *middle row*: W. Hearn, R. S. Johnson, H. V. Bates (Captain), C. R. Bates, E. Smith; *front row*: N. L. Gray (Hon. Sec. & Treasurer), C. F. Johnson, G. T. Bowler.

79. The Westbourne Street billiards team which won the trophy in 1922.

80. Always popular was a pleasant afternoon's row on The Dyke. It was very quiet here in the 1930s by the side of The Rye, with no cows, no football matches and, as yet, no swimming pool.

81. The importance of trout fishing in Wycombe is shown by this diploma of the National Fisheries Exhibition of 1895. It was awarded to J. Thurloe Esq. for two trout taken in the Wye with the fly with weights of 7lb. 2oz. and 5lb. 6oz.

NATIONAL FISHERIES EXHIBITION,
1895.

The Royal Aquarium
AND
SUMMER AND WINTER GARDEN SOCIETY, LIMITED.

J. RITCHIE, Esq., *Chairman and Managing Director.*

This Diploma has been granted by the Royal Aquarium Society to *V. Thurlow Eso.* for *Two Wycombe Trout taken with the fly, Weights Seven pounds two ounces. Five pounds five Ounces. First Award for Best Trout taken from any water other than the Thames.* exhibited in the Loan Collection of the National Fisheries Exhibition, held at the Royal Aquarium, Westminster, March 15th to April 20th, 1895.

82. Trout fishing from a punt on The Dyke. The Wye was a good source of trout in the 19th century but by 1901 it was reported that 'in a year or two the famous Wycombe trout will have become extinct'.

83. Swimming pools became very popular in the early years of the 20th century, with the first being opened at the Dovecote by Alex Stacey in 1910. This was followed by the conversion of the Technical School in Frogmore in 1929, and other pools were built behind the cattle market. This photograph shows the Desborough recreation ground which opened in 1924 and remained in use until 1947.

84. The original Palace Cinema opened in 1909 on the opposite side of Frogmore. A few years later it was burnt down and rebuilt here. The original façade was timbered but after the war it was remodelled. The building was demolished in the late 1980s.

85. The Grand Cinema opened in Desborough Road in 1913, and is here advertising 'The Abduction' and 'Righting the Wrong' with reserved seats at 1s. and the balcony at 9d.

86. The last cinema to be built was the Majestic, which opened in 1930 in Castle Street. The souvenir programme shows a very elaborate proscenium designed like an oriental castle. It was later renamed the Odeon.

Public Houses and Breweries

87. The *Red Lion* in the rain, with the bus from London to Birmingham. This public house can be traced back to 1312 and in 1518 was given to Brasenose College, Oxford. The building dates from the 18th century, but only the upper part of the façade remains; the lower colonnade and the interior were remodelled in 1972 and the portico moved further to the right of Woolworth's building.

88. The original carved red lion was added in about 1820. When the lion needed to be replaced in 1956, Frank Hudson, a local master-carver, was called in. Recent high winds blew the lion from its portico, and a new carving is again needed.

89. When the *Red Lion* was converted into the new Woolworth's store, the town lost a valuable dining room as the handsome Wellington Room, shown in this photograph, was the venue for many special events and regular meetings of the town's clubs and societies.

90. Wheeler's Brewery stood in Easton Street, on what is now the corner with Queen Victoria Road long before that road was constructed in 1902. Robert Wheeler went into partnership with Andrew Biddle in 1808, and the Biddle family had been brewing in Wycombe since before 1784. In 1875 Thomas Wheeler was mayor, Treasurer of the Savings Bank, Chairman of the School Board, Treasurer of the Wycombe Union, a director of Wycombe Bank, and was also running the Brewery.

91. Beneath the broad High Street are a number of brick-built vaults or cellars which included the Wheeler's Brewery vaults shown here. An advertisement in 1736 announced that 'At the Wine Vaults in Chipping Wycombe are sold neat wines ... Port Wine at 6s. per gallon, Mountaine at the same price, Sherry at 6s. 6d., Canary 8s., Neat Brandy at 8s. per Gallon, Rum at the same price. N.B. A person will always be ready to give attendance'.

92.   The *Falcon Hotel* in High Street was a 17th-century building which enjoyed considerable prosperity due to the through coaching traffic, as shown here in 1901. Its position next to the Guildhall made it handy for election sustenance, and in the 1830 poll it joined with other inns to provide dinner and drink for the band, and 27 barrels of beer for the 'refreshment of the population'.

93. At the back of the Guildhall ran Paul's Row, which takes its name from the medieval Poull family, and the inn signs of both the *Angel* and the *Swan* are suspended above their premises. The R.A.O.B. (Buffaloes) Lodge No.1377 met at the *Angel*, while the *Swan* advertises the A.O. dining rooms, and was also the headquarters of the Athletic and Cycling Club and the Ancient Order of Shepherds and of Foresters, according to an 1894 pictorial guide.

94. The crooked chimney of the *Black Boy* was a familiar landmark in the town. This was one of the public houses bought by Wheeler's Brewery in 1854. The inn was demolished in the 1930s during a road-widening development, and the licence transferred to a new house built in Terriers.

95. The *Red Cross Knight* stood just beyond the bridge at Temple End. The name derives from the Knights Templar to whom Ralph Vipont granted this part of the manor in 1227. A public house of this name was opened here between 1866-68 as the Hughenden Road began to be built up, but it was replaced by the building in the photograph in the 1930s, which in turn was demolished in 1986 as part of a road improvement scheme.

96. The *Three Tuns* in the High Street was opposite the *Red Lion* and, though quite small, ran both a coaching and carrier trade. A blacksmith had his smithy in the backyard, and in 1866 Nathaniel Beasley ran a coopering business here. This public house operated a carrying service for many years, which continued until 1931. This photograph was taken between 1895-1903 when C. H. Young was the landlord, and advertises accommodation for 'cyclists with luncheon, dinners, teas, and chop steaks'.

97. The *White Horse* stood near the bottom of Crendon Street, next to Christ Church. Weller's of Amersham, a brewery with six public houses in the town, owned the *White Horse*. This photograph is dated about 1895, and shows the narrowness of the street. The public house was demolished during the road widening scheme which started in the 1930s but was not completed until the 1950s.

98. The *Old King of Prussia* lay on the London Road and was a favourite stopping place for the horse-drawn chair waggons which made their way in the evening to London. By 1915 the owners, Wheeler's Wycombe Brewery, had altered the name to the *King George V*, because of the hostilities of the First World War.

The Brewery, Henley-on-Thames.

MESSRS. W. H. BRAKSPEAR AND SONS

Beg to call attention to their List of

PALE ALES, STOUT, WINES, SPIRITS, AND MINERAL WATERS,

AS SUPPLIED FROM THEIR **STORES**, AT

43, OXFORD STREET, HIGH WYCOMBE.

All Beers manufactured by them are guaranteed brewed from materials of the finest quality, by means of the most modern appliances, and can be recommended for their purity, brilliancy, and keeping properties.

PRICES OF ALES AND STOUT BREWED FROM THE FINEST ENGLISH MALT AND HOPS:—

In Cask at per gallon, I.P.A., 1/6; P.A., 1/4; H.G.A., 1/2; P.X.X., 1/-; P.X., 10d.; Double Stout, 1/6; Porter, 1/-.

In Bottle at per Doz.		Imperial pints.		Half pints.		In Bottle at per Doz.		Imperial pints.		Half pints.
India Pale Ale	...	4s.	...	2s.		Henley Nourishing Stout	...	3s.	...	1s. 6d.
Pale Ale	...	3s.	...	1s. 6d.		Bass' India Pale Ale	...	4s. 6d.	...	2s. 3d.
Light Dinner Ale	...	2s. 6d.	...	—		Guinness' Dublin Stout	...	4s. 6d.	...	2s. 3d.
Luncheon Ale	...	2s.	...	—						Rpt. pts.
						Pilsener Lager Beer	...	...	...	3s. 6d.

Wines and Spirits of the finest qualities, a single bottle of which can be obtained. Finest old Scotch and Irish Whiskies being a Speciality.

MINERAL WATERS.

These we manufacture with great care, and with the most modern machinery, from absolutely pure water, as per the following testimonial of Dr. Moritz, who states: " I consider this a remarkably pure water."

PRICE LISTS ON APPLICATION TO

MR. THOS. H. THEOBALD,
STORES MANAGER.

99. Brakspear's Brewery in Henley had three houses in High Wycombe, possibly including their store in Oxford Street. This 1894 advertisement lists a good range of ales, beers and stouts at most reasonable prices.

100. This imposing building in High Street recently served as the *Grapes* public house before being converted into a shop. Originally it was the premises of John Leadbetter and his son Alfred, who were wine and spirit merchants in the town. They also had a partnership in Frogmore Brewery in 1881, but that concern was sold to Wheeler's in 1898.

Transport

101. High Wycombe was on the route of many coaches and the High Street and Easton Street had a number of hotels and public houses to serve the needs of travellers. Although the arrival of the railway reduced the number of coaches dramatically, the *Red Lion* still provided stabling for 45 horses as late as 1894. This picture of the Oxford-London coach in front of the *Falcon* is dated 1901.

102. The horse-bus was the means of transport for most at the turn of the century, and this one is picking up passengers at the Little Market House in 1900. The service was started by Mr. Weston in 1882 and ran from West Wycombe to Loudwater in two stages, the charge being 1d. for each stage.

103. Equally important was the carrier, and here Worley & Sons of High Wycombe are transporting chairs. This service operated until 1931, long after the formal coach service had been discontinued.

104.   The chair waggons were generally owned by the manufacturers. This is Glenister's waggon loaded up and ready to move off. London was the usual destination and the return trip could take up to 36 hours.

105.   Progress came with the steam engine. Keen's new steam waggon with its trailer set off in March 1904 pulling six tons, and returned from London within 14 hours.

106.   The steam-engine was ideal for collecting timber from the new-fangled railway. Here a load of timber is being transferred to the first steam engine for Plumridge's saw mill.

107. Laying the track for the railways could involve considerable risks, and it was necessary for the workers to be roped together in this hair-raising operation when excavating the Saunderton cutting in 1905.

108. The railway arrived at High Wycombe as a branch line from Maidenhead and opened for traffic on 1 August 1854 when the first train came through. This photograph shows the layout of the station at that time, with the up and down platforms built almost opposite each other.

109. In 1904 a large body of men shifted the down line nearer the platform of the new station, as the doubling meant that the platforms had to be a distance from each other to avoid a bottleneck near the bridge.

110.   The first train on the new direct line to London, a joint venture of the Great Central Line and the terminus at Marylebone, ran on 2 April 1906.

111.   Garages and petrol pumps were necessary when cars arrived on the roads. Davenport's Garage operated from High Street.

Crafts and Industry

112.   This photograph of 1895 shows the fast flow of water passing through Bowdery Lane Mill which lay at the back of Oxford Street on the River Wye. Most mills in the Borough were originally used for milling grain, but later others were used for fulling cloth and finally, in the 17th century, for making paper.

113.   Bassetsbury Mill lies next to the manor on the edge of The Rye and, although not now working, the waterwheel is still in position. It takes its name from Alan Bassett, lord of the manor in the 13th century.

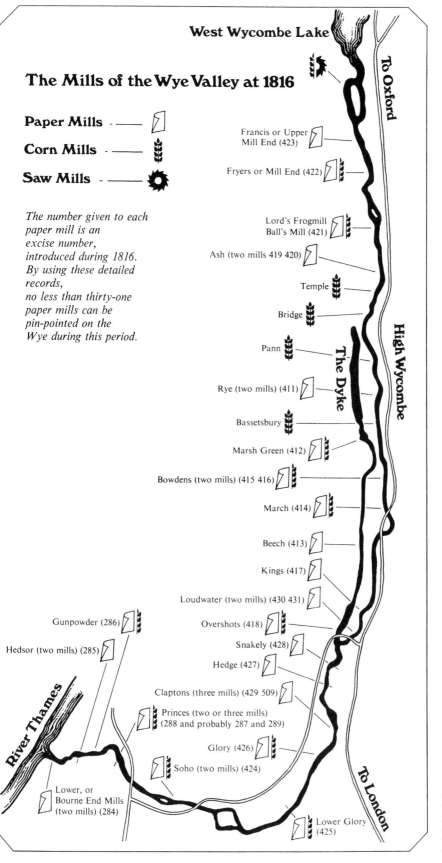

West Wycombe Lake

The Mills of the Wye Valley at 1816

Paper Mills — 🗊

Corn Mills · — 🌾

Saw Mills · — ⚙

*The number given to each
paper mill is an
excise number,
introduced during 1816.
By using these detailed
records,
no less than thirty-one
paper mills can be
pin-pointed on the
Wye during this period.*

To Oxford

Francis or Upper
Mill End (423)

Fryers or Mill End (422)

Lord's Frogmill
Ball's Mill (421)

Ash (two mills 419 420)

Temple

Bridge

Pann

High Wycombe

The Dyke

Rye (two mills) (411)

Bassetsbury

Marsh Green (412)

Bowdens (two mills) (415 416)

March (414)

Beech (413)

Kings (417)

Loudwater (two mills) (430 431)

Gunpowder (286)

Overshots (418)

Hedsor (two mills) (285)

Snakely (428)

Hedge (427)

Claptons (three mills) (429 509)

River Thames

Princes (two or three mills)
(288 and probably 287 and 289)

Glory (426)

Soho (two mills) (424)

To London

Lower, or
Bourne End Mills
(two mills) (284)

Lower Glory
(425)

114. This map, based on the
excise list of mills, indicates
which industries were using the
37 mills which flourished at
various times on the Wye from
West Wycombe Lake to the
Thames.

115. View across The Rye from Bassetsbury Lane at Marsh Green. This was part of the line of watercress beds which stretched from Hughenden Road to Marsh Green, another source of employment in the district. The flooded area has now been drained, and the Express Dairy stands about where the buildings on the left appear.

116. The burgesses of the Borough had the right to graze cattle on The Rye, and cows could often be seen strolling down the High Street after being turned off this grazing area by the Hayward in the evening. They wended their way through the back alleys until they arrived at their home dairy or stable at milking time.

117. The flour mills depended on the grain grown in the area. This 1905 photograph shows Bowerdean Farm nestled in the valley, surrounded by ploughed fields. This landscape has now changed – it is covered with houses and streets, and the public house *Morning Star* stands where the farmyard once flourished.

118. The Rope Walk in Wycombe Rope Factory has a history dating back to Richard the Corder, who died in 1361, and C. J. Young's of Paul's Row were ropemakers as early as 1836. This photograph of the 1940s indicates the length of the process – often 800ft. long rope walks were housed in low buildings which were roofed over but open at the sides.

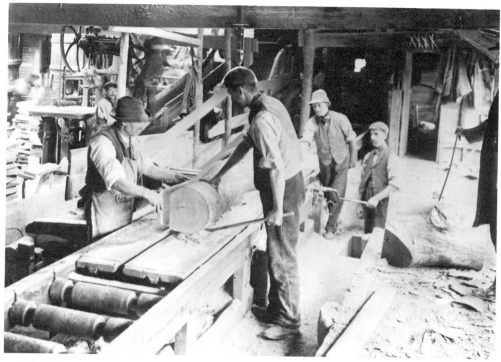

119.   The woods and forests around Wycombe were used for timber. This photograph of Thomas Towerton's sawmills at Stokenchurch shows the conversion of tree trunks into planks using the circular saw, with the man on the right cranking the trunks along in time with the saw.

120.   Mechanisation started in earnest at Plumridge's in Denmark Street in 1904 with the use of this magnificent band saw. This machinery enabled the sawyers to convert into planks trees of much greater size than was possible with the circular saw.

121.   The most popular cottage industry in the early to mid-19th century was the making of Bucks bobbin lace, and a familiar sight was the lacemaker at the door with her lace pillow in position. Here is Mrs. Betsy Ray in her widow's weeds, posing for a photograph *c*.1910. In 1862 William Gilbert, lace merchant of High Street, High Wycombe, reported that he had 3,000 outworkers who regularly made lace for him.

122. The lace industry was struck a death-blow by the introduction of lace-making machinery, but the local women quickly turned to the furniture factories and took over the craft of chair-seat caning and seat-rushing to supplement their husbands' meagre wages. This, like lace-making, could be done at home, often with the schoolchildren collecting the cane and chair-seats on their way home from school.

123. Darvill's mill, generally known as Marsh Green mill, was a paper mill, and papermaking was an important industry on the Wye from the 17th to 20th centuries. Directories show that people living in the area were employed as papermakers, but also as rag-sorters and paper-pickers, who helped in the process of turning the discarded rags or waste-paper into the raw material to be converted into paper pulp.

124.   The firm of R. H. Hulls were engineers and brassfounders from 1880, but had changed in 1909 to W. H. Hulls. The workforce is seen here exhibiting the massive products of their craft. They were employed in Easton Street where private houses were being converted into commercial premises.

The Furniture Industry

125. The bodgers, or chair-leg turners, worked in the beechwoods around High Wycombe, setting up temporary shelters in which to work on the pole-lathe. Outside, two other workers are seen preparing the rough chair-legs ready for completion by the turner for the factories in the town. This view was taken in 1905; the craft continued into the 1930s until mechanisation overtook the hand-craft workers.

126. A turner worked within his thatched hut, using a pole-lathe, a machine unchanged since the 13th century. It was essential that he make identical chair-legs, as they were sold to the factory by the gross and only matched into sets of four when the chair parts were fitted together by the framer.

127. The pit-sawyer worked over a pit dug into the woods. The top-man guides the 7ft. sawblade down to the pitman, whose head just shows below the tree trunk in this 1905 photograph. He returns the saw to the 'up' position. The terms 'top-dog' and 'under-dog' come from this operation, as the pitman's job was the more uncomfortable.

128. The chair-legs were taken to factories in High Wycombe, such as this timber-covered building with chair-waggons being loaded up in the yard. These factories were real fire hazards.

129. Many of the factories were small, employing only one or two men, but others, such as that of Thomas Glenister, shown here in 1902, were vast. This furniture firm was established in 1839 and is still in business. At the beginning of the 20th century it supplied a large number of chairs and stools for the coronation of Edward VII.

130. Chair seats were cut from planks sawn in the saw-pits, and these were in turn shaped or 'bottomed' by the bottomer to make them more comfortable. This was a hazardous process as the adze used was razor sharp; heavy boots and gaiters were worn for protection.

131. The polishing shop was usually on the first floor and was kept warm by a stove, essential to keep the polish flowing. Some chairs went out polished, but many left on the chair-waggons unstained, and were called 'Wycombe whites'.

132.   There are many posed photographs of the furniture craftsmen; this one is of the workforce of Henry Goodearl of West End Road in 1886. Several of the men are wearing their 'breast-bibs' which were wooden shaped supports that enabled them to press down hard when using the handbrace.

133.   A more recent group from Ercol Furniture Ltd. in 1925. This company was started by Lucian Ercolani in 1920, and has grown and introduced the 'Windsor' style of furniture into the modern home.

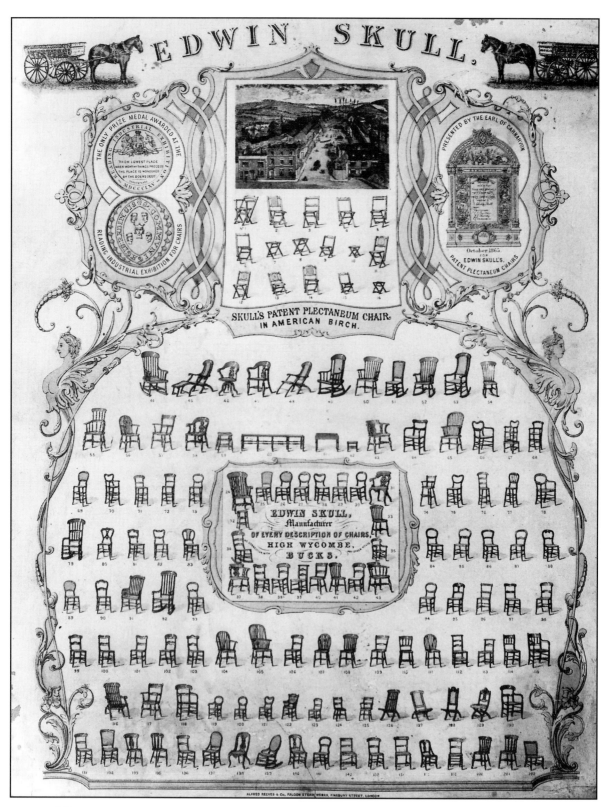

134. This broadsheet of Edwin Skull dates from *c.*1865 and advertises the wide range of chairs he was able to supply. By using a design which incorporated similar items of chair parts into various styles of chair, and by employing mass production from the 1850s, it was possible to have up to 200 varieties of chairs available at short notice.

135. A certificate of membership of the High Wycombe Chairmakers' Protection Society, founded in 1855. The Latin motto means 'We stand for the right to work'.

136. An important worker in the chair industry was the 'framer' who selected and matched the chair parts and assembled them. Here Jack Goodchild, a well-known craftsman in the Wycombe area, is shown completing a bow-backed Windsor chair in his workshop.

137. The fame of High Wycombe and its chairs spread across the countryside, and it is not surprising that an enterprising musician composed a humorous song to be performed in the musical halls of the mid-1920s.

JURKINS OF WYCOMBE

a song
with words and music
by Cecil Sparkes

They sings lots o' songs about varmers and such,
And folks in the country what never do much,
'Cept diggin' up turnips and makin' of hay,
And they tells you, you ought to be thankful to they,
For sending you up all the good thing they grows,
What fattens you up from head to your toes,
But never a word do they sing about me,
Although I supports you its easy to see.

I'm Jurkins of Wycombe, High Wycombe in Bucks,
Where I lives with mi' wife and mi' fowls and mi' ducks,
And I turns up the spindles and makes all your chairs,
Aye! I guess I'm the man at the seat of affairs.

I makes chairs of all patterns and chairs of all styles,
And most of 'em travels some 'undreds of miles.
Chippendale for the ladies what like to look smart,
And good old Brown Windsor for the plain simple heart.
A chair for the wife and the mother-in-law,
I makes 'em so comfy they'll sleep and not jaw.
For newly rich golden seteess carriage hung,
And for lovers, "The Grand" cast iron legs, overstrung.

I'm Jurkins of Wycombe, High Wycombe in Bucks,
Where I lives with mi' wife and mi' fowls and mi' ducks,
And I turns up the spindles and makes all your chairs,
Aye! I guess I'm the man at the seat of affairs.
And whether you're high-born, or proud as can be,
You'd all look very "low" if it wasn't for me.

Markets and Shops

138.   The Little Market House or 'pepper-pot', as it is affectionately called, was built in 1761 to designs by Robert Adam. This drawing of 1880 shows it with joints of meat hanging from iron bars fitted between the arches, and market traders with their small piles of produce for sale.

139.   The cattle market took place in the paved area behind the Guildhall in Paul's Row, but it must sometimes have overflowed into Church Street, for here in 1891 A. Timms the butcher has a fine group of cattle standing before his butcher's shop.

140.   An annual event was the 'hiring fair' which took place around the Guildhall, during which men and women would be hired by employers for the coming season. Each would carry a sign indicating his trade, the carter a piece of whipcord, the shepherd a tuft of wool and the cowmen would stick a tuft of cow's hair in their hats. On being taken on, the future employer would give them a shilling, which they would promptly spend at a local public house or at the fair in Oxford Road. The hiring fair carried on until about 1908.

141.   The cattle market witnessed a strange sale in January 1824 when a man led his wife with a rope and halter around her neck into the sale ring. She was sold to a blacksmith who had offered 10s. for her 'as she stood' and the collector of tolls demanded 1d. for the sale of livestock.

142. As well as the cattle market there were also a large number of stalls selling vegetables, flowers, domestic and luxury goods which stretched from the Guildhall almost up to Easton Street. Fortunately the wide expanse of the High Street makes it possible. No wonder the town was earlier called 'Chepping Wycombe', as the word 'Chepping' means market.

143. A very festive show was put on by McIlroys and by Stevens in Church Street, on the corner with Castle Street, in honour of the 1937 coronation of George VI. G. E. Stevens was a coal and corn merchant, and for many years held out against selling his site to the large store next door. Eventually Stevens sold to Marks & Spencer, and the present building was erected.

144. At Christmas each year, Aldridges in White Hart Street put on a special display which drew many spectators. Turkeys, chicken and game were hung all over the building with even the occasional pig suspended from eaves or from hooks on the walls. This photograph was taken in 1931. Today Country Fashions stands on the site of this shop.

145. John R. Dring, draper and outfitter on the corner of Church Street and White Hart Street, stood in a prominent position. This building was originally an ancient inn called *Chequers*. In recent years it was demolished and rebuilt in identical form following a long enquiry due to its protected status.

146. Navarino House stood on the site of the present W. H. Smith & Sons, and was the main lace depository in the district. In the 1860s, when Thomas Gilbert was in charge, over 3,000 outworkers made lace for the business.

147. When Corporation Street was opened in 1901, Lloyds Bank was built on the left hand corner, and Davenport Vernon's ironmongery and garage on the right hand corner. This new street was built to ensure easy access to the railway station from the High Street, as the narrow Crendon Street was so frequently blocked by traffic.

148. Chas. H. Berry, jeweller, was proud of his date of establishment of 1775, although this was on another site, as the public house the *Antelope* stood here at 12 High Street until 1813. This shop remained untouched until the business was sold in 1987/8, and the present owner has kept its Victorian façade, shown in this photograph of 1894.

149. The small hand-delivery cart of Frank Cross is typical of many of the early part of this century. His dairy was in Kitchener Road, and butter and eggs were available from the roundsman as well as milk. Cross Dairy was in business from *c.*1912-30, and this photograph was taken around 1920.

150.   Goodman's Corner lies opposite the Guildhall at the top of High Street and, in addition to being the post office at one time, has been occupied by various tradesmen over the years. A. Goodman was a seedsman and fruiterer.

The Borough & the 'Foreigns'

151.   The entrance into the town from Marlow was through St Mary Street, one of the older streets with many late 17th- and 18th-century houses mixed in with the Victorian buildings. The church tower can be seen in the distance, as the street leads into Paul's Row and then into Church Street.

152.   With the demolition of 17th- and 18th-century houses in St Mary Street, nostalgia is roused when recalling this archway which led to Lily's Walk, one of the most popular 'lovers' lanes' in the borough.

153. The winding alleys of Newland contained many small shops, rows of terrace houses back to back and numerous public houses. Here lived the workforce necessary for the furniture factories. The name reminds us that the meadows the 19th-century houses cover were 'new land' acquired in the medieval period.

154. The River Wye ran alongside the houses in Oxford Road in the 1890s and even up to the 1950s when the houses could be reached by the bridge and iron posts prevented pedestrians from falling in the river.

155.   Further into the industrial area was Desborough Road, with its shopping centre trying to compete with the town facilities. The various factories, schools, churches and small dwelling houses lead off into what only a few years earlier had been farming land.

156.   From Hughenden the entrance into High Wycombe is through Frogmore, where the fountain played such an important part in the lives of its inhabitants. The original central area had been laid out as private gardens, but in 1877 Mr. J. O. Griffits purchased the site, paved it with York stone and installed the fountain, trees and seats. The fountain was removed during the Second World War as metal for munitions, and more recently the paved area has been remodelled to fit in with the modern view of pedestrian gardens.

157. High Street in the 1840s: an oil painting by E. J. Niemann. This gives an impression of spaciousness which has been lost since the introduction of pavements, street lamps and vehicles. The trees on the left mark the space next to the *Three Tuns* where buildings were erected on a garden area.

158. High Street in the 1930s still shows the elegance of this Georgian thoroughfare. The Guildhall stands firmly at the western end, forming part of the Cornmarket, with the high roof of White Hart Methodist chapel, later demolished to become Murrays Store, rising beyond it.

159. Moving down Easton Street, the building on the right was the *Greyhound* public house, and in the distance is the stonework of the Rupert Gates with High Street. This dates the view to about 1895, and the inn sign on the left is that of the *Cow and Hare*, one of six public houses in Easton Street which are now all gone.

160. London Road, which is now the A40, enters High Wycombe along the old toll road which was constructed in 1718, following the line of the River Wye. This view of 1910 shows the width of the river at that time, as it flowed swiftly from its source near West Wycombe down through the Wye Valley past over 30 watermills to enter the Thames at Hedsor.

161. The river continues along London Road out of town to Wycombe Marsh, crossed by wooden bridges. This photograph was taken just beyond the junction with the road from Wooburn.

162. Crendon Street leads into Amersham Hill, past the railway station and Totteridge Road, which were roughly on the Borough boundaries; beyond this were the 'foreigns'. Amersham Hill was built up with fine large houses from the late years of the 19th century into the 1960s.

163. Amersham Hill leads into Terriers, a small village which was really a group of cottages clustered at the top of the hill, which continued to the toll gate standing next to Terriers First School. The toll road ran from Hatfield to the Bath Road near Reading; its aim was to give easier access to Bath Spa where the fashionable went to take the waters.

BooD Test →

THE RSPB BOOK OF
THE
BIRDWATCHING
YEAR

THE RSPB BOOK OF

THE BIRDWATCHING YEAR

Edited by Sylvia Sullivan

First published 1989

© *Sylvia Sullivan and the RSPB 1989*

British Library Cataloguing in Publication Data

The RSPB book of the birdwatching year.
  1. Birds
  I. Sullivan, Sylvia
  598

  ISBN 1-85336-100-3

*Equation is an imprint of the Thorsons Publishing Group,
Wellingborough, Northamptonshire, NN8 2RQ, England*

Printed in Great Britain by Butler & Tanner Limited,
Frome, Somerset

10 9 8 7 6 5 4 3 2 1

CONTENTS

INTRODUCTION 7

A NORTHERN JANUARY by Wincey Willis 9
From snow-covered moorland to Teesdale and Lindisfarne, Wincey Willis explores
some of the best birdwatching areas near her home on the Durham/Yorkshire
borders.

FEBRUARY IN FRANCE by David Tomlinson 27
Red wine, black woodpeckers and white-tailed eagles are irresistible lures for this
experienced and widely travelled birder.

MARCH AT MINSMERE: THE ARRIVAL OF AVOCETS AND SPRING 43
by Jeremy Sorensen
Warden of the RSPB's most famous reserve, Jeremy Sorensen witnesses the arrival of
avocets and remains optimistic in the face of storm damage.

APRIL: GREEK CYPRUS IN SPRING by Bill Oddie 63
An island renowned for its hunting and shooting, rather than its birdwatching, but Bill
Oddie is delightfully surprised.

THE PYRENEES IN MAY by Rob Hume 81
The mountains of Spain are the home of vultures and birds of prey. Rob Hume leads
a group of birdwatchers through some spectacular scenery and magical moments.

JUNE: A SCOTTISH QUARTET by Sam Kennedy 101
The mountains of Ben Lawers: Lomond in the Gloamin'; Summer daze and Bass
special.

WELSH WOODLANDS IN JULY by John Andrews 121
High summer and the countryside is quiet save for the gurgle of streamlets that wind
through moorland down woodlands and into valleys, but John Andrews sees the
birdlife of the area.

AUGUST AT SPURN: THE BRIDGE ACROSS SUMMER by Michael Clegg 141
Seawatching becomes the 'zen of birdwatching': some exciting vagrants, a misguided
goose and an Antipodean problem.

SEPTEMBER: SWANS OF A DIFFERENT FEATHER by Jim Crumley   159
A song of two swan tribes: one half tame, the other very wild.

OCTOBER: ISLAY, ISLAND OF GEESE by Malcolm Ogilvie   173
Skein after skein of wild geese — thousands upon thousands of wild birds winter on
Islay. Malcolm Ogilvie describes their arrival.

A NOVEMBER JOURNEY FROM THE FENS TO ANGLESEY by John Day   189
From flood meadows through moorland to estuary and cliff — a wide variety of
habitats ensures good numbers of birds.

DECEMBER: VOYAGE SOUTH TO SUMMER by Keith Shackleton   205
Penguins, albatrosses and snow petrels — extraordinary birds in a beautiful and fragile
habitat.

INTRODUCTION

When I was asked to put this book together, my first thoughts were of the people who had imparted some of their own enthusiasm for birds and birdwatching to me. I thought of those who had made me smile and laugh, brought a new turn of phrase, left me sometimes in awe of their vast wealth of knowledge and experience, yet who had a kindly eye for those eager to learn more, and an ability often to leave one with a little food for thought.

Anyone who loves the countryside and its wildlife knows only too well that no matter what the time of year, there is always something of interest to be seen — as timeless perhaps as the changing colour of leaf and hedgerow, the arrival of new birds and the departure of others. The change of the seasons from month to month gives a rhythmical pattern to life that appears infinite — it has been going on since time began and will, we fervently hope, continue unchanging. This book mirrors some of the beauty and delight that birdwatchers find in the world around them, from month to month.

Leaving the choice of time and place, as far as possible, to the individual authors themselves, has guaranteed a wide and unusual geographical spread. And when their contributions came in I was not disappointed. In each I found the spark of recognition, of empathy, whether of mood, or place or bird.

Television presenter Wincey Willis starts off the year in the area close to her home on the Durham/Yorkshire border. Wincey has an active enthusiasm for birds and a practical turn too — she even did a spell as a voluntary warden at the RSPB's reserve on Islay, helping to rebuild the drystone walls. For February, often one of the bleakest months of the year, weather-wise, David Tomlinson takes us to the fringe of the Paris basin, and a taste of the good life — wine, woodpeckers and white-tailed eagles . . .

Then in March we return to England to one of the best birdwatching areas in the country, the RSPB's famous reserve of Minsmere in Suffolk. We savour a taste of a warden's life, as Jeremy Sorensen shares his excitement, watching the arrival of the avocets at the start of the breeding season. I admired his optimism in the face of the terrible damage wrought by the gales of October 1987; the scars will take so long to heal. After so many years of hard work on the reserve, the loss of countless loved trees must have been nearly heart-breaking for him, but with typical generosity of spirit, he claims 'It's not so bad for us living here; we can come to terms with it . . . but I feel sorry for our visitors — to them it's a nasty shock'.

As April approaches, we are jet-setting again, to a place that not everyone would rate high on their birdwatching list — Greek Cyprus, where migrating birds are shot in *millions*. Perhaps after reading Bill Oddie's chapter (and nice words about the RSPB — thanks Bill!) they will change their mind. Bill is a widely travelled birder and his unique blend of irreverent humour and passionate concern for nature conservation make his observations on Cyprus both amusing and thought-provoking: 'I shall never entirely comprehend why this destruction of what I would have thought is surely evidence of God's wondrous handiwork if ever there was one should be so relished in countries which purport to be as deeply religious as those round the Mediterranean.'

By contrast with Cyprus, the Pyrenees between France and Spain is a region well loved by birdwatchers and Rob Hume's evocative descriptions will take you soaring with the vultures, kites and lammergeiers and holding your breath as a wallcreeper flashes moth-like along the grey rockface to its nesting site. Magic stuff and all on an RSPB tour too!

June in Scotland becomes a poetic quartet of impressions by Sam Kennedy, culminating in a view of the Bass Rock, white with gannets, while for July, John Andrews wanders through the Welsh woodlands and uplands in search of pied flycatchers, redstarts, dippers and red kites.

Time moves on to August, and the birds are on the move too — flying down the coast watched by broadcaster Michael Clegg. I can hear his rich Yorkshire tones, brimming with good-humoured fun and see the twinkle in his eye as he describes seawatching as 'having a lot of zen about it'! Any birdwatcher knows *exactly* what he means! You must read too the story of the budgerigars and I can just picture the embarrassment of the misguided Egyptian goose . . .

As autumn commences, Jim Crumley's words of Scottish swans reflect the stately serenity of the birds themselves. It is a piece with a beautiful and ordered structure that harmonizes with both birds and countryside. From the unhurried swans, we gather momentum for the urgent excitement of migration. October heralds the arrival of the barnacle geese on Islay — up to 20,000 of them! Malcolm Ogilvie describes their dramatic landing after they flight in from Greenland to winter on the RSPB's reserve at Loch Gruinart. Islay is a wintering ground for many other birds too, which gave me a marvellous excuse to raid the Society's files of black and white photographs for some rather obscure subjects!

November. The year is nearing its end, but for John Day it is the beginning of a journey. He takes us from one RSPB reserve, the Ouse Washes (spectacularly in flood), right across country to South Stack on Anglesey, another of the Society's reserves. It gives him (and us) a chance to see a good many birds.

From an overland journey to a sea voyage. Although many people daydream of spending Christmas away from home, of going south to winter like the swallows and martins, most of us would probably stop with them somewhere in Africa. Keith Shackleton, however, chooses the Arctic tern as his model and follows it right into Antarctica! I was particularly pleased that Keith was able to write a chapter for this book. His marvellous paintings are deservedly renowned and the simple eloquence that accompanied the illustrations in his book *Wildlife and Wilderness* is again obvious here. Like the other authors in this book he is writing about what he knows and loves. We can share his admiration for the massive ice-sculptures, see the penguins leaping ashore and watch the fur seals and slug-like elephant seals vying for supremacy. Perhaps we can come a little nearer to understanding why there must be international effort to ensure the future of this last, great wilderness. We have but one world . . .

This book wasn't intended to be about bird or wildlife conservation as such, but it is inevitable that those who find pleasure and a lifting of the spirit in nature should care about its future. It wasn't intended to be a book about the RSPB or RSPB reserves, but it is no doubt significant that the Society features quite highly in it. Certainly it was a smashing book to put together; and the contributors themselves enjoyed writing it. I hope you enjoy reading it.

SYLVIA SULLIVAN

JANUARY
A NORTHERN JANUARY
WINCEY WILLIS

Wincey Willis on Islay.

Writer and television broadcaster WINCEY WILLIS started life as a travel courier
before moving into local radio. Her first television appearance was due to her
overriding interest in the animal world. Her cottage on the Durham/Yorkshire border
is home to nearly fifty animals and for several years she ran a wildlife hospital. Wincey
writes regularly on conservation topics and has a weekly column on Oracle on the
Teletext service

As a North-Easterner living in semi-exile in London, I really appreciate going back home. Those who have yet to visit the area still tend to think of slag heaps and back-to-back houses, only populated by grubby pigeons and coughing starlings. It's not like that, honestly!

Vast areas of countryside can be reached in comparative ease. We do have traffic jams, but there are still masses of open spaces to feast the eye and nurture the soul. Admittedly January may not always be the most favourable month in which to indulge your yearnings. The eastern coast is frequently battered by gale-force winds and harsh rain and sleet. It's a hardy life as a northern bird freak. The moorlands are often the first to disappear under a blanket of snow. 'Roads closed west of Bowes' is a familiar winter's cry from the traffic and weather reports.

Despite the severity of the climate, there is still a lot of activity if you know where to look. If you don't mind freezing or dressing really warmly to avoid the problem it is often easier to spot birds and mammals at this time of the year. The deciduous trees are devoid of leaves so silhouettes are more obvious and snow makes a perfect, camouflage-free backdrop. There are some beautiful rivers in the north, and when the frost takes over, the sights can be breathtaking.

The River Tees is one of my favourite hunting grounds. Over the last few years, it has become one of the area's success stories. The quality of a river affects all its wildlife, and the Tees was a major blackspot. Pollution choked the life from its waters, plants and animals became rarer sights each year but tighter controls were enforced and the stricter monitoring of industrial discharges have worked wonders. It is of little use to legislate for controls without the co-operation of the people it affects. Some good work has been done in this area and everyone benefits.

My cottage is on the Durham/Yorkshire border. A tributary of the Tees flows through my neighbours' land. The senior member of the family, who is in his eighties, has seen the decline, but did not give up. When I first moved there eight years ago he took me to see the salmon spawning ground he was creating!

Kingfishers are not that common along the lower valley of the River Coquet, but can be seen with a bit of luck. In very hard winter weather, they will move out to the coast (Michael W. Richards, RSPB).

Confidence paid off, and there are now regular reports of salmon returning to the Tees. It's only a matter of time before they take advantage of his hospitality.

One of my favourite birds is the dipper. I'm always impressed by its tenacity. How can such a fragile-looking creature make its home in the teeming icy torrents? Dippers are to be found well spaced out along the length of the Tees in my area. Defying gravity, they cling to the river bottom, walking upstream, head down in search of food. Even at this early part of the year, this little miracle has reproduction on its mind. The courtship display starts in late January, the splendid white breast playing a major role in the performance. Lots of extravagant posturing, bowing and wing quivering make it look like a wind-up toy. You'll rarely see a dipper far from water, sometimes it even nests under waterfalls.

One of the most spectacular falls in the area is 'High Force'. Breathtaking at anytime but devoid of a mass of tourists its magnificence is so much more apparent in January. Pay a visit and stand in awe of the forces of nature. Strain your ears over the roar of the falls and listen out for the 'zit-zit-zit', the most common call of the dipper. Walk down the banks of the Tees and look out for favourite dipper rocks. At 70 feet (23 m), High Force is the highest waterfall in England. Travel four miles (6 km) west and you'll see the largest cataract in England. Cauldron Snout cascades 200 feet (66 m) down the rock faces. However, it is not so accessible as High Force and at this time of the year the whole of this area can be extremely dangerous. The weather changes dramatically; even a slight change in altitude could mean totally different conditions. High Force often freezes and that's a sight worth freezing yourself for.

Middleton in Teesdale is the nearest town. Over 100 years ago, the area was riddled with working lead mines: now quarries provide the hard rock for road building. On your way to High Force, pause to savour the magnificence of the beech woods in winter. The bare trees allow the winter light to invade the heart of each wood: such a sharp contrast to the dark depths of summer. The smoothness of the bark makes more difficult work for the green woodpecker. Its ground activities are often curtailed by hard frost and it depends even more on fallen rotting wood

This whole area of Upper Teesdale is spectacular and is now part of a National Nature Reserve, which is world famous but the number of visitors increases each year and it is a sad fact that the popularity of the area is likely to destroy it. Not everyone who comes here treats the place with respect. Litter is a grave problem and still people are stupid enough to try and pick the rare flowers. Over-use of pathways is also a problem. Despite the rarities to be found in this area and the unique land formations, drainage and development have also taken their toll. A major cause of controversy in relatively recent times was the construction of Cow Green Dam itself. Completed in 1970, it was a disaster for local conservationists and many sites of vital importance are now under water. Valiant attempts were made to save as many rare plants as possible, by transplanting them to suitable sites.

As the population increases and industry flourishes, the demand for water grows. The creation of a great expanse of water like this causes problems with the increasing number of visitors wanting to partake in water-related leisure activities and the drowning of special flora but it has to be said that the water also attracts many additional birds to the area. One of the advantages of a January visit is the isolation: only hardy souls will be found there then.

Never far out of sight in the countryside hereabouts are the linear monuments to local craftsmen, the dry stone walls. A dying art, it is still a feature of the local agricultural shows. Fierce competition takes place at these annual gatherings. These man-made fortresses shield a host of plants and animals from the worst of winter's ravages. An old stone-waller once told me his secret of successful walling: 'Never put a stone down. Once you've picked it up, find a place for it.' If you've ever tried it you'll know it's not that simple. When partially snow covered, it is apparent how much skill it takes. The ledges of snow highlight the intricacy of the waller's art. The plants cling onto imperceptible rootholds and many birds find food in the myriad of spaces left by the jagged edges. Sit in your car for a while alongside and you'll be amazed at the activity. One of the most deadly predators for its size, the weasel, frequently lives among the cracks and crannies. This animal has suffered for centuries from ill-founded persecution.

for food. Sound seems to carry even further on these cold winter days, and the woodpeckers can sound deceptively close. Tradition has it that the woodpecker used the magic of the small fern, moonwort, to make its beak so sharp it could even pierce iron. In January the ground is often as hard as iron, so it needs it. Ivy clings on through whatever the season throws its way. Every leaf will be searched before the winter's over. The jay's exotic plumage stands out even more against the winter backdrop. If you're lucky you'll witness its frantic search for food hidden around the wood in more abundant times.

Also in this area now is the Cow Green Reservoir. The rarest alpine plants in the country, are to be found here. They are at home, with the fells reaching over 2,000 feet (660 m). The Widdy Bank Fell Nature Trail allows visitors to see these plants which have grown here continuously for 10,000 years. The glacial retreat left a landscape which has remained relatively unchanged since the arctic conditions gave way to warmer climes.

Left *Female great spotted woodpecker; the species breeds on the Rosa Shafto Reserve near Spennymoor* (Dennis Green, RSPB).

Above *A dying art — repairing a dry stone wall: 'Never put a stone down. Once you've picked it up, find a place for it.'* (Neville Turner).

Right *Tiny, but an intrepid predator, the weasel finds shelter amongst the nooks and crannies of the stone walls* (S.C. Porter, RSPB).

In the shelter of the old walls, ash trees can be found. The large, black buds stand out on this British tree. It's the tree that spends the least time bedecked in foliage, always the last to sprout leaves and the first to lose them, heralding the autumn. Legend has it that the ash was the only tree in the Garden of Eden that the snake was afraid of. It is perhaps for that reason that people traditionally made ashwood staffs to protect themselves. Flocks of small finches alight to rest briefly before continuing their almost-ceaseless search for food. The rough pasture hosts the thistle so sought after by our smallest finch, the goldfinch. Incidentally it was this bird which represented the first major success in the RSPB's work. Before the Society's intervention, millions of these birds were trapped for the songbird trade.

Left *A goldfinch feeding on teasel, a favourite food plant. Its fine beak can probe between the prickles to prise out the seeds* (Ardea photographics).

Below *The hardy local breeds of sheep are known worldwide* (Neville Turner).

In this rugged landscape, so often under deep snow, don't be surprised if you meet up with skiers around upper Teesdale. I've often wished I could ski, or at least, that I owned a pair of snow-shoes. It is not easy being a naturalist here. At any time of the year this can be an inhospitable place, but in January you can feel you are in the Arctic. The scrubby quality of the land makes sheep farming the most obvious source of income. The hardy local breeds are known world-wide. Heavily pregnant ewes, like giant walking snowballs, cluster together in any shelter they can find.

How anything survives a winter on the moors, always astounds me. The short-eared owl can often be seen in broad daylight using every available second of hunting time. The vole, its favourite food, is often hidden under snow, so small birds weakened by lack of food, are eagerly taken. The spectacular purple display of summer heather is also under a white blanket. Heather, the plant which so many people treasure as a lucky charm, is not so lucky itself. This plant so essential to wildlife, is rapidly disappearing. In the last forty years, some thirty square miles have

A flock of golden plovers, a breeding bird of the high moors. In winter look for flocks feeding with lapwings on lowland pastures (R. Williams, RSPB).

gone from the North Yorkshire Moors. Sheep farming and grouse shooting maintain the moors. As opposed as I am to killing anything for fun, I must concede that in many areas, it is the finance gained from the activities of the 'Glorious 12th Brigade' which keep the moor alive. It's a shame the money can't come from government.

Good shepherding is also vital. The sheep when controlled, stop the heather from becoming too lank. The correct management of the 'Strip Burning', programme most ensures the regeneration and continuation of this habitat. Fresh new growth springs up rapidly after the burn. The curlew, lapwing, merlin, snipe and golden plover all benefit from the variety this creates. Of course, in January, it is often difficult to distinguish the strips. Prolonged severe frost and snow are lethal to the red grouse. The bird is unique to Britain but a close relative of the Norwegian willow grouse. Heather is the staple diet and to reach it, whole groups of birds can be

Left *The spectacular purple display of heather is under a white blanket. Red grouse feed on the heather shoots, and grouse-shooting and sheep-farming maintain the moors* (Neville Turner).

Below left *Roe deer are shy and timid, but their barking cry can be heard in Thrunton Woods, whose mature woodland is a haven to all kinds of wildlife* (S.C. Porter, RSPB).

Right *The crossbill is among our earliest nesters — its breeding season begins at the end of January* (F.V. Blackburn, RSPB).

seen performing a sort of scratching dance. They also tread during snow storms to avoid being buried. When the surface is frozen they can't gain access to the heather. One extremely severe winter, a few years ago, the grouse were dying *en masse*. One local farmer, who stood to lose a lot of money from the likely poor shooting season to come, took action. He hired a large caterpillar vehicle and drove up and down, cracking the icy surface. The grouse is a true survivor; even when it goes to nest in April, snow is not uncommon.

On other local moors afforestation is a problem shared with many areas of the British Isles. Without careful control it has brought ecological disaster. Hamsterley Forest, however, is an example of the better kind of planting. Travel north of Barnard Castle and you'll soon discover the 5,000 acres (2,025 ha) of Forestry Commission land. The size of the area has done a lot to benefit the wildlife: roe deer, red squirrel, badger and fox are all breeding. For the ornithologist such treasures as the coniferous-loving crossbill, goldcrest and siskin are to be found. Sensibly, many areas of broadleaved woodland have been retained and Pennington Beechwood is one of the highest in the country. The spruce, pine and larch all supply timber for paper, chipboard, fencing and pit props. Visitors

are encouraged here, with car parks and picnic areas in the fields beside Bedlam Beck. I doubt you'll have much need for the latter at this time of the year! The crossbill is a bird which has really thrived in such man-made woods. Its breeding season begins towards the end of this month, and unlike the dipper it is usually enjoying some protection from the elements in the dense evergreen foliage.

Another day, another visit. At the other end of the Tees a totally different scene awaits. Teesmouth seems to be completely industrialized, the ugly man-made eyesores dominate the skyline. Practise tunnel vision, block them out, focus your binoculars on the tidal flats and marvel. In the words of Ian Armstrong, the RSPB regional officer, 'It's a wonderful example of wildlife surviving in spite of industrial development.' Seal Sands is a haven for large numbers of waders. Many migrants use the area as a stopover food station. The spectacular shelduck is present in force, with more than 2,000 over-wintering here. The shelduck, unlike other ducks, has brilliant plumage in both sexes. It resembles a goose in gait and flight, and is often seen flying in wedge formation.

It is only through constant monitoring and campaigning by local enthusiasts that the area is

Many migrants use Seal Sands as a 'stopover' food station. The spectacular shelduck is there in force — more than 2,000 overwinter (Dennis Green, RSPB).

still available for the wildlife. It's such a vital source of food to so many species, that the significance can't be underestimated. The conservationists are to be congratulated on their vigilance. Areas such as Seal Sands are extremely vulnerable to the economic pressures of industry and government and it is especially difficult to resist industrial development in this area of high unemployment.

The Durham Wildlife Trust currently owns or leases about twenty reserves of tremendous diversity, on which good birding is to hand at all times of the year. Many of these reserves are open to non-members, although prior arrangements need to be made if you'd like to visit the Witton le Wear reserve. This 84-acre (33-ha) SSSI is the centre for many research projects. The River Wear follows the southern boundary and included in the area you'll find streams, three lakes and some shallow pools. The mixture of woodland here offers an inviting

variety of food for the many woodland and hedgerow birds present all the year round.

As the area is specifically used for education, many man-made nest sites are provided and well used by everything from tits to tawny owls. The winter is a good time to spot unusual visitors from one of the five hides on the one mile long (1.6 km) nature trail. Waders seek food and sanctuary in the nearby sewage works. A word of warning; the trail can be heavy going in the winter and the riverbank is not stable.

Between the River Wear and the town of Spennymoor, lies a reserve worth joining the trust to see. The 77-acre (31-ha) site, to the north-west of the town is a birdlover's haven. Over 94 species have been recorded on the Rosa Shafto Reserve. It's a great mixture of woodland, scrubland and plenty of low cover. The two ponds attract many of its winter visitors and residents. Great spotted woodpeckers breed here, and can be seen coming to bathe, but unfortunately, at this time of year you'll be unable to see the large warbler community. For me, the only thing that detracts from the reserve is the fact that the shooting rights have been retained.

Naturalists can't have everything! I suppose we have to be thankful that the trust is allowed to lease the area.

Put on your windproofs and prepare to be battered by strong sea 'breezes', if you visit the Blackhall Nature Reserve. The path along the 60 feet (20 m) high cliff will certainly blow the cobwebs away after a large Sunday lunch! In winter it can be quite hazardous, and if you opt for the beach access, make sure you know the tide tables. The back-to-back houses I mentioned at the beginning of this chapter are in evidence near here: once the homes were exclusively occupied by miners and their families. The history of the area is steeped in hard work and hard lives. With such high unemployment now, apparently, a constant part of the North-East, it is good to see local people using their time to preserve what is unique and good about the region. Geologists are in paradise here and the unusual formations shelter many bird and plant species.

When I was a child, one of my treats was to visit Castle Eden Dene, at the north end of the Blackhall area, a place for picnics and for fabulous adventure games. Carved out of the limestone plateau by ancient torrents of glacial melt-water, this valley still has a fast-flowing burn rushing to meet the North Sea. The area is home to the Castle Eden Argus Butterfly, one of four Lepidoptera species first caught here. The three-mile (5 km) valley has a superb mixture of woodland and an excellent variety of bird life attracted by the insect abundance. Badgers and foxes breed here, and although the winter changes the beauty of the area, it does not detract from it.

A valued 'local nature reserve' it is managed by the Peterlee Development Corporation. It was in the early nineteenth century that the Burden family, who owned the dene, started to build a series of pathways. Many local children have had their first taste of 'nature' in this special place. In such close proximity to pitheads, it is a sharp contrast to the harshness of the surroundings. Unfortunately, the closeness of the coalfields is very evident when you see the black beaches at

Despite the weather, it is good to venture out in the limited daylight hours of January (Neville Turner).

Left *The three-mile valley of Castle Eden Dene provides breeding sites for both badgers and foxes. Foxes are on the move in January as it is the mating season* (Michael W. Richards, RSPB).

Below right *Pale-bellied brent flight in; over 1,000 winter on Lindisfarne* (P.R. Perfect, RSPB).

the coastal end of the dene, but in the ravine you'll find a great variety of habitats attracting a good diversity of bird life. The 500 acres (200 ha) encapsulated in this reserve includes dense mixed woodland, limestone cliffs and lovely bridges criss-crossing the burn, while the steep sides of the ravines make it relatively sheltered. It was here as a child that I saw my first sparrowhawk make a kill. It made a profound impression on me, it was one of my first dawnings of the reality of the 'food chain'. If you are the first visitor to the dene after a snowfall you can have a great time identifying footprints. Foxes are on the move in January as it is the mating season and you are quite likely to encounter the real thing, as well as its tracks.

The whole north-eastern coastline has always been special to me. With rugged cliffs and miles of sandy beaches backed by the vital sand-dunes, it is a timeless place. The more northerly coastline is often used by film crews to make period dramas. There are many areas with virtually no evidence of the present day. Durham is a good base to start from, but don't only go south. Sneak over into Northumberland and marvel at the stark rural beauty. Lindisfarne is one of the region's favoured spots for film directors, making January one of the best months

to be there if you don't fancy ending up as a film extra! Winter is hard on Holy Island (its other name) where people have done battle with the elements since the missionaries landed in the seventh century.

Before making your conquest, make sure you know the times of the tides. The island is soon isolated by the rapid, incoming tide. The three miles (5 km) causeway and sandflat access disappears under the icy North Sea. For the birdlover, the limestone cliffs and sand-dunes of the north shore are the obvious destination. The National Nature Reserve is the only place in Britain where you can see the pale-bellied Brent geese. Over a thousand of them spend the winter here. Spoilt for quantity and quality, you'll go crazy! Wigeon, eiders, dunlin and bar-tailed godwit are just a few of the delights, on which to feast your eyes. The tidal ebb and flow gives the vast variety of bird life access to the important feeding areas. It is easy to spot all the different feeding techniques employed by each bird; many species overlap, but are rarely in direct conflict due to evolved specialization. When you sit, feeling colder than you've ever done before, it is sometimes hard to appreciate the appeal of over-wintering here.

Not far away the Farne Islands cannot be left

out of any book covering birdwatching. A world renowned reserve, it is a mecca for thousands of visitors each year and many wonderful wildlife films have been made on these islands. The ever-popular puffin has riddled the area with its nesting burrows; as many as 15,000 pairs use this as their breeding ground. The eider has its most southerly British breeding site here and another of my favourites, the kittiwake, is also found. Incidentally, talking of kittiwakes, when I used to work at Tyne Tees Television in the centre of Newcastle, I was in a privileged position to watch a rarity. From the canteen I could train my binoculars over the river, to see an inland kittiwake breeding colony. They used the old flour mill ledges, substituting this man-made 'cliff' for the natural variety. Every available inch was occupied and it's good to see the tolerance now afforded to a once-persecuted bird.

Made famous by the heroine, Grace Darling, the Farne Islands are not only known to ornithologists — St Cuthbert found sanctuary here in the seventh century and now not only is it a sanctuary for countless birds but also home to our largest wild mammal, the grey seal. It is a carefully protected area with limited access to visitors, and safe from many natural predators.

The Farnes are the most easterly outcrop of the Great Whinsill. Once part of the mainland, they became islands with the rising sea level. The other 75 miles of ancient hard rock is to be found across the north of England. In January, the area is relatively quiet but at the height of the breeding season there is more noise than you'll find at any Newcastle football match. In winter, there are no organized boat trips to the 28 islands making up the Farnes. However, the coastline around this area is always worth a visit and you can save your island hopping for the spring. There is much to see and love about this part of the world. Take any of the tiny, coastbound roads branching off the A1 and you won't go far wrong. Look out for the over-wintering whooper swans, so spectacular in flight. The variety of birds to be

found is too numerous to list, it would sound like an ornithological *Who's Who*. It is hard to imagine a more relaxing yet invigorating place, all with the magnificent backdrop of the Cheviots, but then, I must confess to a slight bias!

When the January sea air becomes too much of a good thing, turn inland from the delights of the Northumberland coast and, west of Alnwick, you'll find Thrunton Woods. The commonest breeding bird in this area is Britain's tiniest bird. The goldcrest is a veritable jewel in these parts. In a severe winter this tiny bird is very vulnerable, an insect-eater that is the first to perish through lack of food. The tiny coal tit is another resident, and along with the treecreeper is constantly on the move in search of food. The crossbill fares better whatever the weather and seems to be on the increase. This mature wood is a haven to wildlife of all kinds, including the magnificent roe deer.

Broadleaved woodlands are always worth investigating and they are relatively few and far between in Northumberland. The pink tinges of the long-tailed tits can be seen in Plessey Woods, south-west of Bedlington. Birch and oak trees are

the most prolific but there are many other native trees in the woods. The nuthatch survives at its northernmost outpost in this area while all the members of the tit family and the now-scarce hawfinch are also represented. Woodlands at Cragside, Wallington Hall and Bolam Lake Country Park are also worth a birdwatching visit: badgers and red squirrels are resident, but in January you're not likely to see the signs of their presence.

Travel upstream, if you can, by the River Coquet and travel through time. Leave behind Castle Warkworth, the impressive example of our war-loving ancestors' fortifications, mentioned in Shakespeare's *Henry IV* for the upland banks of this river flow through moor grass and marsh thistles. In summer you could watch the ring ouzel here. Alder and willow trees dominate the lower valley, while my favourite, dippers, also claim their stretch of river. Kingfishers are not

Like other waterbirds, herons suffer in hard weather, when the water freezes and they cannot fish. Like kingfishers they will move under such circumstances to open water on the coast (M.W. Richards, RSPB).

Jack snipe find winter refuge at Mount Pleasant Marsh (G. St J. Hollis, RSPB).

that common but can be seen with a bit of luck.

There are still many inland areas of great beauty and significance to visit, on the way back to Durham. You could spend the month just exploring the Cheviot Hills with their wealth of wildlife. For millions of years these winter snow-covered peaks have dominated the area. The National Park is rich in specialized flora and fauna. But if you are heading back in a southerly direction go through the now thriving city of Newcastle and across the famous Scotswood Bridge: The Shibdon Pond Nature Reserve isn't far from Blaydon, so famous for its 'races'. Almost 34 acres (14 ha) of birders' delight is there for the taking. One of the good things to come out of the region's coal mining history, are these subsidence ponds. In complete contrast to the coastal solitude, this sanctuary is in the heart of a developed area. It is because such places exist that local people, especially children, can begin to appreciate the importance of conservation,

through education and involvement. I get as excited as the next person, when I see a true rarity, but I still feel a real thrill when I see a kingfisher in an area such as this. My definition of birdwatching, is just that: I can spend a few hours absorbed by a robin's behaviour, experiencing as much pleasure as watching the antics of the Slavonian grebes along the coast. The deep ponds and ditches with reedbeds and marshy areas are full of wonder. Water rail, yellow wagtail, lesser whitethroat, grasshopper, reed and sedge warblers have all bred here, so you must return in spring. For now look out for the regular heron on guard around his favourite hunting site. Tufted duck, teal, shelduck, goldeneye and pochard spend the winter here. Remnants of the moor-like habitat remain, with heather and other associated plants in evidence.

Wetlands as such are becoming less common as each year passes. Economically they are considered useless and pressure to drain them for agriculture or development is ever present. It is therefore becoming *vitally* important to preserve the bits we have left. Mount Pleasant Marsh is another example: is to be found at the busy

The moorlands are often the first to disappear under a blanket of snow (Neville Turner).

A1/A19 junction and owned by the Central Electricity Generating Board, it is a leased reserve. The Durham Conservation Trust is keen to ensure its future. Most people speed by this reserve without ever realizing that its treasures are so close to hand. For access to the actual reserve you'll need a permit from the trust, but it's worth it to see the jack snipe and water rail which are among the winter residents. It's another example of beauty surrounded by ugliness for the CEGB's pylons dominate the site.

In winter, the lure of my log fire at my cottage is a great temptation. I must admit that my bird forays are not always great treks. Since living here, I've seen 65 different species in my immediate surroundings. With just a minor effort on my part I can increase the possibilities of an interesting encounter, by taking a walk across the adjacent farmland. I'm lucky to live in an area where the importance of the hedgerow has not been forgotten. My neighbour grows all his hedges from seed and regularly maintains the existing ones with expert hedge-laying that will last as a living monument to his skills. Corners of fields inaccessible to the plough are all planted out with saplings, providing roosts and cover for many species.

When the end of the year has been particularly bad, weatherwise, January sees a lot of field activity by the farming community. The short daylight hours are filled with the sounds of the tractor, ploughing the heavy soil, to take advantage of the winter frosts. It is a great chance to study the flying skills of those great opportunists, the gulls. I've been lucky enough to sit in the tractor cab and watch at close quarters how skilful they really are. They must have some kind of telepathy, as they soon appear from miles away, as the first furrow is turned.

Another one of the country's characters, who must also be on the same telepathic wave length, is the mole-catcher. This licensed poisoner is always in search of worms, and can often be seen following the plough, competing with the gulls for the prize. The lead gulls change position as they extract the tasty morsels, revealed in each deep-cut ridge. Great parliaments of rooks are fascinating, with their purple-black feathers catching the weak winter sunlight. How do their

How do the nests of rooks, so high in the rookeries, remain relatively intact through strong gales? (J. Lawton Roberts, RSPB).

Little owls do well in my area (S.C. Porter, RSPB).

nests, so high in the rookeries, remain virtually intact, through all the strong winter gales? Since Dutch elm disease robbed our landscape of some of its best rookeries, these adaptable birds have taken over many smaller trees. Rooks also take advantage of lambing time. As farming practice has changed and the lambing season in the lowlands is artificially accelerated, the lambs arrive much earlier than nature intended.

The scavenging crow family takes full advantage of the remains of any stillborn lambs, and the afterbirth of the healthy ones makes a welcome diet supplement in these lean times.

Great flocks of fieldfares descend to the fields to eat anything they can find. I once had more than thirty birds taking advantage of the remaining berries on the bushes at the bottom of my garden. The smaller redwing is also a regular visitor competing for the same food. The skylark's haunting song can sometimes be heard in late January; along with the curlew's, it is one of my favourite bird songs but I miss the call of 'my' corn bunting. In winter he is silent. In spring he takes his post on top of the telegraph pole and sings his head off. The sparrowhawk soon clears

the feeding hordes in the garden, only for them to return again a few minutes later. The kestrel is also well aware of my feeding station and takes advantage when he can. I watch the heron's lazy flight as he flies to his hunting spot on the stream in the next field. Pheasant and partridge grub about in the hedgerows.

When the frost is long and hard, the kingfishers on my local streams suffer great hardship. I often go down and break the ice to give them a helping hand. I was very upset when a pair I knew very well lost their nest hole. The landowner on one side of the river, felled a large number of trees. The following year we had several days of torrential rain and the bank collapsed. Once there were no viable root systems left, the bank became unstable.

Owls are said to be the non-bird-lover's favourite birds: cuddly owl toys and ornaments sell in their millions. Perhaps people are attracted to them because they have forward-facing eyes, so we can easily relate to them. The barn owl, without doubt one of our most attractive birds, is occasionally to be found hunting in daylight during the winter. The older local residents remember seeing them regularly but sightings are now extremely rare. The eastern areas of England have suffered great reductions in the barn owl populations and some re-introduction schemes have been embarked upon. Tawny owls are still to be found in my local woods and although only active at night, it doesn't take long to discover the roost. My nearest tawny suffers mercilessly from the attentions of noisy blackbirds and chaffinches while trying to get a good day's sleep. The little owl does well in my area and I often see one perched on the single telephone line which leads from my cottage to my nearest neighbour's farm. It was at the base of the telegraph pole that I found a dead one a year or two ago, another winter casualty.

I enjoy sharing my home with the birds, and despite the weather, it is good to venture out in the limited daylight hours of January and see the great variety we have in the North-East. With 35 million winter visitors to our shores it's a shame to not seek them out. January was named after the two-headed god of vigil, Janus. It is said he looked back at the old year and forward to the new. Make the most of what January has to offer and look forward to February!

FEBRUARY IN FRANCE:

RED WINE, BLACK WOODPECKERS AND WHITE-TAILED EAGLES...

DAVID TOMLINSON

6.4

David Tomlinson with Bubbles the palomino pony.

DAVID TOMLINSON was born in Kent, where he still lives with his wife and springer spaniel. His interests range from fine wine to fast cars, but his great enthusiasm is for birds and travelling to find them in distant countries. He has worked for *Country Life* magazine for the past fifteen years, where he is the environment editor.

Way back in the late 1970s rumour first reached me, very secondhand, of wintering cranes and white-tailed eagles in France, but it was not until February 1982 that I first set out to investigate. So successful was that brief expedition that I have been drawn back every year since, and February, to me, now means France.

February in Britain is far from my favourite month of the year. The cuckoo's first shout is still weeks away, while often only the lengthening day hints at the changing season. And if it is cold at home in Kent, it is often even chillier at the lakes in France, which, though they may be 240 miles (380 km) closer to the Mediterranean, are sufficiently far from the sea to have a Continental climate, with colder, drier winters and warmer, sunnier summers. The weather makes a great deal of difference to the birds we find each winter, for no two years are ever the same.

Before going any further, I had better explain exactly where the lakes are, and a little about them. The Lac du Der-Chantecoq (Reservoir Marne) and the Lac de la Forêt d'Orient (Reservoir Seine) are almost directly east of Paris. The nearest town of any size to Chantecoq is St Dizier, on the main road which links Paris with Nancy, while Orient is not far from Troyes. Both reservoirs were constructed in the late '60s for the same reason — not to provide drinking water, but to protect Paris from flooding. Sudden rises in the levels of the Seine and Marne had long left Paris vulnerable to floods, so the reservoirs were built to ensure that surplus water could be safely diverted from the rivers. Both reservoirs are very large: Chantecoq, for example, with its numerous bays and deep inlets, has a coastline, if one can use such a term, of more than 42 miles (70 km). Orient is not so large, but it too has numerous bays and inlets, more than sufficient to screen a hunting eagle from view unless you happen to be in the right spot. At the time of writing, a third reservoir is under construction and nearing completion. This new addition lies midway between the two existing reservoirs, close to the little town of Brienne-le-Château. It will be interesting to see whether, when it is flooded, it attracts even more birds or simply spreads the existing bird population over a greater area.

Floods in February affect all wildlife for good or ill (David Tomlinson).

Part of the fun, and not a little of the challenge, of our winter trips to France is getting there. So far nothing has stopped us, but it has, on occasion, been a close run thing. From a birding viewpoint, the expedition starts once the boat has left Dover. Winter seawatches can be bitterly cold affairs, but there are often good birds to be seen from the cross-Channel ferries in February. As you leave Dover, watch out for fulmars cruising the White Cliffs, as this is a species it is easy to miss in mid-Channel. There are always kittiwakes around the boat, even before it has left the harbour. In some years thousands of kittiwakes will be seen during the hour-long crossing to Calais; in other years there are relatively few. You are soon reminded that black-headed gulls are coastal, rather than sea birds by the fact that once you are more than a mile or two offshore, there are none to be seen. Usually a few herring gulls will cruise easily behind the boat, and it is important to look out for great and lesser black-backs, too; both species are rare once you start to travel inland in France.

Gannets can be the highlight of many crossings, sometimes in small, stately parties, with slow-beating, black-tipped wings contrasting with brilliant white plumage, often just single birds, plunge-diving or sitting on the sea. If the visibility is good, and you have quick eyes, you should be able to identify guillemots, razorbills and puffins from the boat. Sometimes you will have good views of small groups of auks, black and white dots bobbing on the sea, but they will drive readily as the boat approaches. Distant flying auks can be a challenge to identify, but not so the flocks of scoters. If they are all-black they must be common scoters, but if you see a flash of white in the wing, then they will be velvet scoters. The latter are rare in February, but much commoner in spring when flocks follow the French coastline as they make their way back to their Arctic breeding grounds.

However often I cross the Channel — and I do cross it frequently — I always enjoy the thrill of seeing the French coastline come closer and closer. It is difficult not to feel a tingle of anticipation at the prospect of the road ahead, and what lies in store. But before you dock in Calais, there are still good birds to see. For a while the ferry follows the coastline, and along this stretch you should look out for divers

Left *The little gull is dainty and attractive: this is an immature bird* (G. St J. Hollis, RSPB).

Below right *The dappling movement of a flock of lapwings relieves the tedium of the autoroute* (David Tomlinson).

(invariably red-throated), which can be quite numerous. And if you see a strange bird fly past, it is bound to be a great crested grebe, for many winter on this stretch of coastline. Calais harbour itself often provides a surprise or two: in most Februarys it has held a small selection of wildfowl — perhaps a couple of eiders, together with a fishing party of red-breasted mergansers. Little gulls are regular in winter, and if you try hard enough you should spot one of these dainty, attractive gulls, best picked out among the crowds of black-headed gulls not by their diminutive size (obvious though this is) but by their distinctive dark underwings.

Once off the ferry, it is well worth spending a few minutes checking the rough ground between the ferryport and the hoverport. Until recently this was a wild, environmentally productive strip of marsh, lagoon and scrub, but the Calais authorities have now reclaimed most of it. Even so, it is a favourite place to find a crested lark, or possibly a ringed plover, oystercatcher or turnstone. Kentish plovers bred here for many years, but I doubt if they still do.

Every year the drive from Calais to the lakes becomes easier as the *autoroute* extends farther south. With motorway from just south of Calais to Laon, the first 190 miles (300 km) are simple — in February this section of *autoroute* is almost deserted, with not a hint of the overcrowded cut and thrust of the M2 and M25 you left behind in England. It is the first reminder of what a big, uncrowded country France is. For much of the drive huge cornfields stretch from horizon to horizon, and apart from rooks and lapwings, there are not many birds to relieve the monotony. Kestrels hunt the *autoroute* verges just as they do in England, while there is always the occasional buzzard to watch out for. These huge fields also attract wintering hen harriers, and every year we see one or two as we speed southwards.

At the time of writing, the *autoroute* finishes at Laon, and the road to Reims can be busy. But once you are past Reims, it is easier going to Chalons, and by the time Vitry-le-Francois appears on the signposts, you know there is not much farther to go. However, the road south of Reims is very exposed, and if it is snowing (which it frequently has done during our February expeditions) drifting snow can be a problem. It only takes one jack-knifed lorry to block the road.

In 1984, it wasn't jack-knifed lorries that were

the problem, but striking lorry drivers blockading the roads. You may recall that in February of that year, the French long-distance lorry drivers fought a bitter dispute which resulted in blockades of up to sixty lorries, all parked nose to tail. Our drive south was a constant challenge of threading our way round blockades, or navigating cross-country to avoid towns it was impossible to drive through. Yes, we got there in the end, but it was an exciting journey, and one I would not care to repeat. In 1988, it was striking British seamen who nearly stopped us, but we slipped across on the hovercraft instead, sacrificing our sea-watch but at least crossing the Channel successfully.

Once past Vitry, signs for the Lac du Der-Chantecoq start to appear and one can start to think about birds again, rather than navigation. This is the home run: over the Marne, then through the forested western end of the lake. This is good barn owl country, and on more than one occasion we have stopped to admire a barn owl perched on a roadside post, or hunting the verge in slow, methodical fashion. If you have caught the 9.00 a.m. ferry from Dover, and

driven quickly, then you will be in time to see the cranes flighting in to Chantecoq to roost, but the February day is short, so normally there is no reason to stop until we reach our *auberge* in the small market town of Montier-en-Der. Over a simple meal — no *haute cuisine* here, alas — much improved by several jugs of M. Gerard's red wine, we discuss plans for the morrow. Shall we go looking for woodpeckers at first light, or watch the cranes come off the reservoir? However many times you have done it before, the prospect of the following day's birding is exciting. Will there be many cranes this year? How many eagles are wintering? We shall know the answers in just a few hours' time.

When you have visited an area on many occasions, individual years tend to blur into each other. Even so, one year does stand out above all others: 1986. Not only was it the coldest year by far, it was also the year the snow came. My diary records the first morning sufficiently well to be worth quoting: 'February 27: An amazingly cold morning: the hotel thermometer had sunk to − 16°C, but at the west end of Chantecoq at first

Chantecoq at dawn (David Tomlinson).

light it must have been at least − 20°, and as cold as I have ever been in Europe. A vicious easterly wind was blowing across the frozen reservoir, chilling us to the bone. The distant howling of timber wolves would not have seemed out of place, for it was more like the Arctic than France. Apart from a few reed buntings not a bird moved — no cranes, no eagle, no wildfowl, nothing . . .' It was a less than promising start, though we did see a beech marten, running painfully through the snow at the side of the road. With such low temperatures, the prospects looked bleak indeed.

Revitalized with hot chocolate, a beverage the French are particularly good at, plus fresh-from-the-*boulangerie* croissants, we were soon out again. By 'we' I mean a group of a dozen or so, of varying degrees of experience but of similar enthusiasm. Our base in Montier can often provide excellent birdwatching, at least by English standards. Hawfinches are remarkably common in Montier, and in cold winters they crowd right into the middle of the town, giving one ample opportunity to admire their handsome plumage and that great nut-cracker of a beak. Other typical Montier town birds include, in

winter, bramblings, siskins, nuthatches and treecreepers, though the latter is not the bird we know from home, *Certhia familaris*, but the short-toed treecreeper, *Certhia brachydactyla*. As far as I know, there is not much difference in the length of toe nails of the two species, but the short-toed treecreeper has a noticeably different call note which invariably attracts your attention.

Follow Montier's little river, the Der, through the town and it will take you down to the racetrack. This is a good place to find green woodpeckers, and there is invariably a buzzard or two to be seen nearby. The French call the common buzzard the *buse variable*, and in this part of France you readily understand why it has earned such a name. The wintering buzzards are a strange mixture of plumages. The standard, chocolate-brown buzzard familiar from home is outnumbered by curiously pale birds, some of which are almost white all over, while others simply have white heads, or pale wings. Rarely does one buzzard look like another, and many are mis-identified as rough-legged buzzards. Rough-legs do occur, though rarely: in both 1987 and 1988 a single rough-leg wintered at the west end of Chantecoq. Common buzzards are as common as their name suggests, and it is not

Above *Another typical Montier town bird is the nuthatch* (Jane Miller, RSPB).

Above *A finch familiar to British birdwatchers is the siskin* (F.V. Blackburn, RSPB).

Below *Flocks of bramblings are common sights in winter. Look for these finches feeding with chaffinches: the white, oval-shaped rump patch is a useful field mark* (Richard T. Mills, RSPB)

difficult to count as many as sixty individuals in a single day.

On the February morning in '86 there were indeed two buzzards on the racetrack, and we flushed a kingfisher and two grey wagtails on the river. The buzzards were sitting, hunched against the cold, on the steeplechase fences, no doubt contemplating the poor prospects for worm hunting that day. Many people find it hard to believe that as impressive a bird as the buzzard survives on a staple diet of earthworms, but it is true. Similarly, the diet of the red kite is somewhat unsavoury, with rubbish-tip hunting a speciality. That frozen morning there were up to four red kites soaring over the racecourse, and over the town itself. Buzzards may be rather good at soaring, but for sheer mastery of the air they are outclassed by the red kite. Watch a circling kite and you will see how its long wings and tail flex to make use of every air current.

Red kites are sufficiently common around the lakes in winter that, after a while, you start to take them for granted, and forget what rarities they are home in Britain, with only a small population in central Wales. However the number of kites do vary according to the winter's weather. In hard winters, such as '86, they are at their most numerous. In '86 we found as many as forty kites congregated on a rubbish tip to the south of Lac de la Forêt d'Orient. So many red kites together was a real treat, and almost made up for the malodorous surroundings.

In 1986, the gathering of red kites was not our only exciting experience of raptors: there were more treats in store for us on the lake itself. Orient was almost completely frozen, with just one small area of open water, crowded with around 800 mallard, a few teal and pochard, fourteen smew and five goosanders. So many birds in such a small area was bound to attract predators, and it was while we were watching the wildfowl that a large female peregrine appeared on the scene, and indulged in a series of stoops on the panicking ducks. Despite, or perhaps because of, such a number of potential targets, the falcon was unsuccessful, and after five minutes, spectacular aerial display, she gave up and flew off. There is usually at least one

Above left *A simple flexing of the tail makes the red kite effortlessly elegant in the air* (M. Wilding, RSPB).

Above *Smew — smallest of the sawbills. The two drakes are immaculate in white with fine black markings* (Hansgeorg Arndt).

Right *Teal, fast and agile in the air, nevertheless fall prey to the peregrine* (M.W. Richards, RSPB).

wintering peregrine in the vicinity of the lakes, though it is not a bird one can always be confident of finding.

For most first-time visitors to the lakes, it is the wintering sea eagles which are the greatest draw. From my halting conversations with French birdwatchers, I discovered that the first eagles were recorded way back in the early '70s, not long after the lakes were first flooded. No-one knows where the wintering eagles come from, but a safe bet would be Germany, for both East and West Germany have breeding sea eagles: so too does Norway, but the Norwegian birds are non-migratory. The French eagles arrive in early November, and usually remain until well into March, with as many as six birds in the area, though a couple of eagles on each lake is normal.

In 1986, we met a group of young French birdwatchers, who told us that there was known to be a single immature eagle wintering on Orient. This was good news, for each year there is the risk that the eagles have not come back, or that they are around but have not been seen recently. Reputations are at stake, for you do not want to admit you have been to France but not seen the eagles. We have, I am pleased to say,

seen eagles every year we have been out, which is now seven years in a row. It was shortly after watching the hunting peregrine that we saw our eagle, but not just one eagle, as we had expected, but three — two full adults with white tails, and one young bird.

For sheer size, there is not much to compare to a sea eagle. The huge, broad wings with blunt ends, and the heavy projecting head are all diagnostic even if you cannot see the white tail (which is only white in adults which are at least six years old). To see your first sea eagle is a memorable moment, and one you never forget. But impressive though it is, the *pygargue à queue blanche* (to give the sea eagle its full French name) can be a most boring bird to watch. If it has a full crop, it will sit for hours doing nothing more than surveying its domain. So it was with our 1986 trio. The three birds flew from a wooded promontory out onto the frozen lake, where they settled on the ice. Despite being teased by a pair of carrion crows, one of which went as far as tweaking the immature eagle's tail, the great birds did nothing except sit, and even the keenest birder becomes tired of watching a static eagle.

Above right *Birding at Orient* (David Tomlinson).

Left *For sheer size, there is not much to compare to a sea eagle. The huge, broad wings with blunt ends and the heavy projecting head are all diagnostic* (Colin Crooke, RSPB).

In seven years of eagle watching, the amount of action I have witnessed has been minimal. In 1982, the first year, I watched two eagles hunting ducks on Orient, but at great range and in poor light. Once, on Chantecoq, I saw an eagle stoop at a feeding flock of bean geese, but I have never been lucky enough to watch a successful hunt. However, on several occasions I have been able to watch soaring sea eagles, sometimes in company with red kites and buzzards which they completely dwarf.

If the eagles sometimes disappoint, then the cranes invariably make up for them. Impressively large (45 in, or 115 cm, from tip of beak to tip of tail), the *grue cendrée* is an elegant, active and very vocal bird. Orient and Chantecoq are favoured resting sites for migrating cranes, and as many as 11,000 birds may mass together on Chantecoq in late autumn. How many remain until February depends on the weather. December 1987 and January 1988 were exceptionally mild, so at the time of my visit in early February 1988, there were no fewer than 1,600 cranes in the area. Most were feeding in and around the western end

of Chantecoq. This lake includes several large islands, and here the cranes find sanctuary, roosting at night, and often feeding during the day. A long history of persecution means that cranes are wary birds, difficult to approach on their feeding grounds. They are protected in France, and I am pleased to say I have seen no evidence of cranes being shot, but they are no less approachable despite the lack of hunting pressure.

In 1986, by contrast, finding cranes was a problem. Snow-covered fields gave them nowhere to feed, while ice-covered reservoirs meant nowhere safe to roost. For two days we looked in vain, but it seemed increasingly likely that we were not to see a single *grue*. This was particularly worrying for me, for on the first night I had rashly bet a bottle of Chateauneuf du Pape, a favourite red wine, with a member of my party who was convinced that we would not find any cranes. I am not a gambling man; I am never tempted by the Grand National or the Derby, and can totally resist one-armed bandits. I only bet on certainties. Despite the weather, I was

Above '*Suddenly, in the far distance, came a hint of distant bugling, the wonderful call of the crane*' (W.E. Oddie).

Left *Black woodpecker, as big as a rook with a flaming red head, are the greatest draw for most British birders* (M.D. England, RSPB).

Right *In February, the colours of the landscape are muted* (David Tomlinson).

convinced we would see cranes, but as time went by and the snow got deeper, the chances seemed poorer and poorer. Lunchtime on our last day, and still no cranes. Then, suddenly, in the far distance, came a hint of distant bugling, the wonderful call of the crane. Was I mistaken? All ears were trained south. Then the marvellous sound came again, and my bottle of Chateauneuf was safe. Two minutes later, a great 'V' of cranes flew over, their trumpeting calls strident in the still, snow-covered countryside. That first chevron of birds was the forerunner of many more, until at least 700 birds had arrived: they whiffled out of the sky like giant long-legged geese, to settle on the edge of the frozen lake, where they preened, danced and continued to call.

If the cranes and eagles are the leading actors on the February stage, there are many species filling the lesser roles without which the appeal of the area would not be nearly as great. In Britain we only have three species of woodpeckers, but there is the chance of twice that number in the vicinity of the lakes. For most British birdwatchers the greatest draw is the black woodpecker, the *pic noir*, as big as a rook, with a flaming red head. I have watched black woodpeckers in Spain, Holland and Germany, as well as France, so it is a bird I know well. Sadly, I have yet to find one in the vicinity of the lakes, despite the fact there is much suitable habitat of mature beech mixed with coniferous forest. I have met a birdwatcher who had just met a birdwatcher who had seen a black woodpecker there, but first-hand records elude me. If you want to try and see a black woodpecker, then your best chance is to go north to the forested hills of the Argonne, a mere 45 minutes' drive from St Dizier.

Similar rumours suggest that there are grey-headed woodpeckers in the area. Again, there may be, but I have yet to find them. However in February there is one species we almost always find: the middle-spotted. A scarce bird through

39

Left *Wildfowl numbers are high in February. Among the species to be seen, gadwall (identified here by the white speculum) are quite numerous* (Robin Williams, RSPB).

Below left *Goldeneye — a particularly handsome diving duck* (David Tomlinson).

Right *Long lines of poplars are everywhere* (David Tomlinson).

much of its European range, the middle-spotted is slightly smaller than the great-spotted (which is the commonest woodpecker around the lakes), with a distinctively different head pattern, and a rosy pink underside. The latter is a good field mark, but hardly mentioned by any of the field guides. Both sexes have red caps. In later winter, male middle-spots proclaim their territories with a far-carrying cry unlike that of any other European woodpecker. When you hear the call the first time you wonder what on earth it is, but it is an easy, distinctive cry to learn, and will often lead you straight to your quarry. By comparison with the wary great-spotted woodpecker, the middle-spotted is much more approachable, though because it tends to feed high in the canopy it can be hard to spot.

In February 1982, firecrests were common in the woods around the two lakes. Observations in following winters suggest that numbers of this delightful little bird vary considerably from year to year. Many people who have never seen a firecrest assume it will be difficult to tell apart from the very similar-sized goldcrest, but the bold white supercilium and black stripe through the

eye make it instantly identifiable — it is a handsome gem of a bird. Firecrests are often found in mixed flocks of tits. Both marsh and willow tits are common, while the handsome crested tit is also resident, and a bird you are sure to find if you spend long enough in the forest. Flocks of long-tailed tits are numerous, but in 1987 we found a single white-headed long-tailed tit, of the northern race. Woodland birding is always rewarding, and it is in the woods that you are most likely to see a goshawk.

Of all the raptors, goshawks are the most elusive. Though I usually see one or two each year, they are never in the same place, and there is no pattern to the sightings. Luck alone decides whether you will see a 'gos'. Hard winters also bring merlins down to the lakes, but they are not a bird I expect to see every year.

Numbers of wintering wildfowl on the lakes are high, especially in the milder winters, and I suspect that numbers reach a peak in February. Certainly you should see 1,000-strong flocks of wigeon, and considerable numbers of mallard and teal. Of the other surface feeders, gadwall are quite numerous, pintail rare and shoveler seldom seen. Numbers of tufted ducks and pochard are usually no more than modest, but are more than made up for by an abundance of goosanders — I have counted up to 100 at once — and good numbers of goldeneye and smew. To see flocks of the last two species, you need a cold winter, but not so cold as to freeze the lakes over.

Every February we see small groups of wild swans, with Bewick's outnumbering the whoopers. At dusk, with the light fading, there is no more delightful sound than that of the wild swans' musical voices carrying across the lake, mixing with the deeper, more gutteral calls of the cranes. Sometimes the chorus of cranes and wildfowl is joined by the wild geese. By far the most numerous of the wintering wildfowl are the bean geese, with well over 1,000 present in a mild February, perhaps as many as 5,000 or more if the winter has been hard. It is always worth checking the flocks of grey geese carefully, for there are usually a few whitefronts and greylags mixed in, and in 1986, when the numbers of geese were the highest I have recorded, we also found a single barnacle.

Reeling off a list of the avian delights of Orient and Chantecoq is one thing, but it fails to convey the pleasure of bird watching in this attractive, rural area. No, it is not beautiful, but it is countryside with charm, and not too many people. In February the colours are muted, the grasses yellowed by frost. Long lines of poplars are everywhere, each carrying footballs of mistletoe to give the landscape a typically Gallic flavour. The extensive forests are well managed, with splendid coppices, yet they are large and wild enough to lose yourself in, or to come face to snout with a wild boar. The lakes may be man-made, but the whole area retains a wild, unspoilt flavour. Once sampled it becomes addictive, which explains why I am sure to continue my tradition of February in France. However, one challenge remains. What is the best way to get the *vin rouge* to a drinkable temperature on a freezing February day? Washing down the cheese and pâté with iced red wine is just not right. Oh well, perhaps we should change to champagne, for this is also the champagne province of France, and there is no better drink to toast a good bird with, either. What is more, it is at its best served well chilled!

THE ARRIVAL OF AVOCETS AND SPRING

JEREMY SORENSEN

Talking to a blackbird . . . (RSPB).

JEREMY SORENSEN has always been interested in birds. He learnt to ring them at school and up to 1967 he had ringed 60,000. In that year he joined the RSPB staff as an assistant warden at the Society's reserve at Leighton Moss. In April 1968 he moved to the Ouse Washes, and since May 1975 has been a familiar figure to visitors to the Society's most famous and popular reserve, Minsmere in Suffolk.

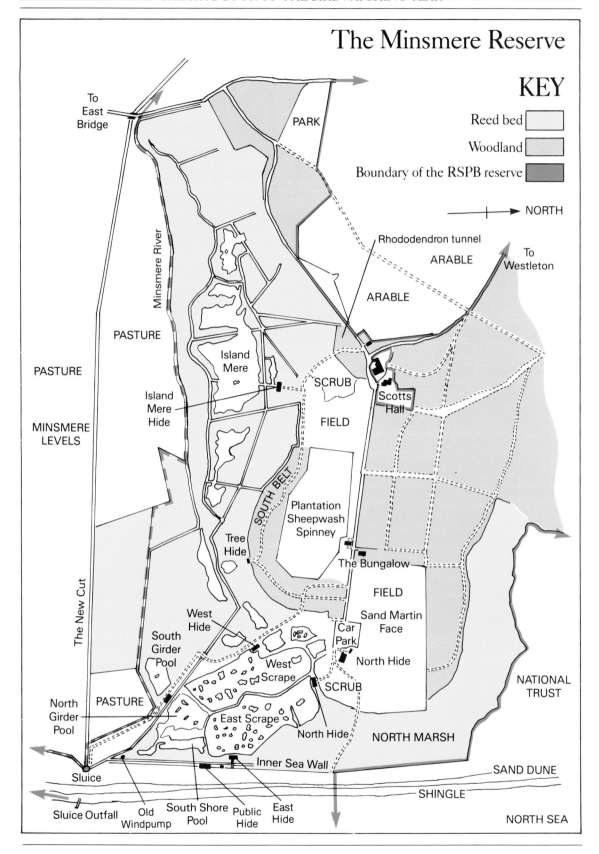

The Minsmere Reserve

KEY

Reed bed

Woodland

Boundary of the RSPB reserve

NORTH

To East Bridge

PARK

Rhododendron tunnel

ARABLE

To Westleton

ARABLE

Minsmere River

PASTURE

Island Mere

SCRUB

Scotts Hall

PASTURE

Island Mere Hide

FIELD

PASTURE

MINSMERE LEVELS

SOUTH BELT

Plantation Sheepwash Spinney

The Bungalow

FIELD

Tree Hide

The New Cut

West Hide

South Girder Pool

West Scrape

Car Park

Sand Martin Face

North Hide

North Girder Pool

PASTURE

East Scrape

North Hide

SCRUB

NATIONAL TRUST

NORTH MARSH

Sluice

Inner Sea Wall

SAND DUNE

SHINGLE

Sluice Outfall

Old Windpump

South Shore Pool

Public Hide

East Hide

NORTH SEA

This is the month of postponed anticipation: looking forward to the spring whilst winter is still with us. Is it because of this that March is a month I enjoy so much? Or is it because of those wonderful occasions during the month when we have the promise of fine things to come? Those beautiful, still, warm days few though they are when everything starts to happen. The woodland birds in full song, the ducks and waders in display, a wonderful kaleidoscope of sounds: that is what makes Minsmere in March.

March is also the month when the avocets come back, those graceful black and white birds that perform such a variety of fascinating and beautiful antics in their display and feeding activities. It is the month when the terns start to return from their winter travels to Africa; the first wheatears perch on the concrete blocks down on the sand-dunes some chilly early dawn, and the first chiffchaff is usually found singing at the top of a tall alder tree down by the rhododendron tunnel on the way to the Island Mere hide.

Today it's dull and raining, raining hard and it does not look as though it is going to stop in a hurry; cold with it too! But I love the rain! That's where one can really score on a reserve: when it is cold and wet; well wrapped up and in a hide, looking out at all the avian activity, a part of it, but without the discomfort of becoming soaked and cold together with steamed up binoculars. So here we are in the West Hide, satisfactorily comfortable and with binoculars in fine working order.

Yes, it's one of those wet, horrible days that people talk about, the kind of weather when visiting a bird reserve is the best thing one can do. Sitting in the hide watching the raindrops drop into the water, always gives me a specially contented feel; seeing the birds in comfort in such conditions. A group of seven teal just out in front of the hide — five drakes and two ducks — the drakes are displaying, calling, bobbing their heads up and down, cocking their tails and preening, lovely! Further back a pair of teal feed contentedly in the mare's tail (a common water margin plant) at the edge of the water, ignoring the activities going on behind them. To the left a little, a couple of shelduck holding territory and, further over, another group of duck a mixed flock: wigeon, shoveler and teal sitting there in the water, some asleep, some fifty duck altogether. About half of them are teal, about ten shoveler the rest wigeon. Behind them a pair of redshank

The drake wigeon are easy to recognize, with their chestnut heads and creamy foreheads (J. Sorensen).

Shelduck are one of about a hundred breeding bird species at Minsmere (J. Sorensen).

are feeding at the water's edge.

Swinging the glasses back to examine the nearby flock of teal more closely, a drake teal stretches his neck, bobs his tail and turns round, spinning in the water, raising his crest and bobbing his head again as he spreads and cocks his tail. Next to him another drake rises a little out of the water touching his breast with the tip of his beak, then, raising his head, he pushes it forward and then back down into the water and spreads his tail to show off that lovely creamy yellow, 'aren't I gorgeous!' The ducks don't look very impressed, just quacking quietly occasionally. But the drakes seem to be very pleased with what they are doing, very proud of themselves, constantly making that rather lovely whistling call. Occasionally a duck lifts out of the water and flaps its wings, to shake the rain off its feathers I suppose. They look happy enough and so am I sitting in the comfort of this hide listening to the water dripping off the roof. It's a good thing there isn't a strong wind blowing from the north-east; with all this rain I would be getting sopping wet as it blew towards the hide: the sensible thing to do in wet weather is to sit in a hide with the wind on the back! However, it's rather pleasant now with the pool in front and the small reedbed

out on the left-hand side. There are two small groups of reeds in the middle of the pool before me with the spread of islands out in front and away to the right. Looking out towards the sea wall, the reed fronds, browny yellow and leafless, blow about, weighed down with all the water, moving about from side to side slowly and heavily.

A group of snipe has got up — 27 birds; very high and changing position, slowly spreading out as they go. Then they drop fast to disappear behind an island, and flying low over the water, appear again, curving round to drop on to the mud, disappearing as they do so because their camouflage is so good. The redshanks call out to the left, *tureluur*, a clean liquid note, enhancing the atmosphere of the day. There are some dunlin flying about; I can hear them calling. That football whistle call of the dunlin . . . yes, I've found the group far over on the East Scrape feeding on some shallow, flooded mud next to a pair of shelduck that are holding territory. A cock pheasant on the bank in front of them is feeding quietly. Another pair of shelduck on this side of the bank, seem unaware of the first pair: at this time of the year they should be strongly arguing with each other. The dunlin just feed contentedly, 29 of them in a small flock.

In the pool at the back of the hide, where the inundated mare's tail meets the pure water's edge, a heron is feeding patiently. He stands half stooped with bent neck forward and still, the feathers at the base of the breast just touching the water and blowing in the wind. Close behind, three drake mallard are standing about untidily doing nothing, (the ducks, presumably, are away laying eggs?) A cormorant glides in to land in the water, and dives to start fishing: it surfaces close to the heron, obviously realizing there is something to be had. It puts its head under the water to look about, ruining the heron's sport. The heron raises its head in disgust! The cormorant's activity is likely to drive all the fish

A view across Minsmere: the reserve covers some 1,500 acres (750 hectares), of reedbed, shallow pools, mixed woodland and heath (J. Sorensen).

away. The cormorant dives and comes up out of the mare's tail with nothing, its head shaking from side to side. The heron is looking utterly disgusted at this, but does not move. Raining hard! The cormorant moves further off now. The heron stabs the water again suddenly, and misses! He shakes his head. Then, beak pointing slightly downwards, he stretches out, very slowly, and suddenly stabs into the water again and this time brings up a fish about four inches long and quite wide, glinting silver. Quite a big fish really: got it sideways, right at the tip of its beak. He throws it sideways the other way round, then flicks it to the tip of his beak tail first and swallows it down, no trouble. I always thought they swallowed them head first but that one didn't. The heron dips its beak into the water again, lifts it up and shakes it; I suppose that smoothes the fish's downward path. Raining hard still!

Moving over to the side window of the hide and looking over the top of the bank that divides the West Scrape and North Girder pools, I can just see the back half of the latter. In it I can see

eleven avocets feeding in a well spread group. Good! that's seven more than yesterday, so they are coming in nicely. They much prefer this pool at the beginning of the season: more succulent brackish water shrimps for them to feed on I suppose. It is quite deep water: the rain as it drops makes circular ripple patterns. With their very long, slate-blue legs, however, the avocets are able to cope, even swimming through the deeper bits. These birds know the ropes, they have been here before and are very likely fully aware how the water levels will develop to their favour. Here they are feeding steadily, some upending to catch deeper shrimps, others sweeping their bills from side to side to catch those nearer the surface. Very efficient, they frequently remove their bills from the water to swallow their prey. The thought of watching their breeding displays in a couple of weeks or so leaves me full of anticipation.

A week has gone by since the day of the heavy rain and we have spent most of today digging out the sandcliff face in the car park to prepare it for the return of the sand martins. We like to have this done by the middle of March before they return, yet to do it too soon is asking for trouble later with the face collapsing from the weathering. It's an interesting face with soils on top of a pale, fine sand, then a line of iron-stone running through at an angle, under which there is a more solid, orange-coloured sand. The deeper we go, the harder it becomes and that iron-stone is so tough we find it best to under cut it rather than try to dig through it. It's well worth the graft. In 1987, 366 pairs of sand martin took advantage of our work and produced over 1,300 young. Quite a sight I recall; with the parents going on bombing runs over the cars in the car park as they worked hard to feed the young in the nest holes, and carting away the faecal sacs to keep the holes clean. Anyway we have finished the job for today, so can rest our aching limbs and I am off to relax in the woods.

On this fine, mild, late afternoon, with a good mix of cloud and blue sky and fairly still air, it is

Avocets feeding in one of the shallow pools that comprise the Scrape, a man-made habitat of shallow pools, small islands and muddy areas that provide rich feeding grounds for many birds and also nesting sites for others (J. Sorensen).

Digging out the sandcliff face to provide suitable nesting grounds for sand martins (J. Sorensen).

easy to hear two mistle thrushes singing. They have a wonderful song, comfortably in the top ten, less detailed than a blackbird's song but so clear, and a more mournful tone that really makes the atmosphere. One is in the South Belt and the other along the road down towards Scotts Hall. Both great and lesser spotted woodpeckers are drumming not too far away. Compare the difference between these two: the very fast, light sound of the lesser spotted woodpecker (not that far off — in the top of an oak I think) and the slower, heavier note of the great spot somewhere deeper in the wood. Behind me a couple of skylarks are singing high in the sky over the field that runs down to the North Marsh. At the side of the road here some early blackthorn bushes just beginning to come into flower. At the end of one of the hard, sharp, almost black twigs, half a dozen of those delicate white, green-centred, five-petalled flowers together with, at the tip, a couple of green leaves are trying to come out. It's so *good* to be about!

On the road a goldfinch (picking up grit I suppose) reveals that lovely yellow/gold splash on the wing, in contrast to the black, white-tipped primaries: what superb markings! Perhaps it's taking in the grit to prepare for egg laying in the not too distant future. It is so attractive, that fine black-tipped beak sat in the middle of that small patch of red, with the gentle almost chestnut-brown colour merging into the white on the breast. It will be run over in a minute if it doesn't fly off as another carload of visitors drives in on the road to enjoy an evening's birding!

Going into the wood to avoid the traffic, one encounters a very different scene from previous years. That storm on 16 October 1987 certainly caused a chaotic shambles. Here I am in the middle of our best oakwood, a huge old oak is torn up by the roots right beside me, three well-spaced standing oak trees are to my left and a close line of three on my right but the ground all around is a tangled mess of trunks and branches: too much sky! In front are half a dozen standing trees, and a huge oak tree not 60 feet (18 m) away has been snapped off half way up the trunk. Funnily enough there is a completely dead pine

Left *Blackthorn blossom* (J. Sorensen).

Below right *The contorted skeleton of one of the many trees destroyed at Minsmere by the gales in October 1987* (J. Sorensen).

tree standing up quite naturally nearby and close to it is a Corsican pine with one of its main branches missing just above the main fork. To the left of the Corsican pine is an oak, its top branches broken and swinging. To my right a once beautiful larch tree has lost its crown; next to it is an oak with a shattered side and next to that another oak tree, reduced to a trunk. It's going to take us years to clear up and sort it out! And I do feel sorry for our regular visitors, who know this wood so well. When they come on their summer visit expecting to see this wood unchanged and familiar, and see this chaos instead, they are going to be heartbroken. It's not so bad for us living here; we can come to terms with it over the weeks and months but to them it's a nasty shock.

Weird that wind: here I am now near the middle of the wood and there are quite a reasonable number of trees standing, nothing like the devastation further back behind me. I wonder what it's going to look like when all the leaves come? That's going to be interesing and something to look forward to. It will certainly look a bit better than it does now with just the buds, the bare branches and all the chaos.

But at least there are some birds; a treecreeper is calling near the ground close by (a long drawn-out, high pitched call not easy for some to hear), a wren is scolding, probably angry about my presence, and three wrens further away are loudly proclaiming their territories. It is astonishing, that so minute a bird has such a strong, angry note, but its powerful song with that trill at the end identifies it easily. A pair of carrion crows are flying overhead, calling *crraah crraah*, quite clearly not too happy about the fact that I am walking through here! A coal tit is singing over to the right in the pine trees while a great tit is sawing away to the background of mistle thrush and occasional bursts of drumming from the woodpeckers. It's a lovely evening.

But this is quite some disaster to contemplate: if you dwell on the damage and think on what these woods once were and look now at the broken branches, uprooted trees and wretchedness, it really hurts. It is probably not too good an idea to contemplate such images too often. I may as well be realistic and take control of the inner feelings and remind myself that it was a natural event, that storm; something that happens in forests throughout the world, so look at the results and consequences with interest. What species of birds are going to suffer? Probably the woodpeckers with many fewer trees. What species are going to gain by it? As the field layer grows up and with so much more light, I expect some of the warblers to do quite nicely. Over the years of course, with replanting and natural regeneration it will recover. But it will not be for a hundred years or more that this wood will look anything like it used to, and even then it will be obvious that once there was a very severe storm.

There is a vast sweet chestnut on my right now as I wander down the ride, ripped up by the rootstock, a great pile of sand ten feet (three metres) high and ten feet (three metres) wide, with its roots splayed out and the trunk sprawled on the ground beyond it. Something like this is worth leaving to rot down because the dead wood is so valuable. Think of all the insect life that will thrive in it, the interesting fungi that will grow on it! There are signs of plenty of bluebells to come with all this light, the beginnings of their leaves just showing. Certainly these next two or three months are going to be very interesting in this

wood; I'm really looking forward to seeing it develop: how many bird species will we find breeding in it, which species and how many of each?

Walking down these rides it's quite clear there is a pretty good population of tits; it must be the peanuts I've been feeding them all winter at the bungalow. Blue tits and great tits are the most numerous, with a sprinkling of marsh and coal tits, and I often come across a flock of long-tailed tits but it's hard to find willow tit.

I have a conflict of interests when walking through the woods; I want to keep my head down to look at the signs from fox, deer, rabbits and the plant-life, and I want to keep my head up to see the birds flying about. It's a good job we have ears too!

I can hear the approach of a goodly flock of small birds, so I shall tarry and await developments. A goldcrest calls, flies across the yellow-edged, primrose-bordered ride into the pines and larches above my head. A coal tit calls, and long-tailed tit too. You certainly need to know the bird calls when in the middle of a wood such

as this: you miss so much otherwise, because so many of the birds in the canopy above are just not visible. It's a good group of long-tailed tits coming, quite a big flock, together with more goldcrests, and two jays screeching harshly not very far away. Tits are hard to count, easiest when they cross the ride: eight, nine, a coal tit followed by a blue tit and more long-tailed tits (one with a very scruffy tail); still more of them on this side and another goldcrest crosses the ride. A bullfinch comes up close to land in a wild cherry: a beautiful cock bird shuffling down to the end of a branch to stretch its head forward and pick off the fresh new buds at the tip, what a gorgeous rose-red breast. Oh! it has dropped down and away. Where did the term 'nipped in the bud' come from? Seeing the long-tailed tits in that larch feeding on the buds, together with the cones and the birds silhouetted against the branches really makes me wish I could paint! I think of George Lodge's magnificent paintings, the way he paints trees and catches the mood. A long-tailed tit is feeding up a very slender branch, a lovely mixture of blacks and greys and almost whites and that gentle buff pink colour.

A treecreeper, crawls mouse-like up the trunk of a pine. It is very white underneath and its head moves quickly up and down as it takes tiny insects from the cracks and corners of the bark. Climbing up the tree, the beautiful brown and cream patterning on its back and barring on the wings, is very hard to see until you get the side view with that very white underneath. Going up the side of the tree I watch the fine curved beak, the eye-stripe and the little, gleaming, black eye. Needless to say, in typical frustrating fashion it goes round the back of the trunk. Treecreepers always fly down and walk up: down he goes to a birch tree, right in to the bottom, examining the knobbly bits by the roots, then up the side he climbs, tail pressed against the trunk, sidling sideways. Once again that white underside really does show up!

Now even some of the long-tailed tits have come down to feed on the ground in amongst the leaves: hear that lovely, quiet, contented ticking call. Two wrens are singing, encouraging each other to keep at it. Tits, flitting from side to side of the ride, feed in the branches of the fallen trees and also in the broken beech tree with its brown leaves still clinging to the twigs. A blue tit feeding on a fallen birch, comes to the top of the trunk and hops over a branch, picking at the insects in the cracks of the bark. That's one thing about

Above right *Spring evening at Minsmere* (J. Sorensen).

Left *The long-tailed tit is a lovely mixture of blacks and greys and almost whites with that gentle buff pink colour on the underside* (J. Sorensen).

birch, it has a nice knobbly bark with plenty of scope for insects. I watch the blue crown and white face, with the dark stripe through it: It's a male blue tit, you can tell by the quality of that blue on the edges of the primaries, a lovely colour. It's feeding busily on the stump now, its back matching the green moss at the side of the bark on the birch stump.

There seem to be two layers of birds feeding at the moment, a flock really close to the ground and a flock right up in the canopy. I suppose the ones feeding at ground level are in a similar habitat, it's just that it's been blown to the ground. A marsh tit way above me in the canopy of a beech tree, flits about, feeding on the tips of the little twigs protruding from the main branches, and now moves to feed on some lichen growing on top of the branch. It examines the lichen closely for food, peering down over the top of the branch. The plumage is a special warm quality of grey on the flanks and breast capped by a gorgeous, shining black crown.

Trudging back to the bungalow to get a meal,

now, the light is going: what an evening! Through the network of branches an orange-coloured sky near the horizon, running to gold close to the setting sun, is shining through a much thicker group of branches and makes a beautiful backdrop to the woodland scene.

Close to the end of March a beautiful, clear morning dawns after the dull, cold weather of the last few days. Away beyond the sluice, out over the sea, the angry clouds contrast white against the deep blue sky, the wind-rippled water of the scrape takes its colour from the sky blue, but the sheltered mirror-like edges reflect the white of the clouds. The pale, warm brown of the reeds make a fine surround to the picture.

On the path down to the sluice, the sheltered puddles at the edge of the dark, muddy, brown track contrast sharply in bright blue with the reeds on the right, low and tatty from the ravages of the winter months. Not a seed-head is to be seen near the edge, they are all in the middle

Main picture *The reeds provide feeding and nesting sites for secretive birds like bitterns and water rails, together with marsh harriers, bearded tits and reed warblers* (J. Sorensen).

Left inset *Goat willow catkins* (J. Sorensen).

Below left inset *Coots in one of the ditches* (J. Sorensen).

where they are more protected from the effects of the wind. Some of the goat willows at the side of the track are laden with quite substantial catkins now, soft silver with lime yellow tips and so fresh, contrasting with the branches, hard and gnarled from the winter. To the left are the small alder trees that we have coppiced to maintain a screen between the path and the scrape. I always examine these carefully ahead as I walk down this path because sometimes a harvest mouse can be seen to drop to the ground some thirty feet (ten metres) in front, wary of my approach. But there are no fruits on these alders at the moment, so we are going to have to wait for this sight until the autumn, when the harvest mice like to feed too on the seedheads of the marsh mallow plants.

Passing the alders, we come to the bends in the path where it passes the sluice gates en route to the South Hide. I always walk along this section head down to see if I can spot any otter tracks in the mud, or to see whether they have put any spraint down? You can often see signs here as they cross the path on their way down the ditch from the tree hide to the sluice, but not today.

Walking past the North Girder pool, I can see 28 avocets feeding and standing about, half a dozen standing on an island that is just beginning to show above the water as the flood waters subside. Today the black and white plumage is conspicuous against the rippled blue of the water. Behind the pool, the large public hide sits astride the inner sea wall. To the right of the hide, the poor man's celery, Alexanders, bright green in colour, is draped along the sea wall. Between the hide and the water, the reeds warm and brown in the sun. In the distance the last of the cloud bank, the lousy weather of the last few days is blowing away.

Continuing to the sluice to check the various gates there and walking up to the Minsmere River I hear a splash: something has just disappeared under the water! I wonder what it was? A moorhen comes up amongst the reeds on the other side. It wasn't a very big splash, I thought it was going to be a water vole. The

Sluices have to be checked frequently — they control the delicate balance of water in the Scrape (J. Sorensen).

Dyke clearing at Minsmere (Michael W. Richards, RSPB).

moorhen is clearly satisfied that he cannot be seen where he is. Rounding the corner by the New Cut, towards the sluice. I can see in the distance the huge shoebox-like concrete structure of Sizewell Power Station. In front of it the grim din of the men and machines working on the 'B' Station is carried on the wind right up to here and beyond. And close by on the other side of the Cut a hare, long-eared and back high, lollops in a random course across the field and away.

I can hear the tide rushing out through the main sluice gates, as I go round the corner to make sure that the water is flowing out unrestricted from the smaller gate. It's bubbling out powerfully round the edges of the sluice flap. I walk further along the bank to check the double gates: the lads did a good job of clearing the reeds from the doors yesterday, it's fine and clear. And on I go to look at Seven Holes' Sluice which takes us past the ruin of the old wind-pump with its bitumen black brick flaking and chipped at the edges to show red underneath, and the mortar green with age. A couple of broken oak timbers stand up skywards; the centre of the wind-pump is now full of elder bushes, together with a couple

of leaning pieces of timber. As I approach the Seven Holes' Sluice I can see four avocets in the South Shore Pool, so that makes 32: things are looking good this morning. The only trouble with this sluice is that when the pipes block, sleeves have to be rolled up and arms pushed down into the ever-so-cold water to ease off the valves, so that the weed can be cleared. Fortunately, not so this morning the pipes are clear.

Walking back to the main sluice, past our long bench seat which arrived on the tide one morning, I have a look at the mud to see if there is any sign of otters in it: a discarded red, blue and white crisp packet meets my gaze — why can't they take it home! And yes, sure enough, a nice sign there in the mud. I can only see three of the claws in the paw mark; that's clearly quite a big otter, walking into the water there. Just two marks in the soft mud today. I can often see an absolute mass of signs here, but of course we are between spring tides now so they get washed off each tide: when it's neap however, you can find a mass of tracks ancient and modern.

Along the strand-line — a colourful shambles of milk crates, detergent containers, an oiled dead guillemot and bits of fishing rope (J. Sorensen).

Walking past the sluice and up the sand dunes, well trodden here, I note the thick marram grass on each side. This is where everyone walks straight from the sluice to the beach. The water from the New Cut can be seen welling into the sea at the end of the sluice: the tide is on the way out.

Just look at the high tide mark though! A load of rubbish blown up on the last lot of easterlies. What a colourful shambles; blue plastic milk crates, yellow detergent containers, white containers with red writing, an oiled dead guillemot, a wooden carton and bits of fishing rope, flotsam and jetsam, a straggling untidy line wending its way along the beach.

I take a careful look at the sluice outfall, a huge, concrete, pipe-like structure jutting out into the sea. A lovely triangle of bright green seaweed on top of the concrete, shelves down to the sea: beyond it is darker brown seaweed, slightly rougher in texture. I can't see any purple sandpipers, but a great black-backed gull sits perched on the triangle at the tip of the sluice and on the upright timbers of the old sluices to the right, a mass of brown seaweed cascades

seawards. Orange, green, blue and grey fishing nets are caught up in the piles, but there's no sign of any purple sandpipers this morning.

I walk along the top of the sand-dunes so as not to miss any birds flying low on either side. An untidy line of concrete anti-tank blocks runs along the top, some square and straight as they were built, others tilting at crazy angles caused by the movement of the ground over the years since the Second World War. Covered in lichens, some are a pale, almost white sage green, others a rather attractive, strongly-coloured yellow with orange patches in the centre. Some five blocks in front of me a cock wheatear bobs on a corner. Seeing me, it drops to fly off low, showing that prominent white rump, curving round to come back up behind me, and adding significantly to the joys of the morning.

A green woodpecker flies up from some sand sedge at the side of the marram as it spots me. It has no doubt been searching for ants. Now it undulates away showing its yellow rump, vivid against the darker green body and wings, and a splash of red on its head. It's not an unusual sight on the dunes down here. It drops down in among the gorse-covered area behind and between the public hides. As I walk on, the woodpecker rises again and undulates over the inner sea wall to fly back to the sand sedge and continue enjoying his fine breakfast no doubt!

Having come over the inner sea wall via the reed tunnel, I am now sitting in the East Hide. Looking about without using my binoculars and listening to the sounds it is evident that spring is in the air! Lapwings roll about in the sky calling, redshanks do parachute display song flights, ringed plovers chase each other about: it's good to be here! There's more too, as I spot two grey plovers and then four spotted redshanks still in winter greys and feeding in the water close together, long fine bills working the water. There must be 250 black-headed gulls today, quite a noise they kick up too. Some are in summer plumage with fine brown heads but most are still

On the edge of the heath (J. Sorensen).

in winter plumage or moulting through. At the back, behind one of the islands, a heron feeds peacefully with fifty or so dunlin in the shallows in front of it. And there are six distinct pairs of avocets, so that is 44 birds altogether: better and better. These birds, experienced mature adults that seem to nest earlier than the others, are already on territory. Three pairs are round Island 40, a good spot for early-nesting avocets.

The water level is kept quite high in early Spring, to encourage the nesting birds to lay their eggs high, then when most of the birds are down we lower the water to provide spare capacity and to prevent nests from becoming flooded in heavy rains. The islands are covered in a short, greyish-green sward from the winter cold, ideal for nesting avocets, terns and black-headed gulls. Over behind Island 39, four avocets stand in a group facing each other, with bills to the centre before they suddenly break up to chase each other about.

By Island 40, life is equally exciting. A female avocet is crouching low with neck stretched and head low, almost touching the water. Her beak is raised and held very still. Close to her left side a

The avocet courtship display is a feast for the eyes (Michael W. Richards, RSPB)

Avocet courtship display and mating
(Jeffrey Taylor/Pamela Harrison).

male avocet is preening with fast, light movements of his beak. The courtship display; I always wonder at the depth of beauty and design that goes into this performance. The male then dips his beak in the water and shakes it to splash the female bird and turns back to his preening. Then he walks round the back of the female to continue on the right side, preen-dip-shake-splash, but he keeps just behind the front of the female bird. Back round, a little closer, to the left side again, preen-dip-shake-splash, increasing in tempo. As he gets a bit too near the front of the female, she pivots a little clockwise, so he is still behind. I've noticed this with experienced female birds — they know that if the male gets careless with eagerness it breaks the pattern and the courtship fails. She is experienced and back

round he goes to the right side much closer this time. So close in fact that he has to stoop under her tail to pass, preen-dip-shake-splash, preen-dip-shake-splash even faster and splashier. It seems to go on for minutes! Back to the left but suddenly he springs up to mount the female from the side, with wings raised. The female is swinging her head from side to side still maintaining the original posture. He bends his legs and they copulate quickly, he jumps off and they run together to cross bills in what always strikes me is a kiss, then the two birds run apart, each in a hunched posture. It is always a beautiful display to watch, and the first of the year for me, a display to look out for whenever visiting the reserve from the end of March through into May. Spring has arrived!

APRIL
GREEK CYPRUS IN SPRING

BILL ODDIE

Bill Oddie and daughter Rosie (C.H. Gomersall, RSPB).

BILL ODDIE was born in Rochdale, brought up in Birmingham and now lives in London, but he has trekked all over the world in search of birds. In between birding, he's managed to write and appear in many hours of television, most of it comedy . . . but now he's even started doing bird programmes as well! Bill has also been a member of the RSPB's council.

I first went to Cyprus in 1983, courtesy of the *TV Times*. Not that the visit had anything to do with television. Well not directly. This is how it came about. Anxious to fill their pages with something rather more riveting than lists of programmes, the *TV. Times* (there's *so* much in it, you know), now and again concoct 'features' in which supposedly well known personalities are allowed to test-drive cars or go on brief holidays. I've done both, with very satisfying consequences. I was allowed to drive a new Vauxhall Nova for a week, and though they wouldn't let me keep it, I was so impressed that I bought one for myself, which I've only just replaced with an Astra after three years of trouble-free motoring. (Free plug for Vauxhall there!) The three-day Cyprus trip was even better. For a start, they couldn't take it back, and, in fact, it was *so* enjoyable I've been returning to the island nearly every year since.

Mind you, I didn't necessarily *expect* to enjoy it. When Cyprus was first 'offered' to me I couldn't help casting envious thoughts towards the quiz show host who was 'testing' Barbados, or the newsreader who was being sent to Disney World (Yes, I *like* Disney World). However, I am not one to ever turn down a 'freebie', especially if there are birds to be investigated, and the great thing about birdwatching is that more or less *anywhere* is worth an exploratory visit. Even if you find nothing at all you can convince yourself that the 'negative result' is scientifically interesting, though of course it's more fun if you *do* find something to watch.

In theory, I thought, Cyprus *should* be pretty good in late March/early April. I had been to Israel at about the same time and it had been brilliant. I had also heard much praise for the birds and beauty of other Mediterranean islands in spring. Crete and Majorca, for example, were advertised by all the specialist natural history tour companies. But why didn't they offer Cyprus? I soon discovered that the fact that Cyprus was not on their itineraries had a sinister significance. The island was unofficially boycotted! Why? Well, quite simply, and sadly, because Cyprus holds the unenviable record of being the country that kills more birds per head of population than any other. The Mediterranean region in general is not

A black-winged stilt admires its reflection. So do I (W.E. Oddie).

exactly kind to its birds — hunting and trapping are tragically rife from Malta to Portugal and all places in between — but Cyprus had the reputation of being the worst of the lot. So, should I support the boycott, or should I go to see for myself?

First, I did a little research. The British Ornithologists' Union had published a quite comprehensive report: *The Birds of Cyprus*. Reading it was the very definition of mixed feelings. The species list was enticingly enormous, and so were some of the numbers of birds seen. Yet all that was overshadowed by the numbers of birds killed. Annually — millions and millions of migrants. The figures were hard to grasp. Estimates of 'a quarter of a million birds "limed" by one village each year' . . . '100,000 song thrushes shot every winter' . . . '35,000 licensed hunters' . . . '1,000 shooters gathered round one lake on the first day of the spring "season"', . . . 'a single "netter" catching over 2,000 birds a year.' It all added up to an undeniable conclusion — several *million* birds killed in Cyprus year after year. And yet, ironically, even the authors of the report could not resist documenting the implied attractions of the island's birds by listing the species 'limed' in one particularly notorious area: 'thrush nightingale, 245 limed, Spring 1968 . . . subalpine warbler 654 . . . rüppell's warbler 446 . . . orphean warbler 1,062 . . . bonelli's warbler 181 . . .' Be honest, these were birds I very much wanted to see . . . but I wanted to see them *alive*. Maybe I should stay away.

Then one day I was discussing the matter with a fellow council member of the Royal Society for the Protection of Birds. He made the decision for me. 'Definitely go,' he advised. 'In fact, we are not absolutely sure what the present situation is in Cyprus, so any new information will be useful.' He was obviously right. Whatever the 'present situation' it was almost certainly still very bad news for the birds and therefore, as an avowed conservationist, I surely had a responsibility to do what I could. As it turned out it was the awakening of a concern that has become something of an obsession.

It has always struck me as a very special miracle that a tiny bird can find its way from southern Africa to northern Europe and back each year surviving weather, predators and lack of

το πιάσιμο αμπελοπουλιών
στα 'βερκά' είναι
απαράδεκτο και παράνομο

any apparent navigational aids. It equally strikes me as a particular obscenity that such a miracle should be pointlessly obliterated by a bullet from a hunter's gun, or have the life squeezed out of it by the fingers of a 'limer' or 'trapper.' I shall never entirely comprehend why this destruction of what I would have thought is surely evidence of God's wondrous handiwork, if ever there was one, should be so relished in countries which purport to be as deeply religious as those round the Mediterranean. Surely it's a heresy? Surely it's a sin? Why don't religious leaders openly condemn it? I do not know. What I *do* know is that I shall continue to do what I can to help condemn and hopefully eventually eradicate the widespread bird-killing in 'the Med.'

Well, that's how I feel now. However, back in 1983 I confess I was looking for an excuse to say 'yes' to a free holiday in the sunshine, some new birds during the days, and free-flowing retsina and lashings of my favourite Greek food in the evenings. Nevertheless, my talk on the plane to the lady journalist from the *TV Times* was not of

self-gratification but of 'investigation' and 'research'. Anyone overhearing the conversation would have assumed *I* was the reporter! I had already requested that I should meet up with Pavlos Neophytou, the secretary of the Greek branch of the Cyprus Ornithological Society, who was also the local representative of the ICBP (International Council for Bird Preservation). In fact he met us at the airport. Even as we waited for our taxi to drive round to collect us, I got a quick run down on the 'present situation'. Pavlos told me it was still very bad. A lot of liming still went on, ostensibly illegal, but the authorities turned a blind eye. The use of mist nets was becoming ominously widespread, though their importation was theoretically banned and bird-shooting was still the country's number one pastime. However, he added '*You* probably will not see any of it!' 'How come?' I asked. 'Well, the main spring migration does not start till about 5 April, so the limers and netters do not bother before that . . . and anyway they are concentrated in the south-east of the Island.' (Some way from

our 'base' at Limassol, which was half way along the south coast.) 'And the spring shooting season does not open till late April!'

So much for my in-depth, on-the-spot investigation! I have to admit it was a bit of a relief. That evening, as I munched my first truly authentic kebab, I resigned myself to having to enjoy the bird-watching instead; only slightly deflated by the implication that I might be a couple of weeks 'early'. I warned my reporter companion that she and the photographer might find me rather elusive over the next three days. It did not seem to bother them. 'As long as we can get a few shots round the swimming pool, we can discuss the article on the plane back to London. We want you to do what you would normally do on holiday.' So I did. I disappeared.

Had they been up at dawn the next day they would have seen me scuttle across the already fairly busy main road outside the hotel, clamber through a building site and emerge in a sort of rough field with a few adjacent allotments, sandwiched between two new 'holiday

Above left *This anti-liming poster is in Greek but unfortunately most of the pressure comes from 'outside': Holland, Germany and the UK. Will the next generation of Cypriots come to see it 'our way'? Let's hope so* (W.E. Oddie).

Left *This little sparrow died by falling from its nest. Had it lived it might well have been blasted to bits by a shot gun. Not much of a choice is it?* (W.E. Oddie).

Right *Hotels like this one on the edge of Limassol have gone up so quickly the birds haven't yet realized they're not really very attractive* (W.E. Oddie).

Left *A male Cyprus pied wheatear. The female looks much the same but is 'dustier'. This is now considered a 'good species' and therefore 'tickable'!* (W.E. Oddie).

Below *The male Cyprus warbler looks like a scruffy rüppell's but moves and sounds more like a Sardinian* (W.E. Oddie).

Below right *A 'wood sand'. Nice to see a bird from home. Even nicer to see a flock of fifty or more* (W.E. Oddie).

developments' that have since merged together to obliterate the site of my first encounter with two species that some birders visit Cyprus specially to see. I must admit it does amuse me that I have heard international twitchers discussing specific 'stake-outs' for the Cyprus warbler and Cyprus pied wheatear. The instructions are sometimes extremely elaborate: 'Drive east out of Limassol. After five miles turn left by a blue Taverna. Carry on for two miles past an olive-oil factory, then take a right along an unsurfaced road. Carry on past a workman's hut (the workman is called Andy) and park by a watermill. Climb the stile — watch out for the dog (also called Andy) — and walk towards a clump of six fig trees, under the smallest of which is a rusty ploughshare. Pied wheatears have been seen using that as a song perch after four o'clock on Wednesdays, and two years ago a pair of Cyprus warblers were mating in a gorse bush 50 yards to the south-east, just by a black and white cow.' The truth is, you would have to stay locked in your hotel room to miss either species — and even then you might see them through the window! The wheatears seem every bit as cheerful singing from the top of a

television aerial as a ploughshare, and the warblers are almost as likely to skulk through the garden lupins as gorse bushes.

Certainly I had ticked them both off before breakfast; along with a couple of orphean warblers — looking like overgrown lesser whitethroats — and a dozen cretzchmar's buntings. These 'blue-headed ortolans' brought back happy memories of a June day on Fair Isle when Britain's second 'Cretz' announced its presence by singing from a dry stone wall a little tune which the finder described as 'Doobeedoobeedoo' . . . which narrowed the identification down to 'very rare bunting or Frank Sinatra!' Add to these, several blackcaps and chiffchaffs flitting around the hedgerows, fantail warblers zipping overhead, and a gnarled old Cypriot gentleman setting out a basket full of 'lime-sticks', and my morning stroll had given me a fair cross-section of what Cyprus had to offer. Pavlos had been wrong in that I *had* seen a 'bird-killer'; though I have to confess he did seem such an amiable old fellow it was hard to muster up the abhorrence I was supposed to feel. Most delightful and encouraging was the impression

A party of little egrets and a squacco heron literally dance at dawn in a roadside pool by Phassouri Reedbeds. For the best views — stay in the car! (W.E. Oddie).

that migrant birds could be literally on your doorstep, even in suburbia. On each of my subsequent trips I have found it to be true — as I shall soon relate.

Meanwhile, back to my 1983 trip. After breakfast I was met again by Pavlos and he acted as my guide round Cyprus' prime birding area: the salt lake and marshes at Akrotiri. I wrote in my note book: 'A superb habitat. Shallow wader pools . . . a tangled quaggy marsh . . . reed beds . . . and a lovely forest which can be crawling with migrants, tho' not today!' Well, maybe not, but we still saw some excellent birds, including a couple of hundred flamingoes 'left over' from the wintering flock which can number thousands, and, one of my favourite Cyprus phenomena, a mixed pack of 'flava' wagtails of various races, liberally sprinkled with red-throated pipits with throats ranging from the comparatively dull stripes of winter to the brick red of breeding dress. There were also the odd little egrets, purple herons and glossy ibis and a fair selection of waders round the marshier bits; short-toed larks and isabelline wheatears on the nearby sand flats; spectacled warblers in the scrub; and

slender-billed gulls over the lake. If this was a poor day — what would it be like on a good one? Already I was beginning to get the feeling that I would want to return to Cyprus, probably a little later in the spring.

Over the rest of that first short trip the feeling was to become a resolution. On the second day, we drove west along the coast road. The scenery became less and less 'spoilt' by holiday homes and hotels, and Pavlos regaled me with tales of counting peregrines and red-footed falcons along the telegraph poles in autumn. We lunched at a Quayside taverna in the picturesque harbour at Paphos, and whilst the others snoozed over coffee I trotted round the corner to discover a heathy headland glowing with poppies and overlooked by a lighthouse with a garden that reminded me instantly of a British Bird Observatory. This too *had* to be worth coming back too.

My final evening clinched it. Earlier in the day

we had paid an obligatory 'touristy' visit to the ancient monuments at Curium, where there is a more or less completely intact amphitheatre overlooking the sea: an appropriately imposing setting for Greek dramas and publicity shots for *TV Times*. Here, in this almost mythological atmosphere I was duly photographed pretending to be distracted by the ghosts of a byegone civilization. In fact, I was eyeing a small wooded gully nearby in which a scops owl was being mobbed by two rüppell's warblers and a thrush nightingale!

Almost struggling in protest I was bundled into the car and driven back to the hotel for more snapshots 'relaxing by the pool.' Relaxing indeed! I had my binoculars stuffed down my shorts (yes, *that* explains the unsightly bulge!) and the car engine left running. The irresistible announcement that the bar was open released me (no press photographer can ignore the call of his

nature!); I scampered to the car and screeched into an impressive 'Le Mans' start and within twenty minutes I was skidding into the carpark back at Curium, just as the last tourists were being shepherded back into the 'charabanc' and the gates to the monuments were being padlocked. Good timing. I had the place to myself. A fence constructed to control a bunch of dozy holiday-makers is no deterrent to a birdwatcher on heat. Within two hops and a small plummet I was over the gate and into the wooded gully. The rüppell's warblers turned to admire my athleticism — whilst I admired their little white moustaches — and the scops owl fled in terror. I clambered down the gully, tumbling through scratchy thorn-bushes and scrambling over ankle-twisting rocks, till I finally emerged at the Curium beach alongside a small road which I could have driven down in the car, had I only realized it. Never mind, birds are so much more enjoyable if you suffer for them.

I like to think I have quite a good eye for a likely bird-spot and this one looked excellent. There was a craggy cliff leading back up to the amphitheatre, and, at the bottom of this, a flat

The lighthouse and garden on Paphos headlands looking for all the world like a British Bird Observatory. No sooner had I taken this picture than six hoopoes flew out! (W.E. Oddie).

area, some of it sandy and uncultivated — pipit and wheatear country, I mused, and some of it grassier — bunting land — whilst round the edges were some low scrub — for the sylvia warblers; and taller tamarisk type bushes — for the phylloscs. Beyond all this was the sea, where hopefully something might fly past. It was already early evening and I only had about an hour's daylight left, and the next morning we were due to fly back to London. But — to quote my notebook — what 'a delightful final session' it turned out to be.

Systematically, I checked each sub-habitat and duly it surrendered its appropriate birds . . . and a little more besides. A quick scan across the sandy flat area revealed six common or northern wheatears and the same number of isabellines for instant comparison. Between them trotted a couple of tawny pipits. Around the rocks flitted three black redstarts and half a dozen Cyprus pied wheatears. Do all wheatears come in sixes, I wondered? But no! Suddenly out popped a single slaty grey female of a species I instantly did not recognize, if you see what I mean.

Five minutes and a couple of pages of notes

Left *Kensington Cliffs, viewable from the garrison at Episkopi — but don't get too near the edge when enjoying eye-level views of griffon vultures, eleonora's falcons and alpine swifts* (W.E. Oddie).

Below left *A superb male citrine wagtail. Considered a great rarity in Cyprus, but I've now seen four there so I reckon it's 'regular' in small numbers* (W.E. Oddie).

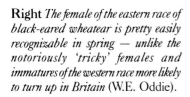

Right *The female of the eastern race of black-eared wheatear is pretty easily recognizable in spring — unlike the notoriously 'tricky' females and immatures of the western race more likely to turn up in Britain* (W.E. Oddie).

later I had pinned it down: a female finsch's wheatear, one of their localized rarities, a few of which winter in Cyprus. This one presumably was on its way out. I thanked it for sticking around for another day and transferred my attention to a little whirl of hirundines quartering the cliff above it. Twenty house martins, five swallows . . . and two red-rumped swallows . . . and what's this? A single crag martin. Four species in one 'whirl'. OK, so now the bushes. In the taller ones, chiffchaffs and blackcaps, more than a dozen of each . . . and in the lower, scrubby thorny stuff . . . a lesser whitethroat and aha! an arch skulker. A Sardinian warbler perhaps? No, it looks too neat and pale . . . a few more minutes needed on this one.

I must admit I rather enjoy conjectural identification based on what you *cannot* see. I will give you an example. One day a few years ago I was birding in an area of southern Nepal (place-dropping I'm afraid) and searching the cover along a riverbank wherein were lurking an almost equal mixture of dusky warblers and eastern race chiffchaffs — two species which can look pretty similar even when seen quite well. There is,

however, one fairly safe way of identifying them: it's only the chiffchaffs that *can* be seen well! If it constantly cringes under cover and refuses to show itself — it's probably a dusky warbler! Mind you, it's a rule best practised only in distant lands where it 'doesn't really matter'. Please do not rely on it too much in Britain, where I certainly would not recommend claiming a dusky warbler 'because you could not see it!'

Anyway, back to elusive sylvias in Cyprus, and the same kind of theory. I know Sardinian warblers have a reputation for being skulky but in my experience they do at least, every now and again, leap up and plummet back in, in a manner that slightly reminds me of a dunnock. To my mind the one that *really* hates to fly is subalpine. Certainly the Curium bird proved the point when, after what seemed like half an hour of both of us crawling around on hands and knees, it eventually revealed itself to be a female 'subalp'.

By this time, the sun was beginning to slide below the horizon but, instead of the birdlife curling up to snooze, if anything things got more lively. As I sauntered to the seashore I became aware of the ticking and jingling of a gathering

roosting flock of 'seedeaters'. There were nearly a hundred birds: corn buntings, serins and cretzchmar's buntings in almost equal proportions. Next, a husky belch made me look up to where a pair of cranes were silhouetted against the evening sky, flying so low they had to bank sharply to avoid crashing into the 'ancient monument'. And finally, as I gazed contentedly at the sun setting over the Mediterranean, a dark wisp on the horizon grew into a cloud and eventually defined itself as a pack of migrating wildfowl. They were a long way off, and the light pretty murky and I resigned myself to having to record them as 'duck sp.' However, they had no such thoughts of anonymity. Instead, they veered towards me and pitched on the sea no more than 100 yards (91 m) away. I 'scoped' them and counted as I panned along. Two shoveler . . . eighty wigeon . . . and . . . no less than 500 garganey, to my eyes the dinkiest of all the ducks! My note book summed it up: 'Lovely'.

So, I was hooked on Cyprus. Since then I have enjoyed two more splendid visits. Both have been in April and both to the relatively unspoilt south-west end of the island, away from the bird-limers and the tourists, and the holiday complexes that I believe encrust the popular beaches of the East. I wouldn't know. I have never been to that part and I don't want to.

The good impressions of my first visit have been entirely confirmed — birdwise that is. There have been some memorable moments: a woody headland alive with over 100 collared flycatchers; a flock of sixteen bimaculated larks so intent on gorging themselves on caterpillars that they refused to move from in front of our car; and a Caspian plover dashing around the headland at Paphos. Some areas have deteriorated. Curium beach is now guarded by a phalanx of tavernas though I dare say it still gets good birds if you get there early in the morning, or indeed late in the evenings. Akrotiri — always a 'sensitive' area due to the proximity of the British RAF base is now even more so after an abortive rocket attack. In a way that's a blessing. Birdwatchers are still perfectly welcome as long as they make themselves known at the checkpoints, but hunters definitely are not. Anyone brandishing a gun is regarded as potentially threatening to the military as well as the birds and consequently the

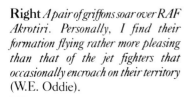

Above left *A spring riot of poppies and corn marigolds so typical of Mediterranean Islands. And if you walk through them you'll flush red-throated pipits and ortolan buntings* (W.E. Oddie).

Left *A rare sight — cranes on the ground. In autumn, huge flocks migrate over the island, including good numbers of demoiselles* (W.E. Oddie).

Right *A pair of griffons soar over RAF Akrotiri. Personally, I find their formation flying rather more pleasing than that of the jet fighters that occasionally encroach on their territory* (W.E. Oddie).

Above *Yes, bird reserves do exist, but are generally rather resented. If you can't shoot the birds — shoot the sign!* (W.E. Oddie).

Left *Red-rumped swallow poses on the taverna washing line. I photograph it with one hand whilst sipping retsina with the other . . .* (W.E. Oddie).

Above right *Another migrant finds a man-made perch perfectly satisfactory. This one is a woodchat shrike* (W.E. Oddie).

Right *Rambo, Cyprus style. Armed to the teeth and ready to do battle with whatever fearsome foe may confront him — like a house sparrow or a small warbler, for example* (W.E. Oddie).

area is perhaps more of a sanctuary than it used to be. It is, however, still threatened by all kinds of developments and drainage, and any British birder visiting it will surely weep at the wasted potential. Just imagine if the area were bought and managed by the RSPB! If only the Cyprus government would realize that if they made Akrotiri an official Bird Reserve complete with nature trails and hides it would actually attract the tourists they are concerned to encourage.

Akrotiri is a great 'site', and so is Larnaca salt lake, and various 'dams' and river valleys along the southern coast, but to me *the* great delight of Cyprus is the fact that migrants can be seen *wherever* you happen to be: in the garden of your hotel, or in the fields and hedges round your holiday villa. During the first week of my most recent visit I was co-leading a party of birdwatchers for Sunbird/*British Birds*. We stayed in a very pleasant hotel perched on a sort of inland cliff just behind Paphos. Every morning or evening some of us would do a quick check of the trees and bushes in the immediate vicinity and every day the population seemed to change. There were always red-rumped swallows

'hawking' over the swimming pool and Cyprus warblers and wheatears jangling away nearby, but with them came alpine and pallid swifts; rüppell's, orphean, bonelli's, subalpine and olivaceous warblers; pied, semi-collared and collared flycatchers; whinchats, redstarts and black-eared wheatears; hoopoes and wrynecks; cretzchmar's, ortolan and black-headed buntings; masked, red-backed and woodchat shrikes; golden orioles and great spotted cuckoos. In fact, the 'morning walk' was in many ways one of the most enjoyable aspects of our trip not least because it indicated just how many migrants must pass safely through the island . . . until, that is, the morning of 20 April. It was the last day of our visit, and the first of the spring shoot.

My previous visits had been too early to coincide with the shooting season. I had heard it described but no verbal account prepared me for the reality. We were woken long before dawn by the crackle of gunfire. I peered out of my bedroom window into the murky morning to see the hotel surrounded on all sides by cars, vans and lorries. I used my binoculars. By the vehicles, under every tree, on every outcrop, sometimes alone, sometimes in pairs, sometimes in packs . . . were gunmen. They wore paramilitary gear: khaki and camouflage, with crossed gun belts bulging with bullets. Every now and then they fired a fusillade. What at, I could not yet see. An unsuspecting tourist might have presumed they had been caught in the middle of a military coup.

It was impossible to sleep. As the sun began to rise, so did I. I got into my car and drove close to the nearest posse of shooters. I parked and watched. They saw me, shrugged and carried on firing even though I was taking photos. I did not feel in any danger except perhaps from stray shots, and I am sure I was not. To be honest, rather like that old limer in Limassol, they seemed pretty cheery chaps. As I clicked away they waved perhaps presuming I wanted a few snaps for my holiday scrap-book. Certainly I reckon they considered themselves pretty photogenic as they swaggered around like a bunch of Rambo look-alikes off to a fancy dress party. In fact, the more I studied them the more I became convinced that this macho posturing and dressing up is a large part of the attraction to the hunters. It's probably also quite a social event too.

Left *Rosie Oddie aged one and a half performs her evening aerobics quite unmoved by her father celebrating the fact he's just found a Caspian plover* (W.E. Oddie).

Above right *If you look hard enough you'll realize most of the swifts that breed under the eaves of the Paphos Police Station are pallids — even if they're too dark to photograph!* (W.E. Oddie).

Right *A desirable holiday villa with uninterrupted views for raptor-watching and hot and cold hopping migrants. And by no means as expensive as it looks!* (W.E. Oddie).

Certainly they make no attempt to creep around or stalk the birds. They yell merrily to one another about what they have shot . . . or more often what they have missed! For the truth is, that morning at least, thank goodness, they did not hit very much.

The smallest birds were generally not shot at all presumably because they stick to the trees and if a shooter fired at ground level he would be more likely to hit one of his mates than a warbler. Ostensibly the quarry species is meant to be turtle doves but if there are not many around — and that day there weren't — anything that risks a flight is used as live target practice. The result is that large numbers of supposedly 'protected' species are blasted from the sky. Nevertheless that particular morning enthusiasm outweighed accuracy — perhaps they were over-excited — and the only birds I actually saw killed were a cuckoo, a pallid swift (which I could not help conceding was quite a shot), and a brace of domestic pigeons which a demented 'cowboy' blasted off the top of the Hotel dovecote! This would be funny if it did not indicate just how totally mindless is the destruction. It is as if those

beautiful living miracles are of no more significance than the old tin cans that the huntsmen eventually resorted to firing at when the birds had sensibly fled or 'gone to ground'.

All in all it was a horribly depressing last day for our birdwatching group who up to then had enjoyed a week of typical Cyprus delights: great birds, excellent food and charming and friendly people. Why, oh why does it have to be spoilt like this? And can we do anything about it?

Well, in a way, it seems my story has come full circle. I began with tales of horrendous bird-killing, and boycotts. It's still going on. So, is staying away the appropriate response? Or are there *any* signs of improvement? Well, there *have* been indications that the Cyprus government and its people are becoming more aware of the distaste with which some of their 'traditions' are viewed. The import of mist-nets has been stemmed and consequently netting has almost disappeared. Liming is still taking a terrible toll though it is largely restricted to the east of the Island and it *is* illegal. It may even be that international protest could persuade the authorities to make more effort to enforce the law. Some of the shooting seasons are still iniquitous and need to be brought into line with other countries. The 'present situation' may be a little better, but it's still bad. A meticulous ICBP survey concluded that in 1986 four and a half million birds were killed in Cyprus. Nevertheless, I do not believe that at this point boycotts are the right approach. Instead, I suggest quite the opposite. Birdwatchers, naturalists, individually and in groups should go. In itself this is a gesture of recognition that there has been some improvement and may act as an encouragement to take it further. However, on leaving we should make two statements. One is a negative: express disgust at any bird-killing witnessed and make it clear that unless the situation continues to improve a renewal of a boycott will follow. The second is a positive: express your enjoyment of the good aspects of Cyprus and point out what a potentially attractive destination it is for all those interested in nature study. This way the government may come to slowly realize that a large part of the beauty of the island is in its birds. Hopefully, they will not want to shoot tourist attractions any more than they want to shoot tourists — which, by the way, could happen if they do not curb the gunfire near to hotels and villas.

Meanwhile, rest assured that conservation societies throughout Europe and Cyprus itself are tireless in attempting to educate the younger generation to appreciate and protect wildlife and in bringing pressure on the government to curb the slaughter. If you yourself want more information or to help please get in touch with the Stop the Massacre Campaign, c/o The RSPB, The Lodge, Sandy, Beds SG19 2DL . . . funny how many roads lead back there isn't it!?

And if you are wondering whether or not to visit Cyprus yourself, I can only quote my friend: 'definitely, go'.

MAY

THE PYRENEES IN MAY

ROB HUME

Rob Hume with young RSPB members (C.H. Gomersall, RSPB).

ROB HUME has kept bird diaries from the age of 12. He learned from years of intensive local birdwatching, but has since watched birds in many parts of Europe and Africa. A member of the national Rarities Committee, his rare bird finds include a 'first' for Britain. He has written numerous papers on birds, and is the author of several books. As well as being the editor of the Young Ornithologists' Club magazine, *Bird Life*, Rob is commissioning editor of the RSPB/AA *Complete Book of British Birds*.

A creak from the little wooden bed, a dull slap of bare foot on polished stone floor, a stab of pain as a toe hits a chair and I grope towards the chink of light that tries to penetrate the inner fog of my sleepy head. It was a late night. And these Pyrenean houses can be very dark with the shutters closed.

'If in doubt, start at the airport' is a tired old joke among worn-out travel writers. For the Pyrenees, starting at the airport is a problem. I have approached from the hazy air pollution, towering concrete office blocks and busy motorways of distant Barcelona, via the hot, flat plains south of Huesca, but when leading RSPB birdwatching holidays always from the west, from the port of Bilbao. This inky-black awakening was after such an arrival, with a long, long coach journey into the night through Vitoria Gasteiz and Pamplona, a town which, from the main road, appears to be entirely composed of new apartment blocks and offices, without a single visible house, and industrial outskirts. No wonder hotheads from Pamplona go out every weekend and shoot practically any bird and animal on sight.

The journey was punctuated by a meal in a roadside inn. Plenty of local red wine — *Don Elias — Navarro Vino Tinto* — cheered us. Six ordered fish — hake — but there was enough only for four. No, maybe enough for five after all. A couple of loaves and all would be well. This is the only bar where I can recall finding a nun enjoying an evening drink.

We had finally reached Berdún around midnight, to the exasperation of all the village dogs, and few of our party really knew what to expect. I had been before, and had stayed in this very room, but familiarity lent only increased anticipation to this first, early-morning view as I swept back the shutters. I knew it would be good.

Berdún is a small village, prosperous again after a lengthy decline, perched on top of a conical hill where the Río Veral, fresh from its short journey from the central Pyrenean peaks, joins the Río Aragon which begins in the hills north of Jaca and runs west and south-west to join the great Ebro, a

The walk through the Foz de Lumbier is guaranteed to give close views of vultures, crag martins and black redstarts (Rob Hume).

river that rises in Cantabria close to the Atlantic but perversely goes the opposite way to empty into the Mediterranean in a bird-rich wilderness of rice paddies and delta. From my window high up on the southern flank of the village, above the ancient walls, I can now see out over the Aragon plain to hills beyond — Portillo del Solaña, the Sierra de la Peña, the pointed peak of the Sierra de Oroel. The hills are pale grey-green, with soft, slightly darker modelling where shade eliminates detail. Nearer slopes are mottled and chequered with a variety of textures, harsh scrub and white sandy gashes of gullies and tracks. The valley floor is flat, and early, low light enriches the patchwork of colours. The hues are strong and beautiful, but slightly softened as if painted in gouache on an absorbent white board. Rectangles of heavy terracotta red, streaks of yellow and grey-green and yellow-green corn give a sharp-edged check, but in irregular, interlocking shapes. Clumps of olive-grey trees and low, dark banks where small, ephemeral streams have cut into soft shale create a pattern which brings to mind post-Impressionist paintings of hot, sharp landscapes.

A long, straight, grey road crosses the valley, leading towards Jaca, and a longer line of white pylons runs dead straight until out of sight. Invisible but essential are the nightingales. The air around the village fairly throbs with the song of them — every clump of bushes, every bushy hedge, every patch of trees has its nightingale, or two, and all compete for attention. The dawn chorus is a mixture of nightingale, spotless starling, screeching swifts and whiplash calls of quails. In the still air before dawn the quails make a remarkable volume of noise, but by the heat of the day they seldom stir. Then it is the drone of traffic, the barking of dogs, the laughter of children, the bells of a few sheep that carry far across the valley plain.

Here I am well south of the great Pyrenees peaks, surrounded by mere foothills where all is parched and the air shimmers with intensifying heat. Most birdwatching trips to the Pyrenees actually concentrate on these lesser hills. From my window I can see a place I know where there may be eagle owls breeding, though I have yet to find them myself. Then there is the hill where I watched red and black kites, griffon and Egyptian vultures, golden and booted eagles and, most

Left *Sitting to write notes of an early Bonelli's warbler, I missed my jinx bird — a black woodpecker* (Kevin Carlson).

Right *Berdun sits up on its hill above the badlands of the Rio Veral valley; at night its lights look like those of an ocean liner far out at sea* (Rob Hume).

Below right *A bee-eater, dazzling in its jewel-like brightness. They are often found perched on overhead telegraph wires* (M. Wilding, RSPB).

special of all, lammergeiers putting the rising air to maximum use. Beyond is the wooded slope where I came closest yet to seeing my jinx bird, when I sat down to write notes on an early Bonelli's warbler only to hear, but not catch a glimpse of, a black woodpecker which flew in front of my companion at the other end of the car. The same pines held short-toed treecreepers and special birds of high European forest, citril finches. That was on a trip around the excellent, clean and well-equipped camping sites of the Spanish Pyrenees. It was, indeed, good to be back, to recall some wonderful birdwatching moments and to anticipate more.

Breakfast in Berdún is taken at Prudencia's, a little bar and restaurant on the opposite side of the village. Reaching it means a walk through the tiny village square and past the old church, on the orange tiles of which stand little gatherings of sooty-black spotless starlings. So often in Spain I have found them aloof and hard to see well. Here they show off and welcome my attention, waving their wings loosely to either side in best starling tradition as they sing and chatter, and produce bell-like and twanging notes almost like some

exotic parakeets or tropical forest birds. Their long, loose, throat and flank plumes flicker in the breeze and the rising sun sends shafts of deep purple from the iridescent upperparts. I struggle to arouse much enthusiasm from the birdwatching group. These birds suffer from too close a similarity to familiar ones at home, rather like pallid swifts on the coast, to be given much attention by people eager to sample the more exotic colour of bee-eaters and hoopoes.

Prudencia's has a balcony which looks north and shows us the other side of our Pyrenean holiday. A deep, severely eroded valley falls away from the village hill, before a narrow cultivated plain. The Veral emerges from the mouth of a narrow gorge, the Foz de Binies, where I know griffon vultures will be circling in a cauldron of heat and wobbling air later in the day. But above and beyond all that rises a long, broken ridge of peaks, for the moment sharp against the pale sky before the midday haze softens the effect. They look close, almost rather small, as if a narrow line of moderate hills is all that separates northern Spain from the greener slopes of France. It is a misleading impression. These are peaks in the

true Alpine mould, big and impressive and many miles distant. Like all big mountain ranges, once penetrated, they have an awesome scale, a mightiness about them that dwarfs all things human. I feel insignificant but the sheer escapism, the joy of being in this gigantic landscape, stirs the emotions. I am not, alas, a mountain climber nor, these days, much of a high hill walker, but to be among the big hills, even if, as in the Pyrenees, I cheat and arrive by road, gives me a thrill rarely equalled in other kinds of places.

My first experience of big mountains was in Spain, not in the Pyrenees but at the opposite end of the country in the Sierra Nevada. Also unexpectedly vast and impressive, even in early summer they blocked my progress with deep snow. I struggled to a ridge and looked out over the peaks. There seemed little appreciable breeze, yet I could hear it, the soft soughing of gentle winds all around, building up in the deep valleys and flowing out over the tops in a continuous hum, almost a howl, that impressed me more than the wonderful view itself. The Pyrenees have the same feeling of extraordinary

Just part of the glorious view from the town of Berdún, over fields with quails, Montagu's harriers, crested larks and ortolan buntings (Rob Hume).

space and solitude, by no means a mere wrinkle on the face of western Europe but a genuine, massive barrier between Iberia and the rest.

There are still stories of bears in these hills, though the sad fact is that under half a dozen survive, and even they are not safe from gun and trap, though the fines for harming one are heavy. Wolves were shot out by 1910 but there are still one or two dog collars of thick leather with inch-long metal spikes, which gave protection from raiding wolf packs, kept as souvenirs. Hunting is immensely popular — so many wild boars had been killed the previous winter that a huge stew was made with the surplus meat and the whole village invited to the feast. When they heard that we were coming with a group organized by a society for *protecting* wild birds, the locals simply laughed out loud — birds are surely for *shooting!*

John and Vivien Boucher started a Painting School in Berdún in 1971. Since then it has widened its appeal and all kinds of groups have stayed in the two houses in the village and eaten at Alberto's and, latterly, Prudencia's. Promoting and maintaining the School is hard work. John books the transport, meets groups at the airport

and gives endless good advice, ably aided by Vivien, and between them they make the stay as comfortable and straightforward as can be. One of the houses has a lounge, with a bar (and incredibly cheap drinks) and tea and coffee, and it inevitably becomes the focus for every group morning and evening. Many bird lists have been called out in that room!

Prudencia provides endless wine — we only pay extra for coffee — and continual culinary surprises, so that one never knows what should be eaten with what, or what might turn up next. There are plates of meat, rings of squid, bread, vegetables, eggs, sausages, heaps of salads, sticky puddings, all brought individually to the table and attacked one at a time, according to whichever is the closest. It is part of the joy of the holiday, for this is, without doubt, always the best and happiest of all RSPB trips.

The village itself is a fascinating place to stay. The coach can get so far along the zigzag approach road then it is necessary to go on foot, up a steep rise and through a narrow gate in the old, buttressed fortress wall where screeching swifts and twanging rock sparrows nest. Berdún is a Celtic name, meaning 'a fortress on high', or a fortified village on top of a hill. There were Arabs in northern Spain from AD 711 though Berdún was never an Arab or Islamic town. It was from these high valleys that the 'Reconquista' began, the reconquest of this part of Spain from the Moors. Before them were the Visigoths, before them the Romans. Before the Roman invasion there were Celts on the site, making it a very ancient settlement. In 1592 there was a pentagonal castle, but it was pulled down in 1725. Though there has been no castle since, one end of the village is still known as El Castillo. There used to be a village below the hill, but it was raided and burned by the English in 1327. The fortress walls used to have three gates, all closed off by massive, inward-opening doors.

Once through the arch you enter the narrow streets and little squares with heavy, solid houses in continuous rows either side, finished in stone or stucco, white or buff, with broadly arched doorways and heavy timber doors (typical of Aragon), huge iron hinges, handles and latches, shuttered windows and balconies with black, wrought-ironwork, baskets of geraniums and caged canaries. The roofs are all wrinkled and warped, in cream, orange and red tiles and many houses have the characteristic Pyrenean chimney pot, a round stone construction topped by a little 'hat' held aloft on thin slabs. The houses are centred on a column with radiating beams and the ceilings have close, parallel beams topped by a series of curved tiles to give rows of long, narrow recesses. The tiles are topped by an earth infill, before a layer of heavy, flat tiles which make the floor of the next storey. On the roofs, the tiles overlap in a series of rows, so that each convex upper surface drains into a concave gutter

Elder-flowered orchids come in two basic colours, yellow and vivid magneta, often mixed together over large areas of high Pyrenean pasture (Rob Hume).

Some grassy slopes near the high passes of the Pyrenees are wonderful places for flowers, such as these splendid Pyrenean gentians (Rob Hume).

beneath. These ancient tiles — wrongly called Arab tiles — both add immeasurably to the visual appeal of the town and give extra opportunities for the birds. Apart from the spotless starlings, Berdún is full of sparrows and hordes of screaming swifts. The roofs are swamped, however, by a multitude of aerials, poles and cables.

Beside the church is a scruffy garden, once a grassy plot which served as *la lonja*, the market place. Beside it now is a very ornate house, owned by a rich absentee. It has its own chapel and mysterious features such as a tall column, embedded in the wall, and heavily carved eaves beloved of swifts.

Apart from this, Berdún and its land is owned by local people, with a wide spread of ownership, unlike many southern Spanish villages where ownership rests with just one or two families. There were once 1,200 people in Berdún — though then all were much poorer — but, in common with other villages, it suffered a decline in the 1950s when many people moved away to find jobs in the industrialized cities. The population is now only 350. Farming quickly

Riglos is an engaging shambles of tiled roofs nestling at the foot of huge cliffs of red conglomerate (Rob Hume).

became mechanized, so reducing the amount of work available locally. Currently its economy is based on cereal production but the effects of joining the EEC have yet to be assessed. One certain fact is that much of the Aragon valley system has such intensive agriculture that anyone going there in the hope of seeing pretty fields sprinkled with poppies and daisies is in for a shock — not a weed intrudes on the perfection of the crops. But in adjacent valleys around Berdún, the flowers are justly famous and colour the shimmering air in the scorching heat of midsummer.

The village dogs are a motley collection, but evidently kept for hunting; after their initial suspicion, they ignore visitors and carry on with their more important business of sleeping and dreaming of wild boars. They are fortunately equally sleepy at night, for Berdún has several scops owls that appear at dusk and call all night long with their monotonous, short whistles, bringing the birdwatchers out into the village streets. Appear is perhaps the wrong word, for it is the calls that make them obvious, and they are sometimes hard to see. Usually, however, given a week or so, most people will catch up with one sitting on a lamp post or silhouetted against the night sky on someone's television aerial.

Graffiti is mercifully sparse here, but there are slogans in opposition to plans to drown the valley beneath another big reservoir. Berdún people are acutely aware of the demise of other such villages along the Aragon and nearby valleys. Not far west is the Embalse de Yesa, a great, green lake which has flooded the farmland upon which the village of Tiermas depended. The whole village is now deserted on its hilltop, falling into ruin and a sad and depressing sight, good for nothing but swifts, starlings and rock sparrows. In the valleys *en route* to the high Pyrenees there are other villages completely bereft of inhabitants, sitting beside a new lake, mourning the loss of the cultivable land. Berdún, with its new granaries and shiny tractors, survives in a depopulated landscape.

Early on a sleepy Berdún morning José can be seen with his mule cart. He used to run a transport service to Jaca, a return journey which took a whole day. Not so very long ago — twenty or thirty years — there was a village barber who shaved all the village men every Saturday and was paid annually in measures of wheat. Now, even the village store is largely redundant, and the noisy rush every morning is caused only by children racing for the school bus.

Our bus arrives, too. Excursions from Berdún can be many and varied. To the south is the Embalse de Sotonera, west of Huesca, where whiskered terns and black-winged stilts, fan-tailed and great reed warblers, calandra and short-toed larks and other species can be added to a holiday list. Also south of the Aragon valley are the hot hills and spectacular conglomerate cliffs of Riglos and Aguëro, where I first saw a lammergeier and compared it with griffon and Egyptian vultures. Riglos has black wheatears, rock and blue rock thrushes, Dartford warblers, ortolan buntings and orphean warblers. Serins flutter about everywhere with their jangling, fragmented calls and woodchat shrikes watch for insects from the tops of fig trees. Crag martins swoop along the face of the cliffs, showing a mastery of flight unequalled by any other martin, sweeping in shallow curves,

stall-turning at the top of each to retrace the previous course, like an endless swingboat. They are like tiny versions of the black, red-billed choughs higher up over the crags. A peregrine soars overhead; then there is a booted eagle; a black kite, then two reds, a third, another black. A whole group of raptors this time — honey buzzards, sweeping from ridge to ridge, peak to peak, on their way northwards for the summer. All the time there is a kind of nervous anticipation, impatience, and an awareness that this is lammergeier country: one *could* be about to appear round the cliff wall at any moment.

Not far from Riglos we visited a refuse tip — from the sublime to the ridiculous, but even here good birds choose rough old places. In the middle of the tip, beautifully clean among the rubbish, is a black wheatear. On wires above are several bee-eaters. There are black kites at no range at all and griffon vultures hobbling about like little old men on the ground.

Narrow streets lead through Riglos village to the little church at the foot of the cliffs — rock sparrows and black redstarts are often on its roof (Rob Hume).

I am reminded of a group of vultures encountered in a higher valley. As we drove up so a column of birds drifted out of a little valley and spiralled out in the clear air. We found an empty car in the middle of nowhere, and vultures all around it. A band of them were too heavy to fly and simply scrambled to the top of a bank and watched us. I could see the flies crawling over their downy heads such was the closeness of their presence. I am not one to think of vultures as repulsive, even on the ground — instead, I found them fascinating. Where was the driver of the mystery car? What were the vultures eating? All we could find was a dead calf, as yet unopened, but presumably the object of the griffons' greedy attention. Long may they find some food. Once, with another RSPB group, in southern Spain, I watched nearly ninety, plus more in the air, at a dead cow by a village rubbish tip. It would be an easy matter to tip offal out for them from slaughterhouses to keep them going in years to come.

North of the Aragon are several deep gorges. Most of them are good for birds of prey, even if only passing by. Griffons breed in several.

Sometimes I have sat on a slope and had griffons fly by so close that I could hear the high whine of the wind through their primary feathers, splayed upwards to increase their stability by reducing wingtip turbulence. The front primary curves up more than the next, the second more than the third and so on, so that the whole wingtip warps rather than sweeps up in a simple curve. This complicates the shape so that a turning griffon, seen from ever-changing angles, can appear to have anything from broad, flat, square-tipped wings to deeply S-curved ones to narrow, upswept ones with pointed tips. Whatever their attitude, they are amazing birds in the air, simply wonderful to watch. They are never better than in a gorge near their nesting ledges, when two, three, even five or six together, will fly side by side, turning and banking in unison in an exhibition of the most perfect formation flying at speeds the Red Arrows would be proud of.

Egyptians are far less numerous, but against a tropical-blue sky, above a sun-baked rock, an Egyptian vulture looks truly beautiful. The body looks dark orange against the light, the wings and tail translucent white with a flush of pink, the flight feathers intensely black. Only on the ground does it become a dirty creature with despicable habits!

These gorges, the hot foothills and the high, snowy peaks are all equally likely settings for the rarest vulture of them all, the superb lammergeier. A tiny dot will appear over a distant ridge. Maybe something about it starts the adrenalin pumping. Could it be? Will it come this way? It does! It is! The dark colour above contrasts with a very striking creamy-white head, always a characteristic feature of an adult. Underneath, if you get a good view, you can see that a lammergeier is strongly coloured, not merely tinged, with orange. As it turns, the charcoal grey or dark brown of the upperside flashes silver in the sun. It floats and drifts with scarcely a muscle moving, then gives a single, deep, slow wingbeat that almost has the wingtips touching beneath it. A lammergeier leaving a perch is always a fabulous sight for me. It will have been motionless for ages, on a rock-face or a tree. Then, without warning, it simply 'falls off', spreads its wings — and goes! No need for powered flight, no wingbeats for this bird — it

Above left *Scrub-covered slopes near the village, with good views of the vultures over the cliffs, and many small birds at Riglos to add to the list* (Rob Hume).

Left *A row of low cliffs above the entrance to Foz de Lumbier provides a regular resting place for griffon vultures — while several other raptor species sail overhead* (Rob Hume).

Right *Griffon vultures, masterly effortless in the air, hobble about on the ground like little old men* (J.L. Roberts, RSPB).

Above left inset *The Egyptian vulture is small by comparison with the other vultures* (P. Van Groenendael and W. Suetens, RSPB).

Left inset *The bird that sets the adrenalin pumping — the lammergeier, or bearded vulture* (Eric Hosking, RSPB).

Main picture *The deep gorge of the Foz de Arabayon is overlooked by a special roadside viewpoint, a perfect bird- watching spot* (Rob Hume).

Right inset *Golden eagle — a great, dark bird* (Dennis Green, RSPB).

The black kite is a scavenger and one of the best places to see them is the local rubbish-dump! (S.C. Porter, RSPB).

flies along, parallel to the cliff, slow and serene, flat-winged and huge, on and on as if it must have a hidden engine somewhere to keep it aloft, slowly sliding on invisible rails, one wingtip always inches from the cliff as it neatly turns in and out to follow the contours of the rock-face.

One memorable evening I camped high in the Pyrenees, in a grassy valley with a rushing meltwater stream — an invigorating place for a wash at dawn — and in the last of the evening light a lammergeier floated across, gave its standard single, deep wingbeat, and alighted on a cliff. There were choughs about, too, coming to the green sward or flying over the peaks, but Alpine choughs, on this occasion, proved impossible to find. I have since seen both species on the same crag. Then, as the air cooled, the sun went down and the heavy scent of the shrubs began to subside, so a nearly full moon rose above a long, sheer crag. Against the pale disc flew two great, dark birds — a pair of golden

eagles taking the last of the evening air before settling down for the night.

In a high gorge, with a group, I stopped to look for something about which I had prior information. This was unusual, as we normally simply go to the best places and see what we can see. But this was to be rather special. An earlier party had come across a wallcreepers' nest in a roadside rock face, a quite sensational discovery. Would it still be there?

The cutting was cold and a very strong wind was driving through it, carrying bits of leaves and grass high into the sky above a rushing river. There was nothing. I could not even identify the crevice in which the nest had been, though we were obviously at the right spot. My group wandered off to a warmer place and I gradually ambled away. No — I must give it another go! Surely the birds would still be in the vicinity? Or had they cleaned out the resources of a little gorge when feeding young, and taken the whole family off to higher cliffs and new feeding areas?

I casually walked back to the right area. Hopes were pretty well dashed. Flick; flick and bob; flick again. From the corner of my eye I had caught a movement — a flash of colour — and there it was, a dancing, bouncing, wing-flicking little bird, all pearly-grey and black and white and flashes of gorgeous deep red, a wallcreeper, head-height and barely ten yards away! It was a moment of real magic. It looked at me and I stared at it, stunned by this sudden turn around of my fortunes. The wallcreeper hopped and jerked and disappeared into a crevice — now instantly revealed as the one so well described to me in advance. I called some of my group across as, at that moment, they reappeared nearby.

'I've seen one — a wallcreeper! It's in this hole just up here.'

If I could hardly believe my luck, the group found it even harder. Oh yes! In that hole, feeding flies to its chicks. Nothing happened. Nothing came out. It seemed an age, though maybe it was only twenty minutes. I was sure it hadn't come out — had I seen it at all?

Just as quick as before, the fabulous bird (I had almost begun to believe that it *was* fabulous, part of my imagination) came out and settled beside its nest. Then, with a quick flicker, it spread its wings, caught the wind and swirled vertically upwards, like a dead leaf, up and over the rock face and out of sight. We gave it a well-earned cheer.

After that, I just had to let the whole group see it. We moved to the head of the valley — where some of us saw a citril finch and all saw a lammergeier — then returned. Now, all follow me and keep quiet — look, that's the nest, just there — and — that's it! A wallcreeper! It came in bang on cue; left again very soon, flew across the gorge, fed, flew, fed again, flicked and bobbed and did all the things that wallcreepers do. It returned to the nest and flickered its wings in front of our eyes. It came in with great beakloads of insects, and it flew in and out of the gorge in superb flashes of colour, like a great burnet moth. What a bird that was!

Above the wallcreeper gorge the hills open out into broader, well-wooded valleys, with beautiful deciduous woods mixed with pines which eventually spread far up onto the more sheltered high slopes. These woods have some special

Pic du Midi D'Ossau rises beyond the border at Cool de Pourtalet, part of a magnificent panorama from the high pass (Rob Hume).

birds such as white-backed woodpecker, though I have yet to see them. There are short-toed treecreepers, crested tits and crossbills, but sometimes the woods disappoint. In fact, the woodland does seem to be rather British in character at times, with stacks of blackbirds, robins and tits.

Higher up there is quite a different world, up in the great hills, amongst the huge peaks such as Pic du Midi d'Ossau and the vast Sierra de Tendeñera range. Even in late May snow may block the roads and in such conditions I have seen snowfinches beside the customs post at Col de Pourtalet. In better weather, however, they are absent and alpine accentors take some finding on nearby crags. It is easier to see water pipits, ortolan buntings and black redstarts, on rocky slopes bright with blue gentians and carpets of yellow and vivid magenta elder-flowered orchids. The cliffs have chamois, if you are lucky. Whatever is there to be seen, the mountains have a tranquillity, solitude and wilderness that is now hard to find elsewhere in southern Europe.

Below the snow and the harsh peaks are alpine meadows, such as those around Formigal, where

Main picture *Slopes near Formigal can be covered with snow well into the summer, bringing snowfinches within easy reach* (Rob Hume).

Above inset *The booted eagle is so-called because of its heavily feathered legs. It feeds to a great extent on reptiles — a large lizard can be seen in the picture here* (P. Van Groenendael and W. Suetens, RSPB).

Left *Black redstart: a male at the nest. Even on the buildings of the ski resort, black redstarts are common, the males often intensely black and well-marked with white* (Kevin Carlson).

Left *The golden orioles take the prize for colour — of all the 'exotics' they remain most impressive, always much brighter, much purer yellow and jet black than any book can do justice to* (D. Green, RSPB).

Right *Lady orchids are frequently seen in areas of spiky, low scrub on hot slopes* (Rob Hume).

burnt-tip and vanilla orchids grow in flowery fields and ortolan and rock buntings sing side by side. Rock thrushes live here, too, looking especially splendid in their song flights and pausing to give more detailed views on stone walls or electricity wires, and there is always a chance of a good bird of prey though the vultures are now often distant specks instead of the close-up views of the lower slopes and gorges. Even on the buildings of the ski resort, black redstarts are common, the males often intensely black and well-marked with white, rather than the dull grey ones so often found in Britain. They sing constantly, with a grating, rasping chatter and short warble that can be hard to pin down. It is the same song that is so common at lower altitudes, when it is mixed with monotonous and equally elusive twangy notes from rock sparrows.

The hotter lower slopes are otherwise very different. Everything is hard and harsh, the grasses yellow and sharp and the shrubs thorny, the soil little more than painfully shattered rock. The green softness of the wetter high ground has gone. Black-veined white butterflies are everywhere and lizards scamper into cover in all directions. A fast, rattling trill is one of the commonest bird sounds, sometimes changing to a slower one more like a yellowhammer — the two songs of the cirl bunting. Such a rare bird in Britain, this colourful bunting is ridiculously common here. Males sit for minutes on end on top of a scruffy little bush, while the females grovel about in the grass below apparently unimpressed by the songs. From even quite small clumps of trees comes a surprisingly similar trill, but softer and looser, a little slower — the song of the Bonelli's warbler.

Loud, rising *'tchu-veee'* notes come from nowhere, cross the sky, and descend to materialize into the song of a tawny pipit: short-toed larks spit out their sharp, spluttery song in high, level, hovering display flights. Rapid, undistinguished warbles from bushes lead to subalpine warblers, the males beautifully blue on top and pinkish-orange on their chins. Chacking calls draw attention to a wheatear — a male seemingly so black and white that I always have a hard time trying to persuade the group that it is just a common wheatear, not a black-eared. 'Surely not! It's nothing like the one I saw at home.' There are always quiet whispers about the competence of the leader, supposedly unheard, at the back of the group. And flutey calls, the source of much speculation on the first morning, become gradually ignored by the party as crested larks are found to be common.

These birds and the bigger ones in the air above — a succession of booted eagles, red kites, black kites, short-toed eagles, vultures — are the essence of the Pyrenees trips, yet properly belong to the lower, more southerly hills and not the high peaks themselves. Especially dramatic are the deep, sheer-sided gorges. Some can be seen from above, others are best enjoyed from within. Either way, to be there by early morning, ready for the exodus of the vultures once the air has warmed up sufficiently to carry them, is a marvellous experience.

The air is rich with scents of flowers and aromatic herbs. The scratchy scrub has many orchids: lady orchid, monkey orchid and the big, strange, lizard orchid. In the tiniest wet patches by the river there are singing Cetti's warblers, their outbursts echoing from the rocks all round. Firecrests manage to be heard above the roar of torrents swollen with meltwater, their thin, high

songs having a great penetrative quality. Blue rock thrushes warble from the walls of the chasm. Dippers zip along the stream, chasing grey wagtails around corners and out of sight. Then the first griffon is up, circling and flapping heavily at first, before levelling out and flying in the way that vultures are meant to fly, gliding and soaring in a perfect display of aerial control. Maybe a peregrine or a hobby circles lazily up above, or a golden eagle is added to the list. Sometimes, if luck is with you, a pair of Bonelli's eagles will circle up and fly off over the hills, magnificent eagles with the power and presence of a really large bird of prey combined with the speed and agility of a goshawk. They are fearsome birds. More likely is a short-toed eagle, sometimes so close that every bar on every feather is etched onto the binoculars, the fierce yellow eye sparkling in the sun. This is another favourite of mine. By midday the sun really burns and the relief of deep shade in a green riverside wood is tremendously welcome, with feet in the river, head in the clouds, orioles singing all around.

Berdún, as a centre, is ideal for all of this and more, being surrounded by good birds and within easy reach of all the best valleys, hills and mountain passes. Even birds of prey are visible without leaving the confines of the village walls. I watched a family of peregrines hanging in a strong wind over Berdún hill one morning. They stooped at pigeons in the streets and came so close to me when chasing a pigeon in a nearby field that I felt that I was literally on the wrong end of a stoop — several times one of the big falcons roared overhead, just pulling out in time, the wind in its wings making a tremendous rushing noise. Their practice was interrupted by a booted eagle, but the big female peregrine soon decided that the eagle must be dealt with in no uncertain terms. In fact, I thought that she must eventually kill it, so close were her repeated stoops and so discomfited was the eagle. At each pass the bigger bird crumpled into a flailing heap, though later it did recover its wits enough to stick out a foot in an effort to keep the peregrine at bay. They were still hard at it after fifteen minutes and far off over Binies, with the whole peregrine family joining in the unceremonious eagle-bashing.

It is always a difficult question when an opportunity comes for travel abroad — whether to go to somewhere fresh, because there is so much of the world to see, or to return to a favourite place because it is simply so very good? When the Pyrenees beckon, the question is put aside. The valleys, the gorges, the mountains, the woods, the birds, flowers and butterflies, all have such a strong attraction that they are irresistible. The first morning view of the Aragon valley with its colourful fields, and the vista in the opposite direction that reveals the snow on distant, romantic peaks, will always bring back memories of birds and places already well known, and conjure up images of more to come.

JUNE
A SCOTTISH QUARTET
SAM KENNEDY

Sam Kennedy in birdwatching garb (Gordon W. McGowan).

SAM KENNEDY lives in Balloch on Loch Lomondside. Educated at Dumbarton Academy and Glasgow University, he teaches Modern Languages at Park Mains High School in Erskine. Apart from his two daughters, Heather and Hazel, his interests include natural history, mountaineering, photography, classical music and gardening.

Left *Looking east to Schiehallion over the Garbh Ghaoir river* (Sam Kennedy).

Ospreys had been elsewhere on Loch o' the Lowes*, angling down to gaff pike in a cluster of hooked claws. They had forsaken a summer squat above the bank opposite for a nest in a flattened stack of branches further along the loch. Great crested grebes staged an impromptu display: after ritual posturing and shaking of their summer manes of orange-to-chestnut feathers, they dived and re-emerged, bills stopped with weed, to paddle breast to breast in a sham greeting of long-lost lovers.

Our journey home late in the June afternoon was indirect and led along the wooded shores south of Loch Tay from Kenmore to Killin. Red squirrels clambered up the masts of birch into the rigging of leaves. A goldfinch posed in a glade where soldier beetles mated on the ferns. Over the water lay the mountains of the Ben Lawers range and the ridge of Meall nan Tarmachan west of Loch na Lairige.

Some years before, I had first ventured into the Scottish hills to look for ptarmigan, and it had been to Meall Garbh and Meall Greigh, the eastern outliers, that I had gone. Fittingly, as we headed up to the snowfields late in April in search of the mountain birds, we had passed Lochan nan Cat. A curlew fêted the spring in song: spilling clear from the sky, it poured in a rapturous cataract over the mountains, and fell and died down the valley. Golden plovers mourned cries across the moorland. Ravens had braved the glacial chill rising in blusters of wind over the summit of Meall Garbh as we had moved east in the lea of the hill to approach Meall Greigh. It was comparatively mild as ptarmigan croaked and cowered along the hillside, then felt safe, and stood erect. Red wattles above a livery of almost uniform grey was summer fashion for the male: the female, cautious and undecided as to winter ermine or spring-time moorland brown, plumped for a seasonal mixture. Over Loch Tay a golden eagle had turned in the sunlight towards the southern banks where we now stood. That first adventure in mind, I vowed an early return.

*Loch o' the Lowes is a nature reserve managed by the Scottish Wildlife Trust.

Above *Soldier beetles mating* (Sam Kennedy).

It was midsummer eve then, and unpromising weather when Dan and I came to climb the satellite peaks to the north and west, Meall a' Choire Leith and Meall Corranaich, and cross Beinn Ghlas to Ben Lawers. In fact I had already fulfilled my initial vow on a June ramble some few years since, when newts swam inelegantly through pools beneath the Tarmachan ridge. A small mountain ringlet graced the hillside meadow cut by the burn and splashed with purple pansies and yellow mountain saxifrage.

We left now in the early morning greyness and by-passed the Hill of the Bird, Meall nan Eun. Red grouse sprang from the heather in alarm, fired repeated rounds of calls and dived for cover. Beyond the confluence of streams we entered lower Coire Gorm; ahead, bilberry blanketed the western approaches to Meall a' Choire Leith. Glints of sunlight patched the valley where June warmth jacked the cloud mass up to clear the lower tops. A swift flew east over Coire Leith, and was gone as we reached the rise onto Meall Corranaich. Moss campion embossed the ridge

in stars of pink. Wastes green yet desolate in the wilderness of time, the mountains stretched on all sides round the Earth, and small life hid and thrived among the large and lonely places.

Meall Corranaich behind us, we dropped to the col below Beinn Ghlas. A ring ouzel left Coire Odhar to contour north around the mountains as wheatears chased crane-flies by the tarn. Unnourished by the sun, wood sorrel nestled stunted on the northern slopes. Snow gentian must have melted into the vastness, but flakes of alpine mouse-ear chickweed were sprinkled about the grassland.

Beyond Beinn Ghlas summit, the ridge fell and rose in a curve, past cliffs undermined by rock-fall. From Ben Lawers, Lochan nan Cat sat in the matt waters tailing down to whiskers of stream joining the Lawers Burn. I moved due east and caught the ridge to the moorland. A snow bunting opted to stay high on the crumbling rock path to the south. Meadow pipits banked over to the lochan, and cowberry and common cow-wheat flourished among wild grasses and heather. Beds of bog cotton and drops of sundew populated the marsh. Small heath butterflies clutched grass-sheaths on the moorland fringe, while cuckoo taunts drifted up the burn from the larch strip.

The Ben Lawers massif had broken the spring lock on a June casket of gems: within were rare and semi-precious stones set in summer mountings. Polished only lightly by the sun, some sparkled on the banks of Lawers Burn: butterwort and thyme in the dampness, birdsfoot trefoil among the boulders. A dipper branched up past alpine lady's-mantle draped along the path. From stone to stone, a grey wagtail flicked downstream to the forest.

I followed and heard stonechat chapping at the entrance to the reserve. The burn flowed through gorges lined with alder, birch and mountain ash into peat-brown pools lathered by waterfalls. A mistle thrush stormed low towards the farm as a buzzard circled and landed in the peaks of the larchwood. Clouds had held tight rein on the sun, rearing loose in high-kicking spurts and gallops over the flanks and saddles of the June hills. The grey high summer crossed the mountains at a gentle canter, and pulled up short in blue pools of sky to the north.

Main picture left *Lochan nan Cat, An Stuc and Meall Garbh from Ben Lawers* (Sam Kennedy).

Above left inset *Ptarmigan hen — a seasonal mixture of winter ermine and spring-time moorland brown* (Sam Kennedy).

Right *Grey wagtail — a frequenter of flowing upland streams* (Sam Kennedy).

Downhill, to the east, common blue butterflies now danced jigs on the meadow. Self-heal and field speedwell flowered in the open; vetches latched onto undergrowth along the fence. A dunnock shied off from the farmyard as swallows trailed pitchfork tails around the steading. Dan had retraced his steps from the top of Ben Lawers to allow me the luxury of a full traverse, and we met up again on the track.

Lark song had trickled onto marsh and heathland; along these valleys adders sneak, a threat to troves of wader chicks and nomad frogs alike. The tide had turned on day and would soon, slowly and imperceptibly, head out upon the year. Midsummer flowed over crests and crags where peregrines slice across the sky, and golden eagles scan the mountains that ripple to the edges of their world.

Lomond in the gloamin'

On a golden evening in June when a ripe sun hung over the parkland, I left home to take my usual walk above Loch Lomond and see the mountains. As I set out, I looked in vain for the curlew flying west over the loch. Fooled again! They catch me every time, the starlings. It may be paranoia, but I am sure they practise. 'Here he comes. Do your redshank impersonation! Go on! That got him last week.' Not a curlew in sight, just the wheezing starling medley and mimicry delivered from a rooftop aerial.

I left the estate and walked towards the North Lodge of Balloch Park. A carrion crow had a brood high in the oak-tree by the gate, and rooks were feeding in the pasture adjoining the road. A strange and welcome sound carried over from the east. Was I being had once more? This time my suspicions were unfounded. Yes! A corncrake slunk through the grain-fields in a line parallel to the hedgerow. As rare as they were tuneless, the calls alone betrayed this private visit. A top-secret agent, he blew his own cover. So undetectable otherwise, in a camouflage of brown and buff, the corncrake yearned and advertised for company of his own kind to share the lushness of the long June days — and was disappointed.

I knelt at a break in the hedge, stone-still and hopeful. The corncrake perched on a post momentarily to reward me with a glimpse. A field

Left *Oystercatchers had bred in the spring* (Sam Kennedy).

Above right *Coots nodded a sedate withdrawal to the heart of the dam* (Sam Kennedy).

away oystercatchers circled over the barley, their high-pitched piping strident in the evening calm. They had bred in spring and the young scurried among the crops, a perfect protective maze.

Belled spires of foxglove towered above dog violets and speedwell on the verge; brambles tangled with broom along the dry-stone dyke. Willow warblers shuttling to and fro from their nest in the grass fought an unequal battle to cater for the endless demands of growing chicks. Caterpillars dangled from the leaf-tips and were snatched as cannon fodder by the parent warblers.

The Campsie Hills glowed across the farmland as the Leven valley dipped darker and cooler out of the sun. I had walked up through the orchid marshes, over the moorland to the hill-fort and on to Carman Dam early in the previous evening. In the saddle between the tops, and this time no imposter, a curlew had risen and beaten a retreat then looped and taxied down the valley-flank. Irked, it yelped to the young to go to ground, and paused for an instant lower on the hill-side. Back over the slopes it flew, calling their names . . . *curlew . . . curlew . . .*

At the reservoir, little grebes had sped away and splashed to a halt as coots nodded a sedate withdrawal to the heart of the dam. I had turned back onto the round hill and veered over to the west. A grey hen harrier had flapped and glided and skimmed the moor where I had seen the curlew. When I dropped down from the ridge in the gloaming I had met a straying urchin, a hedgehog far from hedge or wood.

June is the year fledged: a year brooded under winter snow, hatched from buds and fed on heat and rain by spring. In plumage of oak- and alder-green streaked through with silver birch, June launches summer in the air with wing-flash covert flowers all gaudy under the woodland green. Mud-dull and vulnerable and housed in a yew-hedge further down the valley, blackbird fledglings would shortly leave the nest to join a fat young thrush, breast speckled now and full in feather.

I walked on up the shaded road where hollies flowered white. A wren wove among needles of Scots pine and the beech-hedge bordering the spinney. By the bend on the brow, green plovers tumbled and spun in the field, twisting and

Left inset *Herb-Robert — a familiar member of the geranium family* (Sam Kennedy).

Main picture *Ben Lomond, Loch Lomond and the Luss hills* (Sam Kennedy).

Right inset *Common sandpiper breeds near upland streams. Its constant bobbing movements when feeding make it easy to recognize* (Sam Kennedy).

haranguing a passing carrion crow. Perched in an oak-tree near the farm, a yellowhammer sang its song of summer, a ballad told in many verses. There was still juice to press though, from an evening sun soon to fall behind the western hills. The road led downhill into Boturich estate past the conifer plantation on the east.

Over the fence at the estate entrance, dog-rose bloomed pink beside the hawthorn. Great spotted woodpeckers appeared to have deserted a favourite haunt in the Fairy Glen and doubtless drummed along the lochside alder-groves, digging in piton claws to scale the severest pitch in search of grubs, or returned to their summer base camp tunnelled down a rotting trunk. Often I have seen them rising and dipping in flight down through the bluebell woods, or heard them hammer on the birches in the upper glen.

Meanwhile, moles held a fortress beneath the soil raised in encampments on the edge of the Whin Park. Swallows had plastered nests to the beams in the barn and, in a bid to provide for their offspring, scooped up punnets of insects fresh from the hay-field. Up and down they roved, whiling the evening fruitfully away, flipping and flapping and twittering till the fields cooled and the hatch went down.

Behind the rookery a row of ash entangled the sun in a mesh of branches. The Scots pines etched against the sunset were ebony as the rooks streaming from their tree-top nests in a disgruntled exodus. Lime-trees alternated with horse-chestnuts a short way along the road. A thrush had struck and smashed the many dozen snail-shells strewn around an anvil stone. A rustle and shuffle in the lane, and a roe-buck padded out into the clearing by the stile. One whiff and glance and off he bounded, up the woodland break.

June had raised a tricolour of bugle, stitchwort and campion. Amid bunting of mauve-flowered clover and tassles of dandelion-heads were common spotted orchids in candles of light pink. Opposite-leaved golden saxifrage lined the ditch on the bend as herb-Robert and ragged-Robin stood by. Soon there would be servings of wild strawberry and cream meadowsweet.

A car passed — a Vauxhall Cavalier. Both driver and passenger wore tweeds and smiled as they drove by. I returned the greeting and was unwittingly guilty of generosity. They stopped at the open gate to the silage field. Enjoying the sunset, I thought innocently. 'Grand evening', I'd say when I reached the junction. A rifle-butt leaned on the open window sill, aimed and fired into the field. They seemed pleased and smiled once more in the passing. I looked straight ahead: it was a black car, a hearse for a hare. There is much in a name — 'Cavalier' was right.

As the sun went down calls came up through the woodland fringe, from mallards in the strait. I stood long at the gate till a skliff of moon had taken over watch and stars were posted on all the frontiers of the sky. The mountains west massed black, and magical Ben Lomond lowered over the islands. Pipistrelles split from the cocoon of night and flittered in the weak starlight as I turned on my earlier path. At Over Balloch, tawny owls called from a haunt by the castle and hunted through the dark and into morning to disappear on the dawn.

I left Balloch early next evening, following the short stretch of river north to its source in Loch Lomond. The day had been sultry throughout, and still a hotness persisted. The gap in the riverbank, so often hung with mists and overflown in winter and spring to a sludge of earth and reeds, was crust in the June heat. A coal tit picking a way among the birch and alders could have owned the nest in the oak roots in mid-spring, a fluff cup brimming with life some few yards into the park.

In spirals round the beech and oaks along the loch-side, a treecreeper probed the bark for insects, while red-breasted mergansers swam and dived in the southern loch out from the stream stepping down in pooled ledges and waterfalls, a natural border to the park. Yellow lesser spearwort and pimpernel flowered beside the bramble-wire fencing and the alder-wood.

Loch Lomond had receded and hemmed the mud-banks with summer sand and shingle. Pungent bog myrtle and yellow iris spikes prospered on the rim of the wood. A common sandpiper rounded the shore-line: jetting low to the loch, it quivered and called, then perched and bobbed nervously. Off it flew, cornering a jut on the land to wade and feed in the shallow margins of the loch. Brooches of may-fly fastened on grasses by the waterside and escaped the avid trout cruising and ringing the bay on the evening rise.

Tree pipit — a summer visitor to Great Britain with a distinctive song flight (Sam Kennedy).

From above the gravel pits at Midross a sun-brand scorched across the loch, petering in the few ripples close to shore. Dim and dank by day, the cool wood warmed in the yellow ebb of evening sun. Dusts of sunlight slanted through the rafters: beams of shadow joisted the woodland floor. Warbler song carried on the stillness as blackcaps sang and chiffchaffs called. To the trill of a wood warbler high in the canopy I rose from the water's edge into broken forest and scrub.

There had been darkness in the day: I saw the evidence, chaffinch feathers in chaos fresh around a plucking post. The sparrowhawk soars overhead on reconnaissance, bullets along lanes or shaves the hedgerow to strike by surprise. Ignorant or unmindful of the gore, a tree pipit took to the sky in song, then fluttered back to land. Lit brilliant blue, damsel-flies in tandem wheeled along on rickety wings and drifted into the green banking by the pond. The hills were set to hide the sun easing down behind Glen Finlas ridge.

Sundown brought the paring of moon and a shiver of breeze. A roding woodcock clipped the tree-tops, circled and sought the silent confines of the wood. Pheasant crowing rang across the dusk fields as twilight flushed moths out from the forest edge. Black around the ivied oak-tree on the rise, a bat darted this way and that on a flurry of wings. Sharp in the bleary night, wood owls practised lawless business outwith daylight hours, unharried by the protection racket of blackbird, wren and jay.

June days are long, and I long for June days: slow days when swifts race, dull brown in bright sun, screaming through the evening calm. Pebble eggs on the beaches hatch to dashes of ringed plover chicks, sprinting in bursts along the inland and the island shores. Terns from half a world away have come on ocean winds, swallowing up the seas to reach the summer light lands of the north.

Summer daze

Our plan was more of the same — a return trip to Rannoch Moor to our student quarters in a railway bothy. We had visited these archives before, branching out on occasion to check on

Left *Ants criss-crossed over fungi —* Omphalina ericetorum (Sam Kennedy).

Below right *Dunlin — black-bellied in their summer plumage* (Sam Kennedy).

even remoter sources. Curiosity had taken us to both Corrour Siding and the native pine-woods north of the Glen Lyon hills. Mainly, however, we had delved into the moorland south of Loch Laidon, an inexhaustible library for reference and pleasure.

On our study trip to Loch Ossian, a pall of low mist hung over Beinn na Lap and the peaks of the Ben Alder range. West of the rail-track, the sun glared through the clouds and shafted down in wands of light onto the bog-land and the lower slopes of Leim Uilleim. Dabchicks fussed around the young grebes on the lochan nearest the station, while wheatears jaunted among the rocks. We scattered over the moor in a loose sweep search. A wood tiger moth, garish in repellent guise of black and yellow, occupied a berth on the moorland floor. Ants wandered and criss-crossed over fungi, and cloudberry grew appropriately higher on the mountain-side.

In complete contrast the Black Wood of Rannoch: a definitive work to be flicked through repeatedly. We followed the path by Allt Camghouran where greenshank chicks bolted over the pebbles and grey wagtails balanced on

boulders by the river. Upstream the path turned east to the edge of the woodland. A red squirrel shot across the heather into the cover of the woods past termite mounds of squirrel-red. To prise out much-prized seeds, crossbills climbed round an overhang of cones on the lowest branches of a Scots pine. Overhead a buzzard laboured westwards grasping a glut sack of rabbit. Fact had begun to read like fiction when a golden eagle emerged over the summit of Cross Craigs.

The Black Wood of Rannoch is prehistory and present, a time-warp of ancient loveliness, amber in the sunlight. Fritillaries floated among heathers and alpine lady's-mantle in the forest surrounds. We walked through this thick yet open woodland and saw the black bird of The Black Wood; or rather, failed at first to see it. A capercaillie, detonated in the bracken, exploded in a shrapnel of wings and sounds, spraying and echoing into the distance.

Yes, indeed, more of the same! As we boarded the train at Dumbarton Central, we knew of a treat in store. Few journeys can match the grandeur of the West Highland line as it snakes through the valleys of western Scotland: from

Tarbet along Glen Falloch to Crianlarich, then west and north through Strath Fillan. Beyond Tyndrum it heads for Bridge of Orchy and skirts Beinn Dorain to cross Rannoch Moor to Fort William. See Rannoch station and die!

Documented fact states that Rannoch Moor lies between the Black Mount and Loch Rannoch's Black Wood, and stretches from the Glen Orchy hills to those south of the Great Glen. A browse or deeper summer dip into the moor uncovers vast shelves of manuscripts, some ice-age old. Vellum texts, heirlooms passed down the generations, appear in re-print soft-bound small editions. There are thrillers and mysteries and poetry aplenty, anthologies sorted under 'GOD' or 'ANON'.

When day sleeps lightly and wakens early, that is summer. When the flit and hover and jink of flight is everywhere, that too is summer. When grasses stand high and swaying and the grasshopper chafes a festive song of hide-and-seek, it is assuredly summer, and last year's scattered grains make present and future of the past. From Stob Gabhar to Schiehallion, snipe drum and drum in rising beats. Steeped in mud-water and moss, octopus sundews lure and digest captive insects. Butterflies flash blue and falter to land, wings folded in disguise, among ladders of vetch. Shuffling through the undergrowth, a dunlin herds an anarchy of chicks. It is the best time, the time of thyme, soft summer-time.

To see and hear, a pace away, a snipe squelch and rustle, to catch the curdle of clouds reflected in the dark gloss of its eye, is wealth indeed. To watch its clutch hatch and rise to stand unsteady, then, hours later only, step out into the uncertain murk of survival, is riches untold. When you have charted their progress over days, heard faint life-filled cheeps in the mottled ovals of shell, and seen the product of your waiting, there is poignancy in an unspoken farewell.

Vapour idles over the moor for days, almost immobile, allowing a diffusion of weak sunlight to dull the canvas to monotones. On the fine days, rare and precious, the sun paints an extravagant tableau. It shines the lochans to a finish of chrome, their sheen rippled in the wake of queer grey birds. Coasting half-submerged, head uptilted in primitive quizzical poise and haughtiness, the red-throated diver lives in

wilderness, unsheltered but untethered.

Water-marked, among the rarer works, the Rannoch Rush is found in only two small pools. Others yet are special issue: we happened on a birth, not the heaving writhe of the mammal, but a sober and silent extrication. From the nymph, black and sinister, a dragonfly had flexed and slid, and clung to a stalk of grass above the spent mask and shell of an armoured womb. At rest, this new primaeval creature hung pristine wings to dry in the buffeting wind.

Among the tilted tubes of reed, a poplar hawkmoth clasps a roost. A bull-headed creature with finned wings of greys and greens, it leaves when the bats stir, and returns replete to latch once more to its inconspicuous sanctuary. In the weaving hags and rock and peat puddles which drain the moor to the river, frogs crouch importantly, then reckless, spring to seize a passing meal.

It is not fiction that the river never sleeps, bids endless welcome to the traveller who comes to drink and wander on. It twists to form reeded breakwaters where anxious flights of teal splash down and scuttle to cover. It forks round mid-river rockeries of marsh lousewort and greater butterfly orchid. True to tell, the river is never lonely. At dusk and through the half-light of summer night, red deer steal unheard to its sustaining shallows. It accommodates the restless sandpipers which carry summer on their wings and gorge on the abundance of beetles and larvae. Fantasy, perhaps, that the river is never silent: a million soliloquies; in sum, a hubbub of rumour on which you try and fail to eavesdrop.

The river dances in an iridescent spray of drizzled sunlight as massive boulders bar its forceful passage to the east. On and under the banks, dippers build moss-domes lined with scarce leaves from the few trees nearby. If startled in their rake for caddis deep in the slow twirling pools or causewayed flows, they speed plump and incongruous to privacy.

Perfumed among bog myrtle and fragrant orchids, the emperor moth grub sits decked in emerald finery. Eyebright, bright-eyed, and chickweed, wintergreen in summer white, hide among the heather, where meadow pipits have thrown and placed their fine small pots of nest: late extra broods or second editions fed on

Left *Emperor moth caterpillar — emerald green, it feeds on heather before pupating to become a large, handsome moth, with an 'eye' on each wing* (Sam Kennedy).

Above right *Rannoch Moor — just before dawn. The river, the loch and the clouds showed lilac* (Sam Kennedy).

demand from summer's full supply. In detachable leather binding, the sun-drunk lizards crave the heat. Mostly skim-read, merely glimpsed, they scour the grasslands thick with insects and slurp down moths in daydreams or the unsuspecting spider. They in turn beware the dark swoop of merlin, blue-grey and lethal magic.

An early tome stood prominent among the classics. One June dawn the river, the loch and the clouds showed lilac to a heron lifting into the first flare of sunrise off east. In little time, a lightening storm of yellow and gold enveloped both sky and river as the sun balanced on the horizon. Mist froze in a whale-spout above the foremost low rise of land, and dispersed and evanesced over Loch Eigheach: there the river gurgled, slithered and raced in a golden lava. Day was born a glorious fanfare but became too soon a grey and wizened dirge of winds. From a raised stump of ancient forest, tracts long out of print, a slender greenshank piped volubly while a golden plover in broken plumage of black, grey, white and gold, moved off at a trot and stop, calling with incomparable sadness. Thoughts strayed to volumes not yet come to press, to the possibility of unusual sandpipers, stint or phalarope.

Murder was represented: that deceptive fluttering flight betrayed a merlin. In an obvious plot it turned on whinchats in a swift and tight attack. Different tactics are employed by the peregrine that sailed over and silenced the moor, swung low and spread fear, oppressing all else to a hush of timorous hiding. With few wing-beats it created inordinate propulsion, a momentum dissipated in long glides or spluttering to halt with a stoop and kill.

Meteor summer shoots low through space, trailing seed-head shards and shells across the land. Autumn leaves and geese pass south, 'but thy eternal summer shall not fade'. The Moor of Rannoch gathers fallow winter's harmless must to lie neglected, lost from view. Antiquarian spring discovers and blows dust from the sleeves of continuing sagas, odysseys and natural epics endless as the sun.

Bass Special

ARCHITECT-DESIGNED/SOLID, DESIRABLE STONE-BUILT RESIDENCES/CLOSE TO ALL AMENITIES/NO MOD CONS, BUT BOASTING OUTSTANDING SEA VIEWS/LARGE WELL-STOCKED MARINE BEDS A FEATURE/IDEAL SUMMER FAMILY HOME.

ENTRY BY AGGRESSION.

THE PROPERTY SECTION OF THE GANNET GAZETTE IS PROUD TO PRESENT THE BASS ROCK, MOST ANCIENT OF OUR LISTED MANSIONS, COMPRISING COUNTLESS UPPER AND LOWER CONVERSIONS TEMPERED TO SUIT THE MODERN MARKET, SOME IN NEED OF REFURBISHMENT.

After early viewing in spring, gannets move in on the purchase of the winds from wintering over northern oceans or roving south to the milder seas, return to the Bass Rock in the Firth of Forth to settle and create. And how they create! An infernal din and squabbles attend the ceremony as they bow in to repossess and decorate their precious mounds of putrid vegetation. In this closest of communities each pair lives, often literally, out of others' pockets of grass and sea-weed. All charity begins and ends at home!

Not for the gannet the neighbourly spirit, nor any need to co-operate to survive. Latin temperament and demeanour married to a Viking propensity for pillage typify its domestic ways. Anchored to the nest-site, the air around the gannet is thick with distrust and difference of opinion and interests, perpetual vital petty wrangles.

Right *The gannetry on Bass Rock — the birds nest just out of each other's reach (Sam Kennedy).*

Below *Bass Rock — only 440 yards (400 metres) by 300 yards (275 metres) wide, this tiny island in the Firth of Forth holds one of Britain's major gannetries (Sam Kennedy).*

Weighing anchor, the gannets set full sail, off on billowing spinnakers. They breeze a cool course round the cliff heads, then up, out and over the sea to join the regatta of other small craft. Beneath, cosseting the single egg or brooding squabs, batteries of sentinel gannets thwart the scoundrel gulls all the June days long. With a trailing rudder of webbed feet and braking on flung-back wings, the returning bird alights by the nest. This done, the adults fence in their intimacy with a crossing of bills and excited greetings.

Mid-morning in mid-June, we left North Berwick harbour and eiders diving for crabs or occupying temporary moorings on the rocks. Off-shore, guillemots staged a fly-past or rode the gentle swell. High-rise from the sea in partial white-washed cladding, the Bass Rock drew in throngs from the sky and earned the avian estate agent's tag 'much-sought-after dwelling'.

We disembarked in the cove on the south-east where kittiwakes claimed the lower ledges and screamed above the breaking waves and growling caws of gannets. Plain black-legged gulls, they perched precariously by cupped nests facing the

eastern sea. The footpath wound past the foghorn, up in steps to ring-side seats in the big-top, the gannetry proper.

An initial diversion to the numerous side-shows led us low over the southern cliff-tops. Against a backdrop of guano-splattered rock, cormorants performed a comic double-act, re-creating a hall of mirrors. The spotlight fell from the late-morning sun onto shags preening in hollows worn from the stone. Ochre-chinned and satin-breasted, wine-bottle-green to their tail cockade, the glum-faced shags sat tight to the nest.

Crowds of guillemots spectated from the stone-stands opposite, rising above the inlet. Puffins whirred out to sea and back, a short but colourful turn guaranteed to amuse. A razorbill peered up from the tiniest platform on the rock-face as gannets whirled high overhead, and rafts of auks gathered on the waves beneath.

Up the path past mallow and campion in full bloom and clumps of light-pink thrift, we edged west to enjoy the masters of the trapeze: fulmars skated on stiff blade wings clipping the cliff-edge, shooting high and plummeting deep to the lapping surf. Others ensconced on nests among

Left *Shags — a comic double act. Ochre-chinned and satin breasted, wine-bottle-green to their tail cockade* (Sam Kennedy).

Right *Herring gull — a predator on untended eggs* (Sam Kennedy).

Below *The gannet chick or 'guga' soon loses its white down for a dark, white-speckled plumage. Juveniles become progressively whiter, attaining full adult plumage in their fifth year* (Sam Kennedy).

Grey seals by the entrance to the cave (Sam Kennedy).

tussocks of grass dared a closer approach, prepared to discourage further intrusion with a jet of noxious fluid.

No compère was needed to announce the day's star-billing — a spectacle beyond compare! The gannet colony smelt rank and was deafening, reminiscent of insanitary slum-housing with every ill-natured tenant embroiled in rancorous dispute but sight and sound more than compensated for the stench. The path angled east then north alongside small colonies of lesser black-backed and herring gulls and soon skirted the main gannetry.

Anxious parent-birds screamed defiance at herring gulls diving low across the nursery in search of untended eggs. Others regurgitated a mash of fish to satisfy the black and hungry offspring tucked each beneath a soft goose-down. White gugas like poodle-pups were fat and more than satisfied. The young of previous years, still immature, clubbed together on the periphery or floated past on darker wings, feet dragging as they flew.

Though unmolested now, the Solan goose suffers a hostile press: daubed a fool, or madman, *le fou de bassan;* deemed boorish and awkward, *der Basstölpel;* maligned simply as a glutton: the gannet. Away to the horizon, this sad-faced clown in sinister mask turned acrobat and showman

extraordinaire. Further than a far cry off, troupes of gannets in swirling flurries performed out on the blue-green firth, plunging and folding to spear through the sea and snap up sprats and herring. Back west they would fly laden with a full crop, sea-farers welcomed home with their sea fare.

We returned on the path, passing the nesting gulls and kittiwakes lodged above the bay. All aboard, we rounded the island to head to port. Guillemots stood by the portals to the cave-way on the north. Seals were treading water, deep-green silk waters greyer in reflections from the arches. They eased beneath the surface in smooth slides, popping up again among the feathers shed by the birds we had visited.

The June sun had warmed the fresh sea air and glistened through the spray as the boat had sheared over to the island: the early clouds broke and thinned to patches against the blue. Now on our return, the sea frothed up white and turquoise in the slipstream, though deeper sunlit blue beyond. Sheer-cliffed and summer green, the Bass Rock rose from a plinth of sea behind us: a silent rock it seemed, and lifeless. But we knew better now, having seen over the property and met the residents.

JULY

WELSH WOODLANDS IN JULY

JOHN ANDREWS

Life-long naturalist John Andrews

JOHN ANDREWS is Chief Advisory Officer at the RSPB, travelling widely in the UK and overseas to advise land managers on ways of integrating the needs of birds with farming, forestry and a range of industrial activities. A life-long naturalist, his interests extend to ferns, trees, dragonflies and the history of man's relationship with the countryside as well as birds.

I am appallingly bad at getting up in the morning. To my mind it is delightful to lie in bed watching the early morning sunlight strike in through the windows and listening to the songs of birds, already hard at work attracting mates or defending territories. And, of course, if it's wet then that's an excellent reason for snatching a few extra minutes' shut-eye.

The trouble with the bedroom at Rhyd y groes is that you really cannot tell what is happening outside. A little stream falls down the hillside past the side wall of the house and drops into the river that flows about 50 yards (45 m) away. Their combined noise drowns out not only birdsong but also wind and rain, so that the only way you can judge the weather is by listening for the deep booming noise that the river makes when it's running really full after rain in the surrounding hills. And the bedroom window isn't much help. It's tiny and set low into one corner of the room so that you can only see the sky from it by kneeling down. I am sure the Welsh farmer who built the house put in small windows partly to minimize heat loss and partly because he and his family would have spent most of the daylight hours working out-of-doors, but he would almost certainly approve of the effect which that little window has on lie-a-beds like me, forcing me to get up, stagger down creaking stairs and open the front door to test the morning air.

The house is in a narrow valley, its back wall partly buried in the slope of a hill to shelter it from the worst of the west wind, though it does make it more than averagely damp. The front faces east and the steep opposing hill cuts off the sunshine until quite late in the morning. When the sky is clear, the sun strikes the hillside above the house, shining on heather and oakwood and steep slopes of jumbled rock. However, in mid-Wales rainy days are much more frequent than sunny ones, and this was no exception. The cloud base was down close to the hilltops and the air was misty with a fine drifting rain.

There wasn't much bird song either. July is a bad month for birding here. No, that isn't quite true. All the breeding birds are still around but song has virtually finished. In its place, all the

Once all the hillsides of Wales were covered in broadleaved woodland, but today most of the land has been cleared for grazing (John Andrews).

young birds newly out of their nests are squeaking and chirping — either begging for food or trying to keep contact with the family party. Many of the calls are like each other, and quite difficult to identify. In other words, you have to work for your birds. If you are prepared to do so, you can learn a lot in the process. If you are not prepared to make the effort, you can still have a thoroughly enjoyable day in delightful country, regardless of the weather.

Despite the enforced early rising, I rarely manage to leave the house early. Have a good leisurely breakfast and you do not need to carry so much food to eat during the day. I have never regarded walking as an end in itself. I can cover ground when I have to, but I would just as soon dawdle as not. I enjoy sitting by a track-side and watching things happen, or not happen as the case may be. And not being a committed walker, I don't wear the regulation boots. Wellies are good enough for every hill farmer, out in all weathers, so they're good enough for me.

Anyway, wellies or not, the river below the house was too deep to ford this day. Sometimes by late summer, if the season has been dry, the level drops enough for me to be able to cross little more than ankle-deep in the clear water, but today there was nothing for it but to go the long way round, following the track down through the woods to the bridge a mile away.

Almost at once I disturbed a marsh tit, which scolded me irritably before disappearing up into the green canopy of leaves overhead. By comparison with the blue tits, marsh tits are a scarce woodland bird. The difference is probably because the blue tits are summer visitors up here whereas marsh tits remain year round. In winter, all the blue tits push off downhill and disappear into the lowlands, moving around nomadically over quite large areas. Many of them of course pick up a very comfortable living on the nut bags in people's gardens. The marsh tits on the other hand seem not to move away from their summer territories and the thing is that in winter these woods are cold, wind-swept and very short of food. For a small bird to survive it needs to know its patch extremely well in order to find sufficient food. In fact, they need quite large territories to provide for their winter needs so that limits their population, and it's probably why you never seem to find them at all in small isolated woodlands.

Left *Marsh tit, a relatively scarce woodland bird* (S.C. Porter, RSPB).

Right *Although the Welsh oakwoods look so natural, many of them were planted in the last century to provide fuel. In the winter particularly, sheep find shelter and grazing in the woods. This creates open conditions, in which ferns, mosses and birds including pied flycatcher and wood warbler flourish* (John Andrews).

Below right *Redstart, a member of the robin family, a summer migrant* (J.L. Roberts, RSPB).

Here however there are big expanses of wood with a good variety of feeding opportunities, and I see these stylish and clever little birds quite often.

Turning a bend in the track I came face to face with an Indian file of sheep coming up in the other direction. They eyed me suspiciously with those slightly lunatic slit pupils and then bounced and trotted off sideways amongst the trees. Because the wood isn't fenced at the top where the trees become sparser and eventually give way entirely to open moorland, the sheep can wander in and out at will and their constant search for nutritious greenery makes it very difficult for anything other than ferns and mosses to grow beneath the trees. This is one of the reasons why the woods are so inhospitable to birds in winter — when the leaves are off the trees there is virtually no cover anywhere against the driving wind and rain, and the range of food resources is very restricted. But for birds coming here in the summer, it's a very different story. Once the new leaves have opened on the oaks, food quickly begins to become more plentiful. By the time young birds are hatching in the nests, there are literally millions of caterpillars of tortrix and leaf

roller moths munching away on the leaves, to be busily gathered up by the beakful and transported away to nests all over the wood. In some seasons, caterpillars are so numerous that they practically strip the trees of leaves, and you can hear and feel a constant pattering rain of little green droppings!

The grazing and browsing by the sheep creates an open, cathedral-like effect between the tree canopy and the ground. This suits wood warblers perfectly because they like to nest amongst old fallen leaves and moss where there is little vegetation growing, and they feed in the treetops. They are common here and so too are redstarts, which build their nests in holes, favouring places where a limb has broken away from the trunk, and do a lot of their feeding on the ground. Now, one of them was flying along the path in front of me — a young bird probably not long out of the nest but already flaunting the characteristic rufous tail that gives them their name. It perched on a hazel stump as I stood still, then flew down to the path, pecked at the ground with one economical movement and collected some luckless small insect, before flying up and away to my right. For a few moments I could see it gaining height,

Left *Pied flycatcher, female. Like the redstart, a summer visitor* (S.C. Porter, RSPB).

Below left *The male pied flycatcher in breeding dress is immaculate black and white, but by July they are moulting into a much drabber, more discreet brown and white plumage, very similar to females and young birds* (S.C. Porter, RSPB).

going up the hillside between the oak trunks. Just before it disappeared from view two other small birds zipped across a gap with the characteristic foraging flight of pied flycatchers.

Pied flycatchers are another summer visitor to these woods and they too like the open structure. Much of their feeding is done by picking insects from the ground, the trunk and lower limbs of trees, and by capturing prey in flight. Like the birds I was watching now, they will sit on an exposed perch and then whizz out or down when they see a tell-tale movement, to capture the fly, beetle or caterpillar before whisking back up to another perch. When they first arrive in the spring, there isn't much food about in the hill woods and so then they tend to frequent the valley bottoms, feeding in the alders along the stream-sides, where conditions are just that bit warmer and the spring is a fraction more advanced. At the same time that they arrive, at the end of their perilous journey from Africa, the blue tits also reappear in the woods, having passed a comfortable winter scoffing peanuts in a suburban garden somewhere. Both species like very similar types of nesting place — small holes in the trunk of a tree. So, if for any reason the pied flycatchers are delayed, they may find the blue tits already in possession of all the best sites. Then birds may fail to breed or are forced to occupy unsuitable sites where they often fall victim to predators. But on the whole blue tits prefer woods with much more vegetation in the understorey than this one, so the pied flycatchers usually manage to do fairly well and are very much in evidence in May when the cocks are splendidly smart in their black and white livery.

By this time of year, the males are moulting into a much drabber, more discreet brown and white version very similar to females and young birds, and all ages and sexes suddenly become extremely hard to see. Indeed, it wouldn't have

Right *Old trackways wind through the woods, finding their way to ancient mines and long-abandoned farms* (John Andrews).

surprised me a bit if I had failed to see them altogether. As I watched these two, I wondered how many thousands of miles they would travel between now and the next spring and whether either of them would be amongst the successful few who make it back to breed again.

Eventually, I lost them from view, and walked on down the last part of the track, its ruts running with water, towards the edge of the wood. This track ends with one of the most amazingly derelict gates I have ever seen. Composed entirely of old tree branches wired together, it is thickly encrusted with lichens. The hinges consist of two loops of wire and the fastener is a third one. Every time I open it, lifting virtually its entire weight and lugging it back out of the way, I wonder whether it's going to fall to bits in my hands. But with the proverbial longevity of creaking gates, it has swung for the last ten years to my certain knowledge. The sheep of course ignore it, scrambling through the fence lower down or coming in from the open hill above.

Now I was at the bridge. I find it very hard to cross bridges. Ever since I was a small boy I have found it necessary to stop part way, hang over the parapet and look down into the water below for fish that may be lying in the shady deeps, then cross to the other side and do the same thing again. Leaning on bridges and watching the water go by is one of the most pleasant activities I know and it's also one of the few places where a passing stranger will feel free to stop and talk. You don't have to be a fisherman to do this and I think it probably works because leaning side-by-side over a bridge is a very un-hostile thing to do. There is nothing remotely confrontational about it and anyone who leans on bridges must surely be an essentially trustworthy sort of bloke? Well, perhaps not always. I remember leaning on a bridge such as this one when a character appeared on a bike, dismounted, withdrew a short and efficient fishing rod from the ivy covering the parapet, cast his fly and captured a substantial trout from the deep pool beneath the 'Strictly No Fishing' sign, pushed his still-twitching capture into his saddle bag, hid the rod and was gone again — all in less than five minutes.

After rain, the rivers quickly rise in spate as the water drains off the steep hillsides (John Andrews).

Today there was no one around to stop and speak, but there was a dipper. I heard it before I saw it. First there was a piping call coming from somewhere downstream and then the bird appeared below me, flying fast and low under the bridge arch to plump down on an exposed rock about a hundred yards (100 m) on. Typically, it bobbed, bouncing itself gently as it considered its next move. Its white chest shone brightly even in the dull, hazy light and I could see from the white splotches on the rock that this was obviously a favourite perching place. Suddenly it was gone, casually stepping off into the swirling waters and submerging itself. You have to admire dippers. Most waterbirds are large, tough individuals, physically strong and well-insulated by specially evolved plumage and a thick coat of subcutaneous fat. They belong to families that have very ancient evolutionary lineages and have been honing their underwater skills for a far longer time than human beings have existed. Dippers too probably have been around longer than we have, but they belong to the group of small perching birds which appears to be of relatively recent evolutionary origin compared with ducks, for instance, and of course because they are small, it is much harder for them to maintain body heat under water or cope with powerful currents. Nonetheless, dippers have done it, and done it very successfully. They swim by using their half-closed wings, then grab hold of stones on the bottom to stop themselves being swept away while they rummage for insect larvae that live amongst the gravel and on the undersides of the stones.

The dipper popped back onto the surface and up onto its rock, then down the other side to feed in the shallows, pushing its head under water and turning over the stones with its beak. I watched it for several minutes, appearing and disappearing, and then it set off again, flying decisively upstream, following the bends of the river rather than crossing dry land. I have never understood why dippers have particular preferred feeding places and move steadily from one to the next. To my eye, much of the river looks suitable and I cannot see why they do not spend hours in the same small area. Doubtless they know their business better than I do.

Now, for a little while at least, I was back on the road, walking north up the other bank of the river between close-cropped grass verges. Half an hour or so after I had set out, I was back virtually where I had started, but on the opposite bank of the river from the old farmhouse. From this position, you could see how cunningly its site had been chosen to give maximum protection from the west winds and shelter from the rain. It practically grows out of the hillside and although it is damp, because it isn't regularly occupied these days, it's not difficult to warm it through with a couple of good log fires in the evening. I'll bet its heating costs are a good deal less than many modern houses built in this part of Wales. They're all sited with an eye to an attractive view, so the wind and rain hits them hard and the big picture windows, double-glazed or not, lose great quantities of heat. Farmers see the view every day — they're out there working in it and if they've got time to stop and appreciate it then they can do it with the fresh air on their faces.

Now the road began to climb — a short, sharp pull reminding me that I don't manage to keep as fit as I think I ought to, and that I shall need to pace myself to see the day out. Another ten minutes brought me to the farm at the top of the valley. As usual, I passed through the yard without seeing a soul but three black and white muzzles were thrust under the door of the barn. Sheepdogs seem to be rather complex personalities. Out on the hill they are highly businesslike, working the sheep or walking quietly with their master. But they become distinctly shifty when you meet them out about their own affairs. They'll sidle past you with a sideways look or sculk off into the hedge bottoms. Some of them, incidentally, turn to sheep-worrying if they aren't closely watched; not surprising really when you remember that their herding skill is really hunting brought under control and prevented from reaching its natural conclusion. Anyway, sheepdogs in the farmyard have a third personality — mostly good humoured but definitely noisy watchdogs, and though these three could only show their noses they did their best to let the farm know that there was a stranger about.

Crossing the in-bye, the fields around the farm which are best cared for and most productive of rich grass, I disturbed a couple of magpies hunting for beetles and worms. Higher up, a big

Right *Sparrowhawk, a small but agile woodland hunter, preying on small birds* (D.L. Sewell, RSPB).

Below left *Well-trained dogs are essential to the hill farmer who may have to round up sheep from the open hill several times in the farming year* (John Andrews).

party of jackdaws was engaged on the same business, some youngsters still begging for attention and food, though by now pretty well capable of looking after themselves if no one was prepared to make a fuss of them.

At the end of the fields, the path ran along the side of a little larch plantation that clothed the ground between it and the river below. Looking through it, in a couple of places I could see the bulk of nests up in the branches so I began to work my way through it, searching the ground below each one in turn. Sparrowhawks love larch trees to nest in. They seem to find the nice, regular whorls of branches ideal for siting a nest firmly. The dead lower twigs break off easily and they have little bumps along them where the tufts of needles once grew. Maybe these are particularly good nesting material because they interlock so firmly. If the birds breed successfully in a wood, the female will often return for a second season. Hen sparrowhawks are much bigger than their mates and tend to be longer lived so it's they who choose the nest sites, and you could almost say that the birds have a matriarchal society.

In fact the females weigh about twice as much as the males, which is extremely unusual even in birds of prey, where hens do tend to be the larger sex. It seems that in the breeding season the female's larger body size helps her to produce a clutch of eggs and incubate them while the male, with his smaller size but greater agility can hunt for both of them. Sparrowhawks do most of their hunting in woodland or along hedgerows, often flying low and fast between the trees to come unobserved on a small bird, pounce and grab it before it can get away. They kill by gripping their victim between long strong toes and driving in the needle sharp talons. Being small not only means that the male is highly manoeuvrable, but that he doesn't actually need as much food himself so a greater proportion can be supplied to the female.

Another advantage of the difference in size is that when the female isn't incubating eggs or brooding small chicks, she can be hunting much bigger prey, often taking woodpigeons which are nearly twice her own weight, and this reduces competition with the male who takes smaller birds. But life is never without its little drawbacks.

Left *The thin contact calls of the goldcrest are so high-pitched that they can be difficult to hear* (Robin Williams, RSPB).

Left *A kestrel usually hunts over open country, hovering into the wind* (Robin Williams, RSPB).

Right *Full of nervous energy, the grey wagtail is elegantly slender, handsomely clad in grey and brilliant yellow* (Helmut Blesch, RSPB).

Outside the breeding season the birds are solitary and a hen sparrowhawk is not above catching, plucking and eating a male of the species during the winter months, when, after all, he isn't much use for anything else.

There was no sign of any birds in the wood, apart from a little group of goldcrests whose thin contact calls came from somewhere in the canopy overhead. However, there were seven quite large nests and, though they might all have been old crow sites, lying on the needle litter beneath one of the trees, was a solitary tail feather from a sparrowhawk, pale brown with distinctive dark bars across it.

When I came out at the other end of the plantation, the rain had ceased and above me the cloud cover was beginning to break up. Here the hills close in against the river and on the south side rise up steeply to a little crag. As I watched the patches of blue opening and closing behind the wind-chased clouds, a kestrel which I had completely failed to notice took off from the crag and swung out over my head, losing height as it moved down the valley, then swinging into its hover, head to the wind. All the bird's physical skill was concerned with keeping its eyes quite still in space, so that it could carefully scan the ground beneath for the movement of voles, beetles or a fool-hardy young bird. The kestrel's wings flickered rapidly as it flew forward at precisely the same speed that the wind was blowing it backwards, so maintaining its position in space. At the same time tail and body swung as though it was pivoting from the neck in order to keep its head perfectly stationary. But this everyday miracle of coordination brought it no luck there, and it swung away again, moving half a field further on, before once more hanging itself in space.

By now the path, which had been a tractor's width back beyond the plantation, had narrowed to a sheep track running close to the bottom of the slope and my ears were full of the noise of the rain-swollen stream plunging and swirling along its rocky bed. Here I put up a grey wagtail and it flew low ahead of me before landing on the bank. I watched it trotting about, full of nervous energy, flirting its long tail. To my mind, grey wagtails are among the loveliest of birds — elegantly slender and handsomely clad in grey and brilliant yellow.

Left *Both dippers and grey wagtails prefer nest sites close to or even right above the water, amongst the jumble of rocks and tree roots* (John Andrews).

Right *A great aerobat, the raven's flight silhouette is distinctive — fingered wings, heavy head and a diamond-shaped tail* (John Marchington, RSPB).

As I got closer, the bird took off again, this time rising to fly back over me and slightly dispelling that elegant air because, frankly, grey wagtails often look as though flying is not their favourite activity. Perhaps it was the very long tail blown about somewhat by the wind, that made this one look as though he barely had things under control.

What a contrast with the raven which appeared a few minutes later against the skyline above me. As so often happens, I heard the bird before I saw it, its harsh 'roaac', almost like a bark, carrying right down the length of the little valley. Ravens seem to fly for fun and this individual was no exception. A few slow and powerful wingbeats carried it half-way across the strip of open sky between the shoulders of hill in front of me. Then it changed its wing angle and began to dive towards a gulley on the far side. As I watched, the shape of the bird seemed to alter once, and then again. Raven aerobatics: rolling or somersaulting in flight, just for the fun of it. Ravens are mainly scavengers and their abundance here relates to the availability of sheep carrion. Lots of ewes die in the hills in winter, then there are weakly lambs

and after-birth in the spring, and of course a wider range of food in summer and autumn. Even so, it can be no coincidence that all the members of the crow family are intelligent — some would say cunning. To survive as a scavenger in a cold climate you must need your wits about you, taking advantage of every opportunity as it comes. Is it because they are that extra bit smarter that ravens enjoy playing and, when they are flying, so often seem to combine business with pleasure?

At the head of the valley the river forces its way through a narrow gorge about 15 feet (4.5 m) deep and the path wangles its way along the top of the rocks. All right, it's not a very big drop but, falling down it, you could perfectly well smash an ankle or knock yourself out. The water below is quite deep and cold enough to finish you off. More people come to grief in the hills on silly spots like this than on the sheer high places where they're concentrating on taking care. Fortunately I am totally frightened of high steep places and almost as scared of situations like this, so I tend to watch my footing! And that made me realize that the gap through the rocks here isn't

'A wren churring somewhere amongst the old roots . . .' (Pierre Didier, RSPB).

natural. Some time in the past, it had been cut back and shaped to be wide enough, if not for a little farm cart, then certainly for a pack pony.

I had seen no sign of a proper path back down the valley, nor was there one on the other side of the gorge. Presumably soil creep and the feet of the sheep had obliterated all trace of it. But almost at the head of the valley I came on an old line of hazels and, along the side of it, clear traces of a made-up track beneath the rough grass, rushes and ferns. The lower stems of many of these bushes had the tell-tale right angle bends of a once-laid hedge and from them sprouted a riot of growth — some of the old stems dead and decaying, others throwing up slender new wands with their grey bark shining in the fitful sunshine of midday. This little patch held more birds than I'd seen in the last hour. Chaffinches, a robin, another couple of redstarts, a wren churring somewhere amongst the old roots and decaying limbs, and a willow warbler moving busily amongst the hazel leaves searching for insects.

Another hundred yards and I breasted a low ridge and found myself amongst the ruins of an abandoned farmstead. The rough stone walls still stood shoulder high and I could walk on close-cropped turf from room to room. It had obviously been quite big in its day though how much had been living quarters and how much housing for livestock, I couldn't guess.

Houses fall to ruin quickly in the hills. Seeds of rowan and elder arrive in bird droppings and it only needs one to be washed into a gap in the stonework and germinate for the process to begin. Soon the root system is prising the stones apart. Then frost gets in and helps the process along. A slate slips, and the wind gets into the roof space and blows more off. Now the rain can get at the timbers and they begin to rot. Fern spores drift on the eddies of breeze that swirl in the corners of the rooms, and take hold, growing strong green plants in the sheltered, damp shade. It may be no more than a decade before the place is a paradise for plants, invertebrates and birds. While part of the roof remains, a barn owl may take up residence, drifting silently out as dusk falls to hunt the valley and rearing an ugly, hissing brood of young where once children slept.

But once the roof goes, and the clutter of slates and stones has been grown over by the hill grasses, it becomes extremely difficult to guess the age of the building. Had this farm been abandoned between the wars, or a hundred years ago? And was it with heartbreak or relief that the last people who lived here moved away, perhaps to more fertile, friendly land or perhaps to the mean streets of an industrial town. Now there was nothing left, except a wren's nest built in a gap in the brickwork, the front faced with mosses and a barely visible entrance hole.

It took me an hour to cross the block of hill that lay between the old farmstead and the next valley. The going was steep at first and the top of the hill, though flat, was covered with tussocks of coarse, rank grasses which made heavy going. I found the inevitable sheep carcass — picked clean by the foxes, ravens and crows. For years the hills have carried too many sheep as the farmers have tried to scrape their living from the poor land. But the sheep have eaten out all the palatable grasses so that only tough varieties now grow. The decline in fertility has affected everything: apart from an odd meadow pipit, you'll hardly find another nesting bird up here.

By the time I got down into the other valley, the last of the cloud cover had blown away and the July sun was almost too hot. The character of the valley here was different, with high summer bracken up to my shoulders, and I was glad to pull off my waterproofs and roll up shirt sleeves as I pushed my way through it. Tonight I would have to remember to check for ticks before I went to bed.

The rivers in both the valleys join a few miles downstream but they have quite distinctive characters up here. Compared with the one on the other side of the hill, this was much wider and deeper. By chance, I came suddenly out of the bracken where the river bent and found myself looking down a reach on which a single large duck was swimming together with a brood of downy young. A streamlined grey body, brown

On the hilltops, the soils are impoverished by heavy rainfall and severe over-grazing by sheep. Except where heather remains, there are few birds to be found (John Andrews).

head with a white throat, and a long slender beak confirmed its identity as a goosander. So far as I could see there were at least ten youngsters with her and they were probably all one brood because there was no perceptible size difference between them. Sometimes several broods will combine under the care of one female, while the other females move away. Judged in human terms, you might feel that goosanders make fairly heartless parents but their departure is actually very sensible. Once the young are hatched and water-borne they are relatively safe from predators and the presence of more adults would be unlikely to increase their survival chances. On the other hand, adults need a lot of food so they would actually be reducing the resource available for the young. This strategy leaves one wardening female who can warn of danger while the youngsters harvest all the small fish they can catch.

This duck had certainly seen me as soon as I saw her and she calmly but quickly shepherded her brood downstream and out of sight round the next bend. For my part, I decided on a detour, rather than cause more disturbance with the risk of breaking the brood up. Working my way back

through the bracken, I forded the river by hopping precariously from rock to rock, walked through a scattering of birch trees and found myself up against the fence of a substantial wood. Here, careful effort had clearly been made to keep out the sheep and the effect on the vegetation was immediately obvious. First, the herbage was much taller and more luxuriant. Second, there were young trees coming up — rowans mostly because young oaks don't like growing under the parent trees. A nuthatch was clambering down the trunk of one of the oaks, probing in the crannies with a stout bill. Much to my pleasure, a treecreeper flew in, and landed at the bottom of the same trunk and began to mouse its way up the bark, collecting tiny flies, spiders and caterpillars. Because they climb with both feet aligned with the body, treecreepers can only work their way up a trunk but the nuthatch, typically, had his feet turned sideways so that he could actually hop downwards as readily as move upwards.

As I strolled on through the warm, sun-dappled woodland, a chiffchaff called briefly overhead and there were blackcaps foraging in the shrubby undergrowth. Somewhere high above the canopy of the trees, a buzzard was calling, and I could imagine it wheeling in the warm sunlight. I could also hear a family party of long-tailed tits, and they quickly passed by, moving through the lower branches of the oak trees, each one looking like a little fluffy ball with a long tail. A pair of rather bedraggled great tits were busy carting quantities of caterpillars to the crack of a tree where their brood welcomed them with hungry squeals.

Either I had been climbing without really noticing it or the ground had fallen away, because when I came out of the wood I was half-way up the hillside again and looking across a trim valley floor with small, neatly hedged fields, several with a complement of ewes and well-grown lambs. A tractor was out turning hay in one of the fields. In a wet summer, it can be extremely difficult to contrive the hay harvest and every opportunity has to be taken to dry the cut material, and then to harvest it as soon as a few bright days have removed the risk of it going mouldy once it's baled. The buzzard I had heard earlier was soaring in the middle-air over the fields and I could see a second one away in the distance.

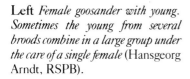

Above left *Where the river bends, it has carved a deep pool out of its rocky bed. Here, goosanders come to dive for fish* (John Andrews).

Left *Female goosander with young. Sometimes the young from several broods combine in a large group under the care of a single female* (Hansgeorg Arndt, RSPB).

Right *Buzzards, along with red kites, ravens and crows, depend largely upon the supply of carrion in the Welsh hills* (J.L. Roberts, RSPB).

Buzzards are economical fliers. When they can, they float on the updraughts created by the wind against the hill slopes or, in fine weather, on thermals of warm air rising from the fields.

I sat down to enjoy the scene and within minutes began to feel my eyelids drooping. I lay back in the sun and stretched.

When I woke, I could feel the damp of the ground soaked into my shirt and a cold breeze on my face. The cloud that obscured the sun was quite small but there were plenty of others hurrying up over the horizon. I got up with a shiver, brushed myself down, and started to stride down the hill to get the circulation going again. Then, round the edge of the wood below me, almost under my left hand, there floated into view the one bird which is the speciality of Wales — a red kite. The returning sun shone on grey crown, russet back and an almost orange-coloured tail. The bird seemed to drift effortlessly through the air, constantly making tiny adjustments in the stretch and angle of its long wings in response to the gusting breeze. Perhaps most noticeable of all was the way it used its tail — it seemed almost like a hand, caressing the

fickle air currents to maintain its speed and direction. Like all raptors, kites have superb eyesight and I was sure this one could see me but it passed close and casually by, intent on its hunting, to vanish from view round the next shoulder of hill. Long after I've forgotten all the rest of that walk, the brief view of that bird will linger in my mind.

As the clouds started to close in again, a party of swifts moved down the valley. In a matter of days, they would be the first of the migrants to depart for Africa, leading a tide of millions more birds which would flow southward over the coming weeks. But for now they were still trawling open-mouthed for the innumerable flies and aphids carried on the wind and I was in no doubt that their movement ahead of the clouds meant more rain was following not far behind them.

At the hill foot I was back on familiar ground, marching down a hazel-lined track with the farmhouse only a mile off, and relishing the prospect of a mug of tea with my feet up. The sky was leaden, but with luck I would make it indoors before the rain returned . . .

THE BRIDGE ACROSS SUMMER

MICHAEL CLEGG

Michael Clegg (Yorkshire Television).

MICHAEL CLEGG was born in Yorkshire and has lived most of his life there. A lifelong birdwatcher, after 29 years and 274 days in the service of various museums he became a freelance broadcaster and lecturer. He has had numerous features on radio, two series for BBC 2 ('Monkey Business' and 'What on Earth') and has also made two long-running series for Yorkshire TV ('Clegg's People' and 'Country Calendar').

Any birdwatching year should ideally contain twelve good birdwatching months, as any forward-looking, optimistic, birdwatcher will tell you. And so it may, but inevitably there will be some periods that are better than others, possibly not even for purely ornithological reasons. Some of these months might even be regarded as one's favourites. That is how it is with me and August.

For me August is the bridge between the high summer of July and the arrival of autumn proper in September and this is why I enjoy it so much. I speak from the standpoint of one who is rather obsessed with bird migration, but likes the 'lottery' element of rare bird occurrence. And August offers plenty of that, especially at Spurn Point, in what is now North Humberside, but was once the old East Riding of Yorkshire.

The trickle of movement that started in July and will reach a torrent level in September, swirls through August at a variable pace but usually casts up a few goodies to make the month special. And these are what put the icing on the cake and create memorable moments. The fickle August weather contributes too — long calm spells, with the sun over the sea making morning sea-watches difficult; sudden switches of wind direction raising hopes when it goes south-east only to dash them again when the onshore breeze dies or turns into a blustery northwester with squally showers.

Long days — short nights, early mornings when you can walk about dryshod in the absence of dew, warmth and the price you pay for it at Spurn when the sea fret rolls in and blots out distant views: these are the attributes of August. Sometimes in the middle of the day heat shimmer over the mudflats and the mirages of several Grimsby towns piled up on each other across the Humber can drive you crazy and make you pray for rain and clear air. On other days when lines of squall showers fall like cold, steel stair-rods you wish you were wearing gloves. But after the rain, the horizon clears to show distant gas rigs in great detail and the passing birds look larger than life. It's all part of August. I am not a theatre-goer or opera buff but I do like overtures — the tasty bits of what is to come later, and August is like that to me.

A fulmar glides past on stiff wings (Michael W. Richards, RSPB).

At Spurn in August there are not many birdwatchers about. Presumably a lot of them are off on summer holidays watching somebody else's birds. But, like the birds, a trickle turn up through the week with a migratory flood of their own at weekends if the wind goes east or a rarity shows up. On the caravan site, where my birdwatching headquarters is parked, the camp is awash with kids. (The school holidays are at their peak and the sand pit is a day-long Olympic long-jump course.) The site is also a favourite spot for retired Hull seamen — ship watchers who can tell you everything about a boat from just a funnel view on the horizon and they often chat while I am watching the sea. I tell them about the birds, they fill me in about the shipping and in between whiles we discuss the fishing industry, erosion, weather phenomena, conservation and other matters of the moment. Many are ex-fishermen from the Iceland and White Sea days and have good stories to tell. A seabird watcher with one eye clamped to his telescope and the other flicking about chameleon-like is a good listener.

For those who do not know Spurn at all, perhaps I should set the scene a bit more precisely. Spurn Point is the four-mile-long (6½ km) sandspit that sticks out from the south-east tip of Yorkshire between the Humber estuary and the North Sea. It is a place of ambiguities, starting with the name. In earlier times the name Spurn Head was used a lot, but I prefer to think that the head itself was actually a now lost part of Kilnsea Cliff. Naturalists, particularly in print, refer to it as the Spurn Peninsula. I like that name — it has a sort of geographical correctness about it, even if it is a bit pedantic. The locals have a tendency to call it 'the Spurn', as if the last stretch of Yorkshire demanded a definite article. Perhaps it does, since Spurns have come and gone over the centuries washed away and reformed by the sea and some of the ancient families could well have lived through a succession of Spurns.

The names of antiquity — Hrafnseyr of the Vikings, Ravenser and Ravenspur of medieval times do offer a good chance for further ambiguity. My own interpretation is in favour of a good Norse association — an ayre or sandspit, as used in Orkney, the Isle of Man, and North Wales with Point of Air; and add to that the raven, Odin's associate, unfortunately no longer with us in Holderness.

Spurn Point is the four-mile-long sandpit that sticks out from the south-east tip of Yorkshire, between the Humber estuary and the North Sea (Michael Clegg).

At the tip of the peninsula, facing Lincolnshire, the point is a jumble of old army buildings, new housing for lifeboat crew families, navigation and pilotage facilities and a dense scrub of sea buckthorn with a fringe of marram grass dunes. When I mention 'the Point' this is the area I refer to. Heading north from the bulbous tip the peninsula progressively narrows until it reaches a stretch where not more than 60 feet separate the Humber shore from the beach on the seaward side. The road runs a little bit precariously between the two. This area is known as the narrows — for obvious reasons. Here, virtually every bird that passes can be seen, whether it is a seabird, wader, passing hirundine or bush-hopping warbler, and the narrows are the great counting spot for visible migration. To some people 'visible migration' seems an odd phrase, but it does make sense when you consider that so much bird movement takes place at night, and is thus, to us 'invisible', 'nocturnal', migration.

The landward end of the spit, now buttressed by a sea wall of dumped earth, and redundant anti-tank blocks from the Second World War, has more buckthorn and marram plus the bird observatory and Yorkshire Wildlife Trust buildings. The whole peninsula is a Trust reserve, and there is a lot of important wildlife other than birds. This area, which is being eroded rapidly by the sea, is, or was Kilnsea Warren, a series of dunes and hollows with even a pond or two before the sea took them. The warren ponds were created by bombs dropped onto the boulder clay-based soil, the explosions creating craters with a puddled clay lining. They dated from 1917 when, to quote the late Wally Clubley who was there at the time 'the clouds parted and there it were — a bloody great Zeppelin'. Two bombs dropped, missing Wally as it happened, and the warren had its ponds which lasted until the 1960s. The Humber foreshore in this area is quite a good saltmarsh sward, much loved by Brent geese in winter. But even this is new. Up to the '60s the area was a spiky jungle of Spartina, cord grass, which having colonized the bare mud, created silt areas which could then be invaded by other plants and the cord grass died back. Now in August the sea lavender and sea aster bloom where there was none a few years ago.

The nature reserve ends at the warren gate but the bird observatory recording area extends along the Humber shore to the Crown and Anchor and Kilnsea village, then back down the lane to the Blue Bell, an erstwhile pub, now a shop. On the seaward side of the road, a couple of arable fields and a lot of rough sea-edge grass complete the area for which a virtually daily bird record has been kept for over forty years.

The caravan site lies just outside the recording area and so does Beacon Lane which runs northwards past the camp before burying itself in the beach a mile further on. From here to Easington's North Sea Gas Terminal the erosion of the recent decades has been impressive. Behind the sandy beach and the ground-down boulder clay cliff remains, a succession of temporary brackish lagoons have formed, the

The caravan site at Spurn — my birdwatching headquarters (Michael Clegg).

latest under the shelter of sea defences, ramparts of granite lumps held in mesh coverings fronting a grassy bank top.

A lot of my birdwatching takes place in the northern extremity of Spurn. The lagoons have a lot to offer, the grassy bank is great for an afternoon sit, and Beacon Lane, with its rutted track and wind-sheared blackthorn and hawthorn, shelters many a migrant, and a good chance of a rarity. The caravan site is bounded by rough wasteland awaiting development, unless the sea gets there first, and this too can produce the goods at times. On the site of the cliff edge is a great sea watching perch and here I sit, an elevated Canute, and enjoy the best there is in birdwatching at times. This tall boulder clay cliff, eroding at about 12 to 18 feet (4-6 m) a year, is, in my opinion, the old Spurn Head of the navigation charts. The rest of the area is so low that 'Head' would be a poor description for it.

Now I know that sea-watching is not every birdwatcher's cup of tea, but it is mine. So let me tell it as I see it at its best. I like the two to three hours up to high water if the tide times allow. Crack of dawn I tend to avoid: the sun glare is

irritating when it makes all your terns black and all your shearwaters sooty. Half past seven to eight o'clock will do quite nicely for starters in August. On some days it is all over by ten, but on others passage will go on for most of the morning. Quite often, if I am away inland birdwatching in the early afternoon an odd fulmar, or a few close-in gannets, will catch my attention and suddenly there is a movement in progress. This sends me off to my perch immediately and I tend to sea-watch then up to six or seven o'clock or even later until the light goes mushy and terns flicker past without a hope of identification. The best sea-watching is, I think, three or four people who pick up every bird and sea-mark it with some precision. Crab-pot flags are great, if you can get the colour arrangements sorted out 'coming up to blue/black, going north passing orange/yellow' is what I like to hear. The opposite is 'out there - straight out from me'. There are times when I am glad I do a lot of of my sea-watching on my own!

Writing it all down can be a problem unless you have a tame scribe along. Generally I am not so lucky so my notes have species name — a line marked ↑ for north, another marked ↓ for south and so on. A double ended arrow ↕ covers 'blogging' the indeterminate messing-about movements and use squiggles thus ੭ for fishing, circling and so on. Sometimes I have used my micro-cassette recorder for sea-watch records but this is murder trying to transcribe afterwards. Bursts of monologue, extraneous comments, deep breathing, coffee slurping, occasional oaths. The whole thing could be used in evidence to support a case for insanity of the worst kind. I usually stick to the notebook.

I like sea-watching so much that I feel I must describe it in full. To me it has a lot of zen about it — a ritual of mind and body, a cultivation of technique and organization — and like the best of zen, a little bit of nonsense. Like when the birds stop moving just when you start watching and you spend the rest of the time playing 'I-spy' with your companions, or even passers-by.

In August one does not expect to suffer frostbite or hypothermia, so clothing is not a problem. But when staring into a reflective sea,

At Spurn in August there are not many birdwatchers about (Michael Clegg).

Sunset at Spurn — too dark for sea watching, but I often watch until the light goes mushy and terns flicker past without hope of identification (Michael Clegg).

under a hot sun, for hours on end some form of head gear might be necessary — it is for me. So here we go. Binoculars, telescope, tripod, notebook, cigarettes and canvas-backed chair. These are the essentials for a Kilnsea Cliff session. Are we sitting comfortably? Right, let's begin.

Field of view extends from the tideline to the horizon, and there is a scatter of crab pot flag buoys to focus and sight on. At this point I think I cannot do any better than to give you a couple of hours from actual day's observations — so let us take 9 August 1987. My first seawatch of the day was from twenty minutes to eight in the morning and lasted one hour.

A cool, cloudy bright morning with a promise of sunshine later in the day, the wind north-easterly force 2-3, and the tide starting to fall an hour past high water. After a few minutes it becomes obvious that most of the birds are moving northwards, perhaps feeding movements

taking them to areas favoured at the early stage of the tide's rise. Possibly the best of the close-in activity has passed and some of the birds are moving out to sea after feeding under the cliff at high water.

A single red-throated diver passing north may well have drifted on the current and be flying back to its starting point. An early autumn arrival, it was virtually in full summer plumage still. Fulmars too, all six of them, went north — perhaps back to nesting ledges around Flamborough Head forty miles (64 km) or so to the north. But where were the six northward-bound Manx shearwaters going? Officially there were no nesting colonies on the east coast — but I wonder sometimes. How marvellous shearwaters are, when it comes to adding a touch of class to a seawatch. If fulmars are the wandering spirits of dead seamen, as in the folk stories, then shearwaters must be officers and some of them even admirals. That swinging, easy flight I find very moving and, if they pass close enough to give the idea that they are looking the land over, you feel that their choice of staying out at sea is a deliberate one.

Left *A Sandwich tern, just starting to moult into winter plumage — the forehead becomes white* (Jan Van de Kam, RSPB).

Below right *A raft of razorbills* (Bobby Tulloch, RSPB).

A steady stream of gannets have an overwhelming majority heading north, 62 compared with two flying south. Again they could be Bempton nesters: most are adults, plus a few late stage immature colony visitors. They are probably making the second leg of their daily fish-carrying convoy of the day.

Common scoters whizz along, hugging the wave tops, four to the north, 42 south; all drakes as far as I can see, moulting birds no doubt, hobnobbing in all-drakes club while their families are still in the Baltic or further north. No velvet scoters to be seen this morning though they are a bit of a speciality at Spurn in July and August.

Three arctic skuas test the passing terns and then drift off generally southwards. I suspect these are just loitering about, living off the tern's catches, and they do spend a lot of time sitting on the sea waiting for victims. A great skua flogs its way south, looking neither right nor left and ignoring the anxiety among the Sandwich terns.

The Sandwich terns, a dozen or so, are 'blogging' — just flying up and down sporadically fishing, with the squeaky-voiced young forever demanding attention from their adult escorts.

Who would be a Sandwich tern pursued by these petulant squawks over hundreds of miles of sea? A couple of little terns are running a fish-ferrying service towards the small colony just north of the site, while a few common and arctic terns 'blog' around and run the skua gauntlet.

A couple of auks rattle off northwards, too far out to be sure of the species and they may well be bound to rendezvous with young somewhere on the sea. In August, little fleets of guillemots and razorbills come in under the cliff at high water and feed their still flightless young. It must be a real adventure for a young guillemot or razorbill, still in down, to jump off Flamborough cliffs at the bidding of its parents and float off down the coast. When you look at these mobile crèches it is impressive to see how solicitous the adults are in tending the little cork-like bobbers. Big gulls, skuas and even large fishes must get some of them, and the risk of a blow of wind is always there but they bob on, forty miles (64 km) from home and still going strong. After being out on the Wash on a mussel boat in the autumn and sailing through thousands of auks, I suspect that might be where the Spurn lot end up.

Not a lot of gulls around, some common and black-headed gulls plus the odd great black-back probably heading up to Bridlington harbour from some Humber shore roost. A little touch of class, through, in the form of three little gulls, all adults with tattered hoods, one heading north and two south. The little gull is a good August bird these days on the Yorkshire coast and increasing in abundance. These came from the Baltic perhaps with early flush of outgoing gulls leaving their nesting grounds. A few kittiwakes today, they seem to be either a feast or a famine here, considering the numbers that nest on the Flamborough range.

Well, that was an hour's seawatch from Kilnsea Cliff. Not the greatest birdwatching hour of my life, but fairly typical. After breakfast I roved over the Humber shore and trekked the lanes looking for migrants, but still came back for more sea-watching from three o'clock to half past five. The day reached its peak between half past three and five o'clock. Three arctic skuas, possibly this morning's trio, drew my attention to a raft of Manx shearwaters sitting on the sea as the tide rose. The skuas buzzed them and about eighty Manxies rose in waves and then settled again with a skua as watchdog. An hour later another arctic skua plus a fine adult pomarine skua lifted them up again. Five minutes later, a sooty shearwater came freewheeling northwards and an hour afterwards a second sooty followed the same track — almost as if it were sniffing out the course of the first. These birds *must* be the departed souls of dead admirals — anything less would be unthinkable.

Not a bad day by my standards, but perhaps the cream was not ornithological; at four o'clock three dolphins rolled past northwards. I could not identify them specifically, white-beaked or white-sided, would be my best attempt, but they did add gilt to the gingerbread. Daylight showed under their bellies as they cleared the surface several times, scooting over the surface like power boats between the wave tips.

Cetaceans, usually porpoises, are a bonus for the sea-watcher and these days in Humber area waters fears are often expressed for their continued existence. This sea area is regarded as a dumping ground for chemical and other pollutants and the conservation group Greenpeace has called attention to the threats to marine life. Strangely enough I have seen more cetaceans in 1987 than for a number of years. Seals, both common and grey, are more regular, off Kilnsea Cliff, though neither species breeds in the immediate area. The commons are probably from the Lincolnshire and Wash populations and the greys may well be Farne Islands animals.

One of the features of August at Spurn is the moult migration of shelduck, out through the Humber, usually in the evening, and off eastwards

Left *The Arctic skua is a pirate of the seas and it will harry other birds such as terns, forcing them to drop their catch of fish* (R.W. Kennedy, RSPB).

Right *A black tern in winter plumage* (Richard T. Mills, RSPB).

Below right *A common wader, the dunlin can be seen throughout the year on Britain's coasts in a variety of transitional plumages — from the dark belly of the breeding season, to a paler and greyer plumage in winter, depending on its breeding area* (C.H. Gomersall, RSPB).

towards their moulting grounds on the Heligoland Bight. On a good evening perhaps 300-400 move out, in parties of between ten and eighty. Down the Humber they come, in waves and chevrons, often passing the ferry to Rotterdam as it passes down the river. When they arrive at the coast they very often show a bit of odd behaviour. A sort of mild hysteria sets in and they dive to sea level, flying like crazy things — falling leaf spins, upside down at times and very often splashdowns. Then after a few minutes sanity returns and they get up and head due east in a very business-like way. Sometimes the departing shelduck, meet flocks of southbound waders and the two get mixed up together. The result might be thirty shelduck departing eastwards led by a curlew or with a bar-tailed godwit embedded in their chevron. The absent-minded waders usually sort themselves out fairly quickly but not without a lot of desperate wing action as they try to match their gait with that of the ducks. The funniest such mix up in my experience occurred on 16 August 1985 when an Egyptian goose set off east with five shelduck. Heaven knows where they had picked up that one! Anyway, off they went

eastwards but fifteen minutes later back came the Egyptian goose on its own. I suspect that was its longest overwater flight since its ancestors were brought over from Africa. (It was the second record for Spurn, by the way.)

Waders at Spurn in August can be very exciting. It is still early days so the numbers may not be large but the variety can be considerable and many of them are still in summer plumage, adults which have perhaps lost their broods or finished nesting early in the Arctic. And then there are the rarities — perhaps the odd American species. These may well be birds who have become marooned on this side of the Atlantic a year or more before and now they drift up and down the palaearctic side accompanying parties of related birds. Or, on the other hand they could be spill-overs from America into Asia, perhaps even Siberian breeders. Whatever their origins, they are pure excitement.

Beacon Lane Ponds, Easington Lagoons and the Humber shore at high water are the best wader spots, but on some days passage down the sea side is dominated by waders. There is something very satisfying about the scurrying,

Above *The turnstone, another small wader, tortoiseshell patterned in August, becomes rather greyer in winter* (C.H. Gomersall, RSPB).

Left *The downcurved bill gives a clue to this bird, a curlew sandpiper* (Dennis Green, RSPB).

Above right *Still in the brilliant grey, black and silver rig of spring and summer, the grey plover, seen here with knot, belies its dull name* (Jan Van de Kam, RSPB).

headlong, southward passage of waders over the sea. Bunches of dunlin and turnstones, sanderlings still in their gingery summer plumage, red knots — so different from their grey winter selves, bar-tailed godwits still cherry bright (outside chance of a black-tailed), whimbrels in neat chevrons whinnying away, curlews in penny numbers, and grey plovers still in their brilliant grey, black and silver rigs. On a good day fifty or sixty of the latter — what idiot called them grey plovers?

On the ponds the dunlin parties include curlew sandpipers — fourteen is my best August total, and a few little stints. In recent years occasional pectoral sandpipers — adult and juvenile one year, a white-rumped sandpiper, and once at Easington lagoons a never to be forgotten semi-palmated sandpiper. That really brought the twitchers in — but next day it was gone. Ruffs stalk about the ponds. Common, wood and green sandpipers flush out of the drains. The shanks are out in force, red, spotted red, and greenshank — surely the wader voice of autumn. A greenshank fluting away as it comes in off the sea in July is for me often the first sign that the

autumn has begun.

If confirmation were needed of that, then the terns supply it. They seem to drain away through August and into September. Spurn is not a great place for terns, a few little terns eke out a precarious breeding season at Easington, and Sandwich terns get up to a thousand or so at peak times, but common and arctic are not all that numerous. Roseate tern is not even an 'every year' bird on my list but August at Spurn can be my best chance for it. The year 1986 was better than usual and two, an adult plus a juvenile on 24 August, was my best record since the 1960s. The odd black tern drifts through in August too but September is better for them in my experience.

A really odd feature of August at Spurn is the appearance of budgerigars. In 1985 a blue one turned up on the 24th followed by a green bird on the 25th. The warden, Barry Spence, regards them as a regular feature, but I found it very odd. Where do they come from and why? Is it the habit of budgie owners to leave their windows open in the summer? Are they discarded pet victims of the holiday season? Or is there in every budgie a kamikaze urge to reach Australia for the

Left *The yellow wagtail is a summer visitor that is starting its return journey to Africa* (Robin Williams, RSPB).

Below right *Another early migrant, the wheatear will also find winter refuge in Africa* (J.L. Roberts, RSPB).

antipodean spring? The mind reels at the thought! I missed the 1986 budgie, which was last seen with a sparrowhawk in hot pursuit . . .

Birds of prey in August are a mixed bag, with immigrant kestrels reaching a dozen or more some days. These are often rather miserable souls which dot the overhead wires along the peninsula as they scan the ground for prey. Disturbed by passing cars, in situations where rodents are hard to come by, no doubt quite a few starve here. Apart from kestrels and the occasional sparrowhawk, better suited by the small bird hunting available here, an odd merlin may turn up in August. These are probably European birds rather than members of the declining British population. Marsh harriers, the odd buzzard, the occasional osprey and hobby are the most likely raptors. The hobby has been a bit of a speciality of recent Augusts, and I must say I cannot see too much of them — as they harry the hirundines and cause panic among the wagtails.

The hobby and the swift are to me something of an August combination: under the right conditions swifts pour down the peninsula at perhaps 3,000 an hour with a steady flow of outward-bound swallows and sand martins plus a few early-moving house martins with them and then, a grey-blue blur looking momentarily like a giant super-swift cleaves through them. A black-hooded moustached head, a rusty flash at the thighs, and it's a back view of a rapidly receding raptorial missile. Sometimes, for fun, one will double back over the Humber mud and raise the waders in a cloud of fear.

Every August, God willing, there will come some sort of a 'fall' of passerine migrants. It may be a one-day event, a good night crossing from Europe followed by a clear night on which everything moves on, or better still a bit of fog or rain will ground the birds for a day or two. This is the time of year when twitchers far inland sniff the breeze for a taste of an easterly, when the shipping forecast is more important than the news, when prayers to the powers of birdwatching might be answered. The floppy wryneck, a host of warblers, chats, starts, flycatchers and shrikes are the likely arrivals overnight.

Early in the day I open my caravan door and look out onto the area of close-cropped grass where the tourers and tents park at busy times. If it is running with yellow wagtails and hopping with wheatears I am well pleased. If a redstart sneaks surreptitiously off the gun emplacement and under a caravan my interest quickens. A whinchat or two in the weedy heaps beyond the site, a pied flycatcher in the lane and I am off into a dream of what might be waiting out there after breakfast. You will notice my priorities include food first, because I have a theory that the best birds of Spurn are usually seen in mid-morning after they have slept off their night's travels and are ready to get up and feed. After a couple of boiled duck eggs and a pile of bread and butter I am ready to face the world.

Bush to bush down Beacon Lane, check the hedges round the cottages and along the road to Spurn where the tall hedge has a stagnant little, insect-filled ditch below it. This is often where a concentration of warblers show up. More willows than yesterday, the odd garden warbler or blackcap perhaps. Whitethroats — are they the Beacon Lane regulars? Lesser whitethroat — was it there yesterday? Sedge warbler in the usual wet ditch, but perhaps a reed warbler on a wire fence.

It must be new. Sometimes in August there's a goldcrest or two — forerunners of the October rush, or in recent years early siskins that peel off from the hedge top and go whining over the fields. While they have certainly increased in England in recent times I suspect that this tendency to show up on the coast early in the autumn may mean hard times over in Europe. Are their forests producing less seed? Is it our acid rain that might be causing it? I feel a twinge of nationalistic guilt at times.

Cars whizz down the lane towards the observatory; the east wind moves more than just birds. Birders on holiday, twitchers answering the call of the wild, cause instant leave of absence (a sick relative, a sudden whim, tend to bring a lot of observers on a perfect August day when a fall might be due).

The 'Big hedge' site of so many good occurrences, the 'canal bushes' that springtime warblers love, the bank of tall plants and shrubs that runs towards the observatory and ends in the Heligoland trap are all searched minutely. And down at the point, the scrub round the trap next to the parade ground is sure to turn up something

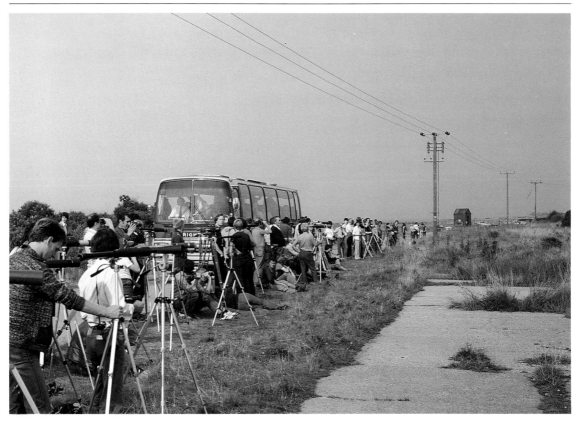

if there has been a fall. The rabbit-mown turf and broken brick of the old parade ground appeals to wheatears, chats, wrynecks, black redstarts and other ground feeders very strongly. Others have seen hoopoes here — for me, so far, only two spring birds elsewhere on Spurn.

A funny place the Point in August — go down at crack of dawn and nothing shows, return at half past ten and it can be alive with birds. Swallows line up their young on the cross bars and guy wires of the trap and stuff them with food, migrant willow warblers, surely among the most discreet and humble of birds, in August fight like wildcats over a choice bit of feeding ground in a bramble bush. Turtle doves and the occasional juvenile cuckoo seek out the taller trees and moribund elders. And from time to time something truly memorable takes place. We ate our lunch one day on the gun emplacement overlooking the point buckthorn area, while an icterine warbler scolded, four feet (1.2 m) away from us, a banana-yellow adult with smart avocet-blue-grey legs. Strange birds, icterine warblers — I remember one in August at Wells Wood in Norfolk which attacked blue tits invading its

Left *A rarity has turned up. Birdwatchers line up to glimpse a booted warbler, an unusual vagrant from eastern Europe. Spurn Point always offers the chance of the unexpected* (Michael Clegg).

Below left *A female whinchat. By late summer migrating birds will often be in transitional plumage, making them difficult to identify. Males may have forsaken their bold breeding colours, and juveniles add further confusion* (D.G. Doig, RSPB).

Right *The bird observatory at Spurn enables birdwatchers to examine closely migrating birds. This wryneck, after being ringed and measured, was released again within a few minutes of capture* (Michael Clegg).

patch of ripe brambles. A yellow virago, that one.

Looking through my notes I see that 28 August 1987 was warm with sunny periods and a bit of patchy haze over the sea. The wind was westerly force three or so, but had been easterly the day before. We arrived at about half past ten. The first sign was whinchats dotted around the bushes near the bird observatory: things were looking hopeful. A scattering of wheatears along the peninsula and it was down to the narrows. Here a wryneck flopped into some buckthorn, looking as always like a big brown moth and not inspiring confidence in its ability to get to Africa. A pied flycatcher tucked into a buckthorn-fringed hollow looked better suited to the migration business and flicked about collecting the insects which shared its shelter. Whitethroats turned up at intervals but some of these were no doubt local breeders, which seemed to be at full strength that year.

The Point fulfilled the early promise of the day, with a juvenile barred warbler making heavy hops from a hawthorn to the ground and back just by the Point Heligoland trap. I sat down to watch this for a while and suddenly became conscious

of a bird actually in the trap, self-caught as it turned out. It was another wryneck hopping along behind the wire in a fairly bemused manner — surely this was not the way to Africa. Not being organized for bird-ringing I set it free and off it went into the nearest bush. A mob of willow warblers, a lesser whitethroat and a couple of garden warblers tracked us through the buckthorn. On the way back a red-backed shrike stuck its head up as we passed and added itself to an already good list for the day. Hirundines were passing most of the time as well, at least 220 sand martins, nearly 200 swallows and five house martins and later in the day 32 swifts hurried south — a bit on the late side!

The good spell continued over the next three days with another barred warbler up the lane, one or two red-backed shrikes and a nice scatter of wrynecks, several of which were caught and ringed. Quite a classic situation for late August. On the morning of 1 September I had to leave Spurn and as I waited for the bus to Hull an icterine warbler ducked out of the caravan site hedge and flicked across into the garden opposite. As it happened, it was one of four seen that day, but I did not know that until later. Green-olive above, yellow on the breast and silvery-white below, with a greyish wing patch and grey legs, it hopped about in the elder bushes. It seemed a fitting end to August and a harbinger of all the good things that would come later when the migrant trickle became a deluge — and that is how it turned out.

It may seem that my Spurn Augusts are an all-action chronicle of birds passing — would that it were so. But on some days the highlight might be a mammal, or migrant butterflies and moths, and sometimes nothing more than lying in the grass watching a family of common lizards. But one thing is certain there is always a highlight, something to stay in the mind and when I read my field notes I can see it again in my mind's eye. The aquatic warbler — a streaky mustard-coloured sprite that led us a merry dance round Beacon Lane ponds; a storm petrel — a different kind of sprite, like a scrap of charred paper, fluttering along with an inquisitive arctic skua following its erratic passage.

As you may have gathered, I do a lot of my birdwatching on my own, but at Spurn the bird observatory is a constant focus of news and observations and I take full advantage of that. Barry Spence, the warden for over twenty years, his seasonal assistants, long-staying birdwatchers and ringers, as well as the transient twitchers are all major parts of the scene. I enjoy a bird in the hand for ringing as much as a bird in the bush at times and the observatory offers this sort of experience.

On Kilnsea Cliff, my sea-watching Valhalla, there is a magnetic quality about a hunched-up figure glued to a telescope end. Sit there for half an hour and the world will come and talk to you. Curious youngsters in groups materialize from nowhere, retired mariners abound and share their nautical knowledge. It was one of these fellows who absolutely stumped me one evening. Shelduck were passing, heading off towards Heligoland in waves in a very satisfying demonstration of moult migration. I explained what was happening to my fellow observer and ended up by mentioning that the ducks would be in Germany by tomorrow. He thought about it for a moment and then came out with a question that still haunts me. 'What's their hurry?' he said. There's no answer to that — is there?

SWANS OF A DIFFERENT FEATHER

JIM CRUMLEY

Jim Crumley in the Edinburgh countryside.

JIM CRUMLEY was born in Dundee in 1947. A journalist by profession, he became chief feature writer for the *Edinburgh Evening News*. He is now a full-time freelance writer. He is also Scottish area reporter for *The Great Outdoors* and was chairman of the Scottish Wild Land Group, which he helped to found in 1982.

My September is a song of two swan tribes. One is half-wild, one is wholly, uncompromisingly wild.

One, the confidant of man, sits pretty and preposterous and queues for his all-seasons' crumbs of comfort; one, the shunner of man, flies south from the Arctic rim on wintering wings, lingers listlessly, flies restlessly north again at the first green flag-waving of spring; one, whose young have just begun to flex their first flight muscles in September (trialist duck-panicking, coot-cowering sorties ruffling the pond's feathers), and one whose young have just accompanied them for a thousand landless miles; the mute swan and the whooper.

My September is also a song of their watersheets. One is a fat-of-the-land farmyard pond, an oasis of astounding fertility in the swan desert of West Lothian a dozen miles from Edinburgh, one an ocean-wind-rinsed lochan, eagle-scoured, diver-crooned, 700 feet (230 m) up on a Skye hill.

They are as chalk and cheese as nature permits in Scotland, but their common bonds are their harboured swans and the hold they have over me. I know them both as I know my back garden — indeed the mutes' pond was almost in my back garden for a while, and my regular Skye pilgrimages invariably come to rest near the whooper lochan. They are places of many intimacies, of well-won familiarities, where the only thing which fails to surprise me is that for all their familiarities they continue to surprise me, and to repay my vigils by their shores.

On one of these, I slipped out into a mellow September afternoon, stepped quietly from the hawthorns to the dregs of the flag irises, sat and stilled . . .

. . . I have never seen the pond so crammed with bird life, almost all of it lulled by the hour and the mood of the day into a kind of stupefied torpor. Almost all, because there can never be a lasting profound calm where there are coots in abundance, ill-natured, foul-mouthed little presbyterian demons of birds which abhor stillness as determinedly as nature does her

vacuum. There are at least three breeding pairs here, at least one of which is responsible for three broods, at least one of which is eight strong — make that irresponsible for three broods. I have no idea how many coots are on today's water, only that they muster collectively and individually a persistent series of forceful intrusions on the pervading spirit of calm.

Mute swans exert calming influences of their own, the more swans the more profound the calm, or at least the influence. It has always seemed to me that while other birds can charm or captivate or flaunt aristocratic arrogance (an absurdly human judgement that!) or overpower with spectacle, nature has tumbled all her wildest superlatives into swans. Here and now there are ten — cob, pen and family of eight, the young a fawn and tranquil phalanx chaperoned and shepherded by the douce dazzle of the parent birds.

It is a phenomenon of this pond that year after year the swans hatch every egg they lay and nurse and cajole every chick through the long and fraught flightless months, but here there is a conspiracy of benevolent forces which foster swans uniquely in this all but swanless county. One of these forces is a well-disposed human population, some of it hyper-active, some of it hyper-passive. My first encounter here was memorable for its conversation. He was a pond-side local, a farm worker with no ornithological inclination save for an instinctive Burns-like thirling to anything and everything which nature ever invented.

'Do the swans do well here?' I had asked him. He looked back in a long, blank silence then said, 'Do what well?'

'I mean are they disturbed much?'

'Disturbed? Whae'd disturb swans — an' what fur?'

'Lots of people do, though admittedly for no good reason. Fishermen for instance.'

'Na, there's nae fushin' here. Nae fush. Ahm catchin yur drift. Na there's nae fushin', an there's nae ither buggar fushes for swans, we a' see to that. Aye, ah suppose y'ed say they do well enough.'

'How many young?'

'Seven every year.'

'*Every* year?'

'Aye.'

'Seven every year'. . . except for the last three years now she has hatched eight, raised eight and fledged eight. (Mute swans normally lay between five and seven eggs, but up to twelve have been recorded.) (Jan Van de Kam, RSPB).

'And how many usually make it to flying?'
'Ah've tellt ye. Seven.'

His simplistic arithmetical confidence was unshakably based on unthinking ritual observation day after day, season after season 'Fur mair nor twenty years' as he told me later. He assumed on the same basis that hatching and fledging were likewise matters of ritual unswayed by alien influences, a tribute to the benevolent forces. I tried to argue otherwise with him, explaining the uniqueness of these circumstances, the failure of other swans elsewhere, but he would have none of it. He turned exasperated to the pond and demanded my evidence which proved him wrong, and there was none, except that three days after my arrival, she hatched eight! For the last three years now she has hatched eight, raised eight, and fledged eight.

So eight more gather beyond my feet on a September afternoon of coot-scratched glass calm, jostling in the degrees of their boldness for accustomed scraps, the adult birds stand-offish

The fat-of-the-land farmyard pond — mute swan breeding site (Jim Crumley).

and wary, but just as eager to exert their pecking order priority if the pickings prove rich.

Already the young birds have stamped their personalities on my vigils. Always there is one — identifiable for the moment by a whitening stripe by one eye — which is first to the feed; his blunt head-on confrontationist approach leaves brothers and sisters bickering in his wake. Another is faster, nimbler in pursuit of scattered morsels, avoids the bickering, the only one of the family to square up to the bold one and call his brazen bluff. Another lags furthest out, feeds least from the handouts, and 'up-ends' more than any of the others. She will fly the wildest of the brood.

Today there are no flung fragments, however, and the swans re-group and paddle after the parent birds, prospecting the shore for other hands that feed, pausing again and again to preen. Mike Birkhead and Christopher Perrins in their book *The Mute Swan* (Croom Helm) hint at an astounding statistic which explains why preening so preoccupies swans:

> . . . nobody has ever counted the feathers of a mute swan but people once counted those on a whistling swan (Amman 1937). This latter bird, which weighed 6.1kg, had 25,216 feathers weighing 621g, one-tenth of its total weight. Presumably mute swans, some of which are twice the weight of this bird, have even more feathers.

If the implication of that equation is 50,000 feathers, the ritual which roots a single swan to the spot for half an hour or often more — preening everything from tiny throat feathers to eagle-sized primaries — assumes a critical significance.

It is a ritual of some grace. The pen stands now on a partly submerged rock. (I have no idea why swans find such a perch, unless it offers them a stance surrounded by the relative security of water, but even then, the rock is often no more than a yard from the shore. Whoopers and

Adult mute swan with this year's young. The cygnets gradually assume white plumage over the course of three years (Michael W. Richards, RSPB).

Bewicks do it too, and mute swans far tamer than these on my West Lothian pond do it in the heart of Edinburgh.) The light has mellowed yellow in the late afternoon, and with her tail whipping up a small whirlpool of circles in the water around her, she stands high and deep chested, her neck straighter than it will be at any point in the next half hour, tucks her bill into her throat and begins. The neck starts to arc as she works down its length, sifting, scattering, scuffing, soothing, smoothing, smooring the white fires of her plumage back into a semblance of decorum.

The almost limitless flexibility of the mute swan neck begins now to extend its repertoire, as she tackles the lowest of her neck feathers and the highest of her breast. To ease the process, the neck is first laid thickly off to one side, then permits two more thin curves so that her bill, now pointing above the horizontal from her inverted head can penetrate deep into her breast down. With each new stage of the process, the bird's profile lowers and widens, so that by the time she has gravitated through the whole range of her feathered anatomy to the underside of her tail, she is a low-slung and barely recognizable assembly of curves, as far removed from the heron-like beginnings of the ritual as your

imagination or a swan's physiognomy can conceive. Throughout, her balance has not wavered, nor a foot shifted an inch.

The ritual is more important now than ever. The young swans do not winter here, but leave in dribs and drabs for the firth, or perhaps across it to Loch Leven. Either way, it is an adventurous time of year for mute swans. The young must be taught to preen and fly, and in the aftermath of the moult the adults must groom for the winter freezes which may also compel them to contemplate the firth.

The cob rears suddenly and opens an expanse of wing which never fails to surprise and impress for its breadth, its length, its power, its brightness. As he subsides, one of the young — the wild, shy one — adopts his attitude, flapping clumsily at first but then with more and more fluency, and almost involuntarily, it seems, begins to hurtle over the pond on heavy feet. As she crashes aross the water, the hysterical laughter of dabchicks and the indignation of riled coots mark her progress, but suddenly, and for the first time, she is airborne, clearing the far hawthorns, her wings singing at each beat, hardly rising above

the horizontal in flight, the exuberance of first flight almost visible. She flies for perhaps a minute, two rough circuits of the pond, a shallow climb above the farmhouses, scattering swallows from the wire, glides, brakes, touches down thrust-feet-first, subsides to a perfect, instinctive controlled landing.

By the end of the afternoon two more have flown, but her flight was the ice-breaker and the most facile, and I suspect then that she can be as wild or as tame a swan as she chooses — a survivor.

As the sun dwindles down through the quickening September evening, the pen leads her young back to the nest island, the nest itself now a bedraggled and scattered parody of its vast nursery snugness, but still a symbol of some security. As they climb from the water, a small panic of bloody-nosed young moorhens speeds away from the island to be rounded up by their parents and — once the swans have settled — led back to the deep shadow of the island rocks.

The cob stays late out on the water, ink-black against the pale-fired sunset pond, a leisured regal procession around his small kingdom, ducks deferring, coots chittering from reedy discretion, swallows skimming across his bows. He sails at last to my trackside, and with the last of the pink light on him, mounts the same rock as his mate had done three hours earlier, begins flamingo-tall, to preen.

★   ★   ★

It is at this point that many birdwatchers are consumed by roosting notions of their own, and slip with the sun below their own horizons, but I have long since learned to love the hour of the half-light of any season, shivering gladly in the gathering folds of the night cloak. In any case, gloamings of early September are hardly a penance of discomfort.

I have never managed to summon the dedication of the dawn riser, but the slow dusk-into-dark dwindling of the landscape suits my frame of mind, and justifies my philosophy. The dawn-watcher has no logical sense of a vigil completed. His tranquillities inevitably fail him as the morning grows and the world wakes, and whatever the joys of his dawn hour, he is

confronted irrevocably with anti-climax.

The dusk watcher and his day, however, wind down with his roosting charges, and the unveiling of nightlives is a furtive low-profile progression which harmonizes with his mood. He retires replete because he has worked with the grain of the wilds, not against it. He marks his hours with the chimes of roosting pheasants, the passing of the laws of daylight with shuttered suns, the dawn of the moon regime with the echo of tawnies. It is good because it fits.

So now on my swan pond it is the owl hour. These are well-treed acres, the county as rich in badgers as it is bereft of swans, and from the tall pond-fringing beeches, a wheezy young tawny owl splutters out a reedy hoot, a thin unpractised asthmatic bout, untranquil on the evening air if you like your owl vowels rounded, but music to my pondside ears because it is of its time of day and its month of the year. The adult reassurance from a distant pine sparks off a sweet-and-sour conversation which will last an hour.

Meanwhile, there are liberty-takers afloat, relishing the sudden swanlessness. With the mutes safe on the island there is conspicuously

Above left *The cob rears suddenly and opens an expanse of wing which never fails to surprise and impress* (Helmut Blesch, RSPB).

Right *The cob stays late out on the water, ink-black against the pale-fired sunset pond, a leisured regal procession around his small kingdom* (Jim Crumley).

Left *The sun dwindles down through the quickening September evening* (Jim Crumley).

Below left *Mute swan in aggressive display — whooper and Bewick's swans do not arch their wings in this way* (Michael W. Richards, RSPB).

Right *Coot, an ill-natured, foul-mouthed little presbyterian demon* (S.C. Porter, RSPB).

more room for lesser pond dwellers, and the shyest of these take their ease now in streaming single file from the furthest reeds — a family of little grebes. The soprano horse laugh of the adults is a favourite song of the pond, a good-humoured cackle which mercifully has no juvenile parody I have ever heard. There are none of their boisterous daylight ploys now, and even the coots seem resigned to muted bickerings, chipping away doggedly at anything which threatens to sound like a protracted silence.

If anything out-populates the coots hereabouts, it is mallards, and these gather now in new-found bravado around the island's base, and — in a clear gesture of collective challenge — about the feet of the preening cob. Even I, a mere unwebbed non-wildfowl, can see the gesture's folly. I can only guess at how a standing swan seems through mallard eyes from somewhere around ankle height, but it must be daunting enough. When the swan then spreads a furlong of wings and casts off with every apparent intention of stepping on your head, there would seem to be some merit in retreat.

Mallard scatter in every direction but mine,

while the cob, serene even in anger, makes a token neck-lowering dash at the slowest as in retreat, they sail off into the unfathomable blackness of the far shore. Almost at once, the mallards reassemble in good order, step ashore to stand and preen one-footed, the incident already obliterated, I fancy, from memory.

The swan's re-entry has persuaded the grebes into reedy exile, but undaunted coots and moorhens still steam over the pond on small jerky missions which quite escape my understanding. The island swans have laid their necks far back over their shoulders, their heads pillowed deep in the most sumptuous of feather-bedding.

There is a far shore commotion of mallard and coot and tufted duck and others unidentifiable by sound, which may or may not mark the prospecting of the neighbourhood foxes, but from this distance in this light, there is no telling. Perhaps the dawn-watcher will find a pool of feathers, a stain of small slaughter, in which case, he will be one up on me.

This is the same September, two weeks later, this is a small hill of Sleat in the south of Skye, the month turned traitor with typical West Highland frailty. Yesterday it snowed. Today my panorama — Knoydart, Rum, and close Cuillins — is dusted white, and flayed by a snotty-nosed termagant wind. There is no escaping the abuse of its tongue-lashing.

I have been watching for twenty minutes now the lochan half a mile (1 km) to the west, 200 feet (60 m) below, where there are five whooper swans, with the Arctic still on their wings. I would like to be closer. I plot a course to come on their watersheet undetected, and having plotted, begin a wide arc to the south, an arc fankled by peat hags but also shielded by peat hags. Whoopers this wild, this restless, this newly arrived from the far north, are wary beasts, and I want photographs of them at ease, not running fearfully for cover.

More important than the photographs, I want to lie close and watch, to eavesdrop on their soft trumpet-talk, to learn from them and of them in one of the wildest corners of their kingdom. So I follow my chosen path far below the lochan, then

Whooper Lochan, Skye (Jim Crumley).

turn towards it blind, guessing, faltering, praying I won't put up hind or hare to give my game away.

I have come in too high. Damn! The lochan is suddenly below me, but my God of the Wilds smiles and in the instant of my skylining error all five whoopers are tail-high, heads deep in the water's peaty depths. There is only one course of action now, and that is a 100 yard (100 m) crawl through peat hag and hollow, to a heathery ramp climbing gently to the lochan's shore. A pair of goldeneye at that end of the lochan could be a problem if my discretion fails me.

The last five yards (5 m) are the worst, gingering an inch-at-a-time to the crest of the bank, so slow, so soft, a slug couldn't have done it better. My eyes clear the heather, to find four yellow-ringed eyes staring back, five yards away. Freeze! — but the goldeneye is not born which would ever mistake a photographer for a slug, and this pair clatter their panic straight over the swans.

My chin gouges a groove in the peat. I hold my stillness until my eyes ache from trying to focus on the heather forest before my face, until every limb I own screams for the release of movement — any movement. I know that the swans' attention will be focused not on the retreating ducks now circling high between the lochan and the eagle crag, but on the source of the threat which persuaded them to retreat — my source, my threat.

I raise an eye to confront ten swan eyes staring uncomprehendingly at my moor-coloured stillness, and, having advanced in their bewildered curiosity, only twenty yards (20 m) from my shore. I raise the camera, focus, fire, a calculated routine of minimal movement and sound, yet still there is enough of both to provoke a degree of unruffled hysteria bugling through the swans like a new wind through fallen leaves, and from the pen, a threshing retreat. I have achieved precisely what I set out not to achieve, which was to unsettle the birds, to be an alien in their midst.

While they chorus and cruise, withdraw,

Whooper swans beat a threshing retreat (Hansgeorg Arndt, RSPB).

advance, stiff-necked and tense, the camera hisses at each new opportunity, until they settle beyond its reasonable scope to feed at the furthest point of the loch, but always with one adult gaze riveted on me — a disconcerting knowledge to be tolerated as an enemy within and held at a distance by wild swans whose approval I crave. That is the outrageous arrogance which is the prerogative of my species, to plead for favours from wildness, the language we have long since lost (a few still have the words on their tongue — I have seen wildlife writer Mike Tomkies work miracles with its speech), to seek kindred-spirit-hood newly dismounted from my car with these, newly dismounted from the Arctic.

Another thought crams into mind, which is the frantic pace of whoopers' summers in contrast to the leisured ease of the mute swans of my Lothian pond. These whoopers probably flew north from here in mid-April, to migrate, to mate, to nest, to lay, to incubate, to fledge, to turn and fly again, to find the Arctic or something depressingly like it awaiting their journeyings' end on Skye in September.

The mutes were nesting before the whoopers had left, the cygnets on the water before the whoopers had laid, yet these three young whoopers had just flown down from Iceland with only Faroe to pause for breath while the young mutes were still toying with the idea of a first circuit of their nursery pond. Through the glasses I fell to watching the whoopers feeding and preening, to marvelling at their evolution, to dissecting the vagaries of the swan tribe, and the similarities.

The whoopers relaxed again now, an hour of camera-free stillness later, begin to advance haphazardly down the lochan, so that the camera once more has possibilities. The adult male suddenly rises on the water — he has found a barely submerged rock, and in the manner of all his tribe, proceeds to preen with only his feet and two inches of leg under water. It is a less elegant, less flexible routine than the mute, and I begin to wonder whether the whooper's characteristically straighter neck is also a less flexible grooming aid.

There follows one of those golden moments which is the privilege of the seeker-in-stillness. As his mate approaches him, apparently

unobserving for her head is immersed deep in the feathers of her back even as she paddles, he rises higher, and unveils a heraldic spread of wings, a vast embrace. For perhaps two seconds, she lies furled beneath his stupendous unfurling, then he subsides, she uncoils, straightens, consults the whereabouts of her young, turns and shepherds them closer. These two seconds are as vivid in my mind as anything my wildest hours and days and years have ever divined. They will last my lifetime. The camera, for once, was primed, ready, and produced one souvenir worthy of the vigil, the peat on the chin, the shivering hours; the reward, the privilege.

The light begins to dowse. The one Knoydart peak I can see from my heathery wedge begins to fade into the evening sky. The camera's hour is almost done. I contemplate calling it a day, but there are instincts at work now which I cannot name and never question. They say 'stay' and 'still' when logic argues the reverse. I have many causes to be grateful for the urge to linger through the last hour of half-light when there is little to see but the shifting mood of wildness as the laws of daylight peter out and the laws of darkness

peter in. My glasses are still on the swans, and I am only vaguely conscious of a gentle splashing at my back where the lochan bends out of my restricted field of vision. I suspect the return of the goldeneye, but as the splashing persists, there is a sudden change in the attitude of the swans, a muttered bugling from the adults, a stiffening of necks, a swivelling of heads, a slow advance a dozen yards down the loch, a concerted discretionary halt.

I can rise on one elbow, and crane as far round my left shoulder as my unswanlike neck will permit. It is enough. Five red deer hinds and three calves have walked into the shallows 50 yards (45 m) away, as unsuspecting of me as I had been of them. My low-lying stillness and the ocean-born wind are in my favour, and I venture rolling over twice to a better vantage point. The light is too far gone for new photographs, and even my new position denies my cramped right arm enough leeway to focus the realigned telephoto. I simply lie, watch and memorize.

They wade and drink and mutter. The swans, as far down the lochan in the other direction, paddle and feed and mutter. Something beyond

Above left *The adult male suddenly rises on the water — he has found a barely-submerged rock* (Arthur Gilpin, RSPB).

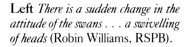

Left *There is a sudden change in the attitude of the swans . . . a swivelling of heads* (Robin Williams, RSPB).

Right *Whooper swans winter in Scotland and other parts of the British Isles but their breeding grounds are in Iceland, Scandinavia and Russia* (P.R. Perfect, RSPB).

my perception may have passed between the two, or perhaps some flaw in my stillness or fickle wind trickery betrayed me, for the leading hind suddenly stops, stands, stares, ears forward, nose working. She holds that attitude, curiously reminiscent of the whoopers' first questioning glare five hours ago now, barks a command and leads a bounding retreat to a heathery swell. There the herd pauses, skylined, as wild as the wind, turns again to trot across the hill to the glowing dusk.

The western sky pales and clears. An early moon has risen beyond the Cuillins. Owl cries drift up from the wood above Ord, and the psychology of the hour compels me homeward. The whoopers barely mark my standing now, no more than a conspicuous movement by the male so that he sits on the water between his young and my silhouette. The water is the colour of milk, a trick of the light which has the curious effect of darkening the swans. Again I recall the mute cob on *his* pond at sunset.

My path lies beyond the peak from which I first watched the lochan, so I must re-thread the peat hags, and climb, before the long moorland descent to the car. There is little enough need for discretion now, so I simply walk the shore of the lochan towards the whoopers' bay. I pass within ten yards (9 m), an event which is marked only by one more discreet shift of position by the male. Always, he is between me and the young, always the female behind them. He is head-up, alert, wary. She is head down, but still visibly wary. The young, shapeless slumps, lie submerged in as deep a roosting slumber as any swan of the wild is permitted, which is shallow enough.

I pause and turn — like the deer in retreat, it occurs to me fleetingly — on the summit. From this angle the water has darkened and stilled, like black glass, flattering the rising moon. The swans are lost from sight behind a rise in the ground just above the lochan, but high above the crag, where the sky is palest, an unmistakable silhouette is on the air, a spread-eagle of wings, a slow spiralling climb, a long stiff-winged glide across the face of the crag, then a soaring climb to a second bird, and within moments, a third, beating hard from the south.

The three birds of prey — male, female and young female — fly around each other, back-flipping, talon touching, a mesmeric routine of astounding aerobatics on the grand scale, the bumbling aerial turmoil of a golden eagle master-class. They are teaching the young one to fly.

Yet even this mastery, this instinctive fluency in one so young as this year's eagle is overwhelmed by the young whoopers' feat. Not even an eagle is asked to fly a thousand miles (1,600 km) at ten weeks old.

The eagles wheel their threefold might across the sky — again I am compelled to sit and stare and be still, for eagles choose their stage with an unfailing eye for landscape grandeur and even within eagle repertoires there are few arenas to match this with the Cuillins trailing wisps of cloud shroud, and far Rum's own Cuillins for an afterthought in the wings.

The final act is a quiet clamour down on the lochan and the heart-stopping sight of the swans low over the moor, contouring the low hills and dropping down for the coast, the halflin moon on their wings. They had tholed my presence for half an unflinching day, but it seemed that the eagles overhead were a last, unsettling straw. It is barely credible that the swans considered them a threat — there is little to perturb a swan other than a man with a gun or a string of pylons — but that awesome silhouette in triplicate and the natural unease in new surroundings (and exacerbated no doubt by my own long intrusion) has tipped some balance of instinct and discomfort . . .

When I turned again from their low flight, the eagles had gone from the sky, and when I sought out the swans again in turn, they too had found their sanctuary in the mustering gloom. I had moon and snow-beacon to light my path down to the empty shore — the inland shore shunned by swans this wild.

OCTOBER
ISLAY, ISLAND OF GEESE
MALCOLM OGILVIE

Malcolm Ogilvie on Islay (Margot Perrows).

MALCOLM OGILVIE worked for the Wildfowl Trust, Slimbridge from 1960-86, studying and writing about geese and swans. He paid annual visits to Islay to count the geese and in May 1986 went to live there as Director of the newly formed Islay Field Centre while continuing to write and lecture about birds. He has been a frequent contributor to radio programmes such as *The Living World,* and has written seven books, the most recent being *Flamingoes.*

It was early morning on a bright, but decidedly windy, October day, with a near gale-force northerly wind blowing in my face. I was standing near the entrance to a shallow sealoch on the north coast of the island of Islay. As I gazed to the north, peering into the blustering wind, I could see a skein of geese approaching. They were flying very low over the sea, seemingly skimming the surface and lifting over the rolling surf as it crashed noisily onto the sandbar that nearly closes the mouth of the loch. There were about a hundred birds in the skein, strung out in two thin lines, swaying up and down as if to match the restless waves. The low-angled rays of the sun, dodging between hurrying clouds, caught their backs and I could see flashing patterns of black and white.

They came steadily on. There was no slackening in their purpose as they drew level with the land. They flew on, undeviating, straight into the mouth of the loch and on towards its head. As they approached me, I looked beyond them to see another skein, and then another. These were smaller, no more than twenty birds in each. The gap between the flocks was a few hundred yards: the skeins were in sight of each other, following in purposeful flight as they neared their final destination.

Then I heard geese calling from well above me, and there, several hundred feet up, was yet another skein which I had missed as I concentrated on the low-flying birds. These were coming from a slightly different direction, some way to the west, but on a heading to bring them, too, to the head of the loch.

This loch varies between about three-quarters of a mile and a mile and a quarter in width (1-2 km) and runs for nearly four miles (6 km) almost due north-south. It is very shallow, with great expanses of sandflats lying exposed at low tide, a river channel wandering lazily through them. Its mouth is guarded on either hand by high yellow dunes, contrasting with the blue sea beyond and the white surf on the sandbar. At its head lies a strip of saltmarsh backed by several hundred acres of low-lying pastures, reclaimed from the sea in the early part of the last century. These pastures form the heart of the RSPB's Loch Gruinart reserve. This is the wintering place of thousands of barnacle geese from East Greenland, and I was here watching their autumn arrival, as they made their landfall after an over-sea journey of some 800 miles (1,300 km).

Bird migration is a subject which has always intrigued mankind. The very concept of fragile, feathered flying animals not only covering long distances over inhospitable sea and desert, but doing so almost as regularly as clockwork, finding their way unerringly from breeding place to wintering grounds, induces a sense of wonder which undoubtedly contributes to the fascination which birds hold for man.

The subject is made even more mysterious because it is so seldom seen taking place. Considering that tens of millions of birds fly to and from and over Britain in the course of a year, the number of times that one actually witnesses this migration in progress is remarkably small. This, of course, makes those occasions when one does see it even more memorable. And here on Islay, every October, one can watch the arrival of the geese and, in a very small and incomplete way, begin to gain an understanding of what bird migration involves; the forces and the skills, both physical and innate, which have successfully brought these birds on their annual journey south.

The barnacle geese do not normally arrive on Islay *en masse*, in great sky-darkening flocks of thousands. Instead they come in a steady stream, just as impressive in its different way, as the inexorable migration goes on for hour after hour, all day, and on through the night.

Soon after dawn on that blowy October morning, I counted the number of barnacle geese feeding on the Gruinart Flats, as the grassland area at the head of the Loch is called. I found a total of just under 4,000. The day before there had been only a few hundreds. I had been watching the weather forecasts and keeping an eye on the numbers of geese over the previous few days. Although I had been fortunate enough to see the unforgettable spectacle of the barnacle geese arriving on Islay the year before, I was determined not to miss any opportunity for watching it again.

Above left *As the geese approached me, I looked beyond them to see another skein and then another* (C.H. Gomersall, RSPB).

Left *Then I heard geese calling from well above me . . .* (M.W. Richards, RSPB).

Since acquiring Loch Gruinart as a reserve in 1984, the RSPB has been managing the fields for the geese (C.H. Gomersall, RSPB).

As the first few skeins flew past me, I turned to follow their flight. The high-level birds had already set their wings and had begun a long glide in order to lose height. As they neared the end of the long stretch of sandflats, they turned into a short spiral as they swung round to land into the wind. The low-flying birds flapped steadily on until they, too, were approaching the last few yards. Then a quick glide, their legs dropped down, and a last-minute twist brought them head to wind.

All the birds landed on the sandflats, which the ebbing tide was quickly exposing. Only a few hundred yards further on was the inviting green of the pastures. Since acquiring the reserve in 1984, the RSPB has been managing the fields for the geese, ploughing and reseeding the old pastures so that there is plenty of good young grass waiting for them each autumn. Yet the birds landed short. Food was not their priority; not yet. These newly-arrived birds had other needs which clearly they held as more important than food. They wanted to bathe and to preen, and, above all, they wanted to sleep.

As soon as each skein came in to land, the birds started immediately to settle their feathers after their long flight. Wings were flapped and shaken, body feathers ruffled and relaxed again, and heads were rubbed over the preen gland and then thoroughly over their plumage. Small pools and freshwater streams meandering over the sandflats became busy with splashing and flapping geese. There was a great deal of calling, too, probably between members of families as they sought and found each other. Barnacle geese migrate in family parties, and it is vital that the young do not become separated from their parents, who have not only brought their goslings on this, their first migration, but will show them the best places to feed, guard them and look after them through their first winter.

Gradually, the bathing and preening geese ceased these activities, walked onto firmer ground, tucked their heads under their wings, and went to sleep. They needed to recover from the rigours of their long flight. They had probably been flying for some ten to twelve hours non-stop. There is no evidence that they ever come down and rest on the sea, and nothing much for them if they did. One can only surmise at the effort required to fly continuously for such long periods, but the evidence of these sleeping geese suggests that it is considerable.

This pattern continued throughout that October day. Each time I looked to the north, there were further skeins coming into sight. A remarkably high number seemed to have the perfect course which brought them straight into the mouth of the loch, and I wondered how much last-minute correcting had brought them there. Other skeins continued to arrive on different bearings, though, some coming more from the west, others from the east, presumably seeing the island some distance away and changing course accordingly.

There was hardly a pause in the steady stream of geese coming in from the north. A few large

Small pools and freshwater streams meandering over the sandflats became busy with splashing and flapping geese (Pamela Harrison, RSPB).

skeins of several hundred birds came along, as did some groups of no more than a handful of individuals, presumably single families or even pairs, but most flocks were between about thirty and a hundred. For long periods, there was always another flock (or two or three) in view as one passed me, though every so often would come a longer gap. In the middle of the day, the migration slackened off somewhat, only to pick up again towards evening. There were also occasional heavy squalls of rain, borne down on the wind. During these, few geese seemed to arrive. Perhaps they had been able to take avoiding action and either arrived before the squalls, or slowed down until they were passed.

Although the main migration was of barnacle geese, other birds, too, were on the move, taking advantage of the favourable conditions for migrating south from Iceland. Several flocks of whooper swans came powering through the sky on their great wings. The grey-brown cygnets were obvious in some of the groups, flying in family parties and dependent on their parents in exactly the same way as the geese.

Whooper swans are among the largest of

Left *A few groups of pintail appeared, their wings beating nearly twice as fast as the geese* (M.W. Richards, RSPB).

Below *White-fronted geese: large numbers of the Greenland race winter on Islay* (John Marchington, RSPB).

Above right *The good green grass was only a few wingflaps away* (John Marchington, RSPB).

migrant birds, powerful and majestic fliers certainly, but towards the upper limit of weight for flying long distances. All flight takes a large amount of energy and migrant birds lay down supplies of such energy in the form of layers of fat which they can burn up during the long journey. This, though, means extra weight, and, being already very large, heavy birds, whooper swans are not able to carry as much extra fat relative to their size as smaller birds, and thus the distance they can fly in one journey is shorter, too.

A few groups of pintail appeared, one flock actually flying alongside a skein of barnacle geese, their wings beating nearly twice as fast, the long tail feathers of the drakes streaming out behind. The pintail which breed in Iceland, migrate to Britain and Ireland for the winter. Very few spend the winter on Islay, and these migrating flocks would not stay long before passing on further south.

Greenland white-fronted geese, too, were on the move, though as yet only a few hundred. Their main migration tends to be later than that of the barnacle geese. These geese breed on the west side of Greenland and while some move across the icecap to spend a few weeks each autumn in Iceland, others gradually move south down the Greenland coast before heading out over the North Atlantic direct for Scotland and Ireland.

As I left the area, shortly before it got dark, I counted the barnacle geese bathing and sleeping on the sandflats as well as those now feeding on the adjacent pastures. It seemed that a few hours sleep was sufficient, and then hunger pangs awoke them. The good green grass was only a few wingflaps away. My count reached 11,000, which meant that at least 7,000 geese had arrived during the day, at a rate which, during the peak periods, had comfortably exceeded 1,000 an hour.

That particular goose arrival, in 1987, was an early one, taking place on 10 October. More usually the geese come around the 18th-20th of the month. They do not fly direct from their breeding grounds in East Greenland, but instead leave in the middle of September and make the comparatively short, 200-300 mile (320-480 km), hop to Iceland. There they spend the next few weeks feeding on pastures, before the

Barnacles grazing (John Marchington, RSPB).

approach of winter drives them further south. A deep depression crossing Iceland a few days before had brought about the early onset of winter by pulling in strong northerly winds which, in turn, brought heavy snowfalls, covering even the lowland areas and so depriving the geese of their food. The belt of northerly winds had then extended south towards northern Britain forming a perfect migration corridor, with a helpful tail wind of some 40-50 mph (64-80 kph). These conditions would similarly have encouraged the Greenland whitefronts present in Iceland to leave as well.

The second stage of the migration for these geese is a minimum of 600 miles (965 km), which would take them to the northern tip of the Outer Hebrides, but is more usually as much as 800 miles (1,300 km), which is the distance from southern Iceland to Islay. At their normal cruising speed of 30-40 mph (48-64 kph) such a journey could take up to 24 hours, but it is probable that the birds try to time their migration to take advantage of strong tail winds, as on this occasion.

In the days immediately following that major

arrival of geese, the winds changed, conditions in Iceland ameliorated and no more birds came during the next week. The total wintering population of barnacle geese on Islay is around 22,000, so roughly half the population arrived on that one day. It was not until the more normal arrival period of 20-21 October that most of the remainder came. So, too, did the bulk of the 7,000 Greenland whitefronts which were to winter on Islay that year.

The barnacle geese which arrived early stayed on and around the RSPB reserve at Loch Gruinart. The ample new grass enabled them to put back any weight lost during migration, while the goslings still had some growing to do. There was plenty of grass available even for 11,000 or more geese and it would not be until much later in the autumn that substantial numbers would leave the reserve and spread out over the rest of the island.

Only a few of the whooper swans stopped at the head of Loch Gruinart on their arrival. Most continued and I later found several flocks round

Loch Gorm, a substantial freshwater loch a few miles away. This is a traditional autumn stopping place for whoopers on Islay. They use the loch for bathing and roosting, and fly to feed on nearby barley and oat stubbles. Sadly, only small numbers of whoopers stay on Islay for the winter. The majority move on south to spend the winter in Ireland.

The geese, whooper swans and pintail had been the visible part of that urgent migration from Iceland. Soon afterwards it became apparent that other birds had come, too. Redwings were plentiful on the island, feeding in flocks on berry-bearing trees and hedges, and hopping, eyes alert, over lawns and fields. A gyr falcon, of the dark race which lives in Iceland, was seen a number of times flashing across the moors.

The highlight of that October's birdwatching on Islay, though, was a harlequin duck, a species which in Europe is confined to Iceland, though it

Harlequin drakes — a species that breeds in Iceland and a very rare vagrant to Great Britain (W. Suetens and P. Van Groenendael, RSPB).

also occurs in North America. This individual, a young male or perhaps a female, was only the eleventh to be recorded in Britain. It stayed about ten days before perhaps deciding that it was a long way from home. Normally this species hardly migrates at all, merely moving between the rivers in Iceland where they breed and the coastal waters where they spend the winter. One can only speculate, but it seems most likely that this individual became caught up in the great waves of birds leaving Iceland on those fierce northerly winds, and Islay was its first landfall.

Just as the harlequin is a vagrant, lost and well away from its normal range, so vagrant geese also appear on Islay, though invariably they are in the flocks of barnacles and Greenland whitefronts. Two snow geese and two Canada geese were present among the first arriving flocks of barnacles that October. The former were white phase lesser snow geese and the latter members of one of the small races of Canada geese, no bigger than barnacle geese themselves.

Both these goose species breed in North America and stray regularly to West Greenland. Thus it would be quite possible for them to get

caught up in the flocks of whitefronts and come with them to Islay. To get caught up with the barnacles, though, they would first have to cross to the east side of Greenland or reach Iceland. The possibility that they have merely escaped from some wildfowl collection much nearer home must always hang over them.

Loch Gruinart is certainly the heart of the goose areas of Islay during the autumn, but the much larger sealoch, Loch Indaal, which runs in from the south-west and almost cuts the island in two, is the focal area for ducks and waders. It, too, has an area of saltings at its head, and large expanses of tidal sandflats. Later in the winter these are used as a roost by many thousands of barnacle geese which fly daily to graze on the surrounding farmland.

The saltings and sandflats support populations of waders, especially curlew and oystercatcher, and a wintering flock of up to 150 bar-tailed godwits. Each October, though, migrant waders of many different species can be found feeding on the strandline or spread out over the flats. Sanderling, knot, grey plover and little stint fly in to join dunlin and ringed plover, many of which

are probably resident. Whimbrel and greenshank are regularly seen, too, with the occasional greenshank staying on for the winter.

Loch Indaal is extremely important, too, for its wintering divers, grebes and ducks which arrive in October to feed on the abundant fish and crustacean life with which the loch abounds. There are several small burns flowing into the loch, bringing fertility from the surrounding land. There are also three small villages and many houses scattered around the shores, whose sewage products also add to the nutrient levels. However, it is probably the presence of two distilleries that has done most to make Loch Indaal quite so attractive to these water birds!

One of the distilleries has been in operation for about 200 years, the other for at least half that time, and throughout that period they have daily poured out hundreds of gallons of washings from their fermentation tanks and stills into the loch. These contain nitrates and phosphates as well as small particles of barley so it is little wonder that marine life flourishes in the sea and on the bottom of the loch.

The main duck species is the scaup. Over 1,000 will spend the winter in Loch Indaal, one of the largest flocks in Britain, and it is during October that they first arrive in strength. They, too, probably come from Iceland where they are one of the commonest breeding ducks. Here in the loch they are usually to be found feeding and loafing a short distance offshore near the principal village of Bowmore, and with them can be found a selection of the other species.

A few days after the barnacle goose arrival described above, on a day with little or no wind, I drove round to Bowmore and parked on a very convenient layby raised some 50 feet (15 m) above the level of the loch. The layby was created with some rather untidy tipping of spoil resulting from the construction of a small electricity generating station. It may still be something of an eyesore, but there is no doubt as to its usefulness to birdwatchers! Mounting my telescope on a window clamp I could sit in comfort and scan the loch for what it held. The sea was ideally mirror smooth and every bird on it showed up perfectly.

I soon located the flock of scaup floating in a straggly group on the flat surface of the sea a few hundred yards offshore. I counted the number of

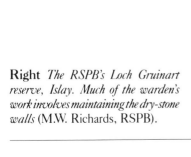

Above left *The oystercatchers are among several species of wader that feed on the saltings and sandflats of Loch Indaal, Islay* (Jan Van de Kam, RSPB).

Left *A large and elegant wading bird, the bar-tailed godwit winters in a flock of up to 150 individuals* (R.T. Mills, RSPB).

Right *The RSPB's Loch Gruinart reserve, Islay. Much of the warden's work involves maintaining the dry-stone walls* (M.W. Richards, RSPB).

Left *A Slavonian grebe in its drab winter dress* (J.D. Bakewell, RSPB).

Below *Long-tailed ducks — two drakes and a duck: half a dozen of these most elegant birds winter in Loch Indaal* (Bobby Tulloch, RSPB).

Right *The reserve's fields are grazed by cattle, so that the grass will be at a suitable length to attract the geese to feed* (C.H. Gomersall, RSPB).

birds present, thankful that for once they were not actively diving for food. When the objects of one's counting are spending more than half their time underwater, it does make for difficulties in getting an accurate answer. There were just over 700 in the flock, a high number for the middle of October and strongly indicative that they, too, had arrived with the same strong northerly winds a few days before. Although many of the birds were yet to come into full winter plumage, it was apparent that, as usual, the majority were males. Such an imbalance in the sexes among flocks of wintering ducks is quite usual for many species. Somewhere else in the wintering range would be flocks containing a majority of females, thus restoring the overall balance of roughly one to one throughout the whole population.

Dodging in and out of the scaup, and this time disappearing beneath the surface with infuriating regularity, were several much smaller, slighter birds, dark-capped and white-breasted. They were Slavonian grebes, yet another species which had arrived here from Iceland. They had shed their summer plumage of chestnut, with black and yellow head plumes, and were now in their more drab winter dress. As I scanned away from the scaup flock, I could see others dotted about, and though their constant diving precluded a really accurate count, I was reasonably happy that there were at least 25 present, perhaps more.

My eye was next caught by one of the most handsome of all ducks, a male long-tailed duck with his pure white head and flanks, dark chest, and long, long central tail feathers adding about an extra third to his overall length. Half a dozen of these most elegant birds winter in Loch Indaal and this one, and four others which I spotted shortly afterwards, were the first arrivals. The long-tailed duck has a more or less complete circumpolar breeding distribution within the Arctic, though the nearest breeding area is in Iceland, again.

There were eider ducks in plenty on the loch. These are resident on Islay, with a healthy breeding population around the coasts, and plenty of young to be seen most autumns, especially in Loch Indaal. The males were still coming out of eclipse and there were still rather few in their full finery of black and white, tinged with pastel green and pink.

Left *Eiders are resident on Islay, with a healthy breeding population around the coasts* (Ake Wallentin Engman, RSPB).

One of the more puzzling ducks which occurs year round on Islay is the common scoter. There is a flock of between about eighty and 150 on Loch Indaal in every month of the year, with the peak in mid-winter. Yet, in the middle of summer there can be nearly a hundred present, with the males displaying vigorously to the females as if preparing to breed. A few pairs do breed on the island, though fewer than ten, and it is a mystery where the summer flock fits in, unless it is comprised of birds which are not yet old enough to breed. Scoters do not mature until they are at least two or three years old. At any rate, that October day, sure enough there was a flock of around 85 on Loch Indaal, the males all black except for their prominent yellow bills, the females browner with conspicuous pale cheeks.

Below *A great northern diver in winter plumage — a passage migrant probably from Iceland or Greenland* (C.H. Gomersall, RSPB).

I now turned my attention to some of the larger birds which I could see across the loch. Several were cormorants or shags, both of which breed on the island, but others were clearly divers, and it wasn't long before I had located up to five each of all three species, red-throated, black-throated and great northern. The first-named breeds on many Islay lochs, but the other two are passage migrants and winter visitors, the black-throated perhaps from breeding sites in northern Scotland, the great northern very probably comes in from Iceland and Greenland.

Loch Indaal had yielded up its usual splendid range of species on this near perfect day. When a gale blows, particularly from the west, then it is a great deal harder to either locate or count the birds. There was still a surprise to come, though. I had a glimpse of a rather smaller bird, a grey back and perhaps a chestnut head as it dived. There are several pairs of red-breasted mergansers breeding round the loch, and a late summer moulting flock of 200 or more, but this bird seemed wrong for that species. Sure enough, when it surfaced, there was a smew, either a young one or a female, with the clear white cheeks surmounted by a chestnut cap. This is a comparative rarity on Islay, though there had been one in Loch Indaal all the previous winter.

Islay in October is not just about migrant waterfowl, though. The range of habitats includes woodland of many types, both mature deciduous and recent conifer plantations, lowland bogs and upland moorland, sea cliffs and much fertile farmland. In every month of the year one can reckon on finding over a hundred different kinds of birds on the island. Certainly over a hundred species breed on Islay, probably somewhere between 105 and 110 each year. And in the course of a winter weekend, the century of species is comparatively easy to achieve. Yet October remains supreme. In October 1987, a keen birdwatcher, anxious to beat the total of 105 achieved by his friend the previous week, notched up 111 species. Yet he missed several that were known to be present! My best estimate for the week he was here is 120.

October sees the first gatherings of tit flocks in the woodlands. Extensive areas were planted during the nineteenth century around four main houses on the island. These have matured into superb habitats, where oak, beech, sycamore and

Redwings are winter visitors that descend in large flocks with fieldfares to strip the hedges of berries within a few days (R.W. Kennedy, RSPB).

ash rub shoulders with noble fir, Douglas fir, western red cedar and the occasional giant redwood. Here, from October onwards, I have encountered one flock after another of blue, great and coal tits flitting from tree to tree, accompanied by treecreepers and goldcrests. Long-tailed tits, too, can be seen bounding one after another across the clearings, calling all the while.

The redwings which came from Iceland in early October 1987 were just the precursors of a much larger movement which took place later that same month. Around the 19th and 20th, redwings and fieldfares began to appear in some numbers, to start with on the fields in the south-east, but later over the whole island. Where the first redwings had certainly come from Iceland, these later waves were arriving from the east with fieldfares and can be assumed from this, and from their generally lighter appearance, to be Scandinavian birds.

In most autumns, the movement of fieldfares

and redwings is comparatively small. Few of either species winter here, and the great majority of birds passing through Scotland towards wintering grounds in Ireland and south to Iberia, seem to miss Islay altogether. Not in 1987, though. Flocks of hundreds could be heard passing overhead each night, the skies filled with the chackings and seepings of the birds as they kept contact in the dark. During the day, it seemed as if every pasture and coastal grass strip on the island was covered in hopping thrushes, the comparatively few berried hedges having been stripped in the first few days.

It was difficult to estimate just how many thrushes were present on the island at one time, let alone the number which were passing through, but it must have been several tens of thousands each of fieldfares and redwings. And every so often, as one moved around the island, one saw flocks of song thrushes, and blackbirds, and it was similarly apparent that chaffinches were present in very large numbers.

There are many stubble fields and kale fields on the island in the autumn, and these become home for flocks of skylarks, linnets, chaffinches and twite, searching for seeds and every so often flying up in panic as a merlin or a sparrowhawk hurtles past. A flock of about a dozen Lapland buntings was found in one stubble field at the end of the month in 1987. The straw was long and concealed almost everything from view. But if one walked out across the field, birds lifted in all directions, flying round, circling and dropping again out of sight. Calls of all kinds filled the air, including the distinctive '*chew*' of the buntings.

October 1987 had begun with a large-scale migration of many different species, principally wildfowl and other waterbirds, from Iceland. The goose arrival was rather earlier than usual, but it is about as predictable an event as these things ever can be. Just the precise day or few days when it will occur cannot be foretold. And the great majority of the birds involved are coming to Islay to spend the winter. This is the terminus of their long journey: Islay provides the habitat, the food, the sanctuary that they seek.

The month ended with a spectacular, indeed colossal migration of Scandinavian birds, principally thrushes, which was certainly out of the ordinary. No-one here could recall anything quite so massive taking place before, yet no-one can possibly say that it will not happen again. These birds were not destined to stay on Islay for the winter. Only a few weeks later and the vast majority had moved on. But who knows? All of these many tens of thousands of birds which had probably never been to Islay before have now some experience of the island. Perhaps some will retain that memory and return next October, too.

October is undoubtedly one of the finest months of the year on Islay, and certainly the greatest month for bird migration. Seabirds stream past the south-west corner of the island *en route* for the open Atlantic; gannets, shearwaters and petrels passing in their thousands. Major arrivals take place of the great variety of passage and wintering ducks and waders coming from many different parts of the Arctic. And every once in a while, hordes of Scandinavian thrushes pause on their journey further south.

Above all, though, October is the month when nearly 30,000 geese fly in from their breeding grounds in Greenland to give Islay its unique character for yet another winter. And it is in October that one can actually see that migration, experience that arrival, as the geese make their traditional landfall at Loch Gruinart after their long flight from the north. This is when one can come closest to an understanding of all the processes which combine to produce such a phenomenon and at the very least achieve some sympathetic appreciation of the underlying instincts and abilities of the birds which make it possible.

A NOVEMBER JOURNEY
FROM THE FENS TO ANGLESEY
JOHN DAY

John Day (RSPB).

After eighteen years with the RSPB, JOHN DAY resigned as head land agent to be the Society's senior warden in the Lake District. John, who has a degree in biology, has undertaken original research on bitterns and marsh harriers. He has written several scientific papers and numerous articles about wildlife conservation. He lives near Haweswater, Cumbria.

My journey started early one morning in late November from a village not far from Cambridge and in the heart of the fens. A low bank of mist hung over the river, spilling out over the glistening black, peaty soils and running in thin lines down the ditches. As a weak sun began to break through and the mist to dissipate and vanish, the horizon receded across the great flat expanse of arable farmland until the lantern tower of Ely Cathedral became visible above the clustered roofs of the town. The road wound across the fens like a causeway. Peat shrinkage, helped by drainage and constant exposure by cultivation, has caused the level of the fields to fall several feet below the surface of the tarmac. Turning down a narrow bumpy road beside the raised bank of the river, I arrived at my first birdwatching objective, the Ouse Washes.

This great floodplain is a 20-mile-long (32 km) strip of grassland, half a mile (1 km) wide, which bisects the black fens. It is enclosed by two slow-flowing rivers, each in turn contained by tall, grassed banks. This was the final chapter in the draining of the fens, started by the Romans and finished by a Dutchman after the Civil War. Cutting off a 50-mile (80 km) loop in the Great Ouse river, these channels transport water from the heart of East Anglia more swiftly to the sea, enclosing a strip of fenland in the process which acts as a relief valve for the floodwaters which spread over it each winter. Cattle-grazed in summer, and home to countless wetland birds in winter, the Ouse Washes has become the most important inland wildfowl refuge in Britain.

This year the floods had arrived early after a wet summer, and the previous month, as the water slowly rose across the four-foot (1.5 m) lateral fall of the fields, there had been frantic activity. Cattle in their hundreds had had to be gathered into small herds and driven up to eight miles along the banks to the gathering pens, where for many days a continuous shuttle of lorries had been arriving to take them away. Now, all was quiet except for the wind rustling the dead leaves in osier willows and the mournful cries of

The Ouse Washes in winter: a great floodplain that provides important breeding and wintering grounds for many birds, the RSPB, Wildfowl Trust and Cambridge and Isle of Ely Naturalists' Trust all manage reserves on the Washes (M.W. Richards, RSPB).

the lapwings in a nearby field.

Crossing the river by the bridge alongside the squat bulk of the pumphouse, I set off down the bank. The turf was short and springy after the summer grazing, and I soon arrived at the wooden birdwatching hide, put up for visitors to sit at ease out of the wind and watch the birds, gaze out over the water across to Littleport and Ely or just eat their sandwiches!

A group of wigeon was feeding nearby at the water's edge, the drakes with their smart chestnut heads and yellow foreheads. Noisy self-confident birds, they grazed and squabbled, one bird sometimes chasing another when its feeding area was violated. From time to time the flock was joined by other small groups, heralding their arrival with noisy greetings; their whistling calls, once heard, are never forgotten, the spirit of the long-vanished great fen.

Further out, teal were grubbing in the shallow water at the ditch edges where accumulated spoil made submerged linear banks under the brown floodwater from which the grass stems and thistle tops emerged forlornly. Here, too, shoveler were feeding, dipping their beaks in the water like miniature vacuum cleaners, and straining out small insects and water snails.

Below the osier bed, in which a wandering party of long-tailed tits was busily examining each leaf and twig, watched by a cock reed bunting, ran a small ditch. Its course took it between the heavily overgrown reedgrass and nettles beneath the bushes, and the short-grassed bank beyond. Seeing a movement at the edge of the mat of tall vegetation, I focused my binoculars and saw a thin, red beak, soon to be followed by a beady red eye, and the head of a water rail. It stood for some time, clearly suspicious of the open space on the other side of the ditch, but eventually satisfied that all was well, it scuttled down into the dyke and began to feed. Moving cautiously along the depression, its smart black and white-striped flanks, grey breast and russet brown back were clearly visible. Unerringly and with extreme rapidity it picked insects off the surrounding leaves, sometimes running forward to claim a special prize, but always keeping close to cover.

Suddenly, it dived back into the thick tangle of grass, and looking about, I saw that the wigeon too had stopped grazing and were looking away

down the bank. Then they were up, and calling noisily. They flew a short distance to settle on the water. A large, brown bird was flying down the bank, now flapping, now gliding, with wings held in a shallow 'V', its head turning from side to side as it scanned the ground ahead. Some distance away from my viewpoint, the female marsh harrier veered away, probably suspicious of the hide, and crossing the river and the road beyond, quartered a beet field, putting up a flock of woodpigeons, and began to work her way down a fen drain until lost to view behind the trees. Marsh harriers are mostly summer migrants, breeding in the reedbeds of the coastal marshes and broadland fens of Norfolk and Suffolk, where there are now about forty pairs. A few birds, mainly females, do overwinter, and some of these range far inland, especially in autumn.

Slowly the ducks relaxed, some started washing and preening, while others, in twos and threes, flew back to the waterside and resumed their interrupted feeding. Further down the water's edge, where the grassland graded into wet, sedgy ground, a group of snipe was feeding. Unseen by the harrier, their beautiful brown and gold striping matched perfectly the colours of the sedge clumps, and now only their jerky movements betrayed them as they probed the mud with their impossibly long beaks, seeking out worms beneath the surface mud.

The Ouse Washes is famous as a haven for waders and duck in winter, with up to 42,000 wigeon having been recorded and lesser numbers of pintail, teal, mallard and shoveler. But it is also known for Bewick's. These wild swans breed in the Russian Arctic, setting out in early autumn to cross Europe and spend the winter mostly in Britain and Holland. The largest numbers are usually to be found here on the fens where over 2,000 have been counted. So far, none had been visible from the hide, and deciding that it was time to go, I took a last look across to the opposite side where a kestrel was hovering, hunting the numerous voles crowded into the remaining strip of grassland by the rising waters. As I watched, a small group of swans, previously hidden by the strip of willows, swam into view, their plumage dazzling white against the brown water. Seven adults and three young, the latter recognizable by their grey colouring and the

Above left *Wigeon share their grazing on the meadows with the cattle in the background. The reserves carry livestock at certain times of the year to ensure that the grass is managed to provide optimum breeding sites and feeding grounds for the various bird species* (C.H. Gomersall, RSPB).

Left *Shoveler were feeding, dipping their beaks in the water like miniature vacuum cleaners . . .* (John Marchington, RSPB).

Right *Water rails are shy and skulking by nature* (M.W. Richards, RSPB).

Bewick's swans are one of the Washes' winter specialities, travelling from arctic Russia each year (S.C. Porter, RSPB).

absence of the yellow upper beak which distinguishes the adults. The shape of the yellow colouring is unique to each bird and, with practice, can be used to identify individuals. They breasted the water gracefully, moving down the flood stream. They had probably been out earlier on the arable fens, feeding on discarded beet tops or waste potatoes made soft by the mid-November frosts, since they showed no interest in feeding now. As the swans moved slowly into the distance, it was time for me to leave, passing a charm of goldfinches, dismembering the teazle heads and flying from one stand to another with high twittering calls.

At the bridge, I paused for a final look. A heron was flying slowly down the far bank, its rounded wings seeming to gather pocketfuls of air with each laboured flap as it looked for a quiet place to fish, and high above, small groups of duck flew in tight packs, tracing pencil lines in the sky as they headed purposefully for unknown destinations. I pointed the car to the north-west, towards the Great North Road, to Newark in the east of Nottinghamshire, then Chesterfield with the twisted church spire, and on to my next stop,

deep in the hills and dales of the Derbyshire Peaks.

The next day dawned cold and clear. Frost sparkled on the fields and rimmed the leafless twigs of the ash and hawthorn as I motored up the side of the reservoir and parked in the conifer-shrouded woods at the end of the road.

Donning walking boots, and packing wet weather gear in the rucksack, since sudden squalls can catch the walker unawares in these hills, I crunched up the frozen track past the woods of Douglas fir, spruce and larch.

The thin sibilant calls of goldcrests could be heard in the trees, and a woodcock rose silently from a patch of ground kept damp and frost-free by a hidden spring, and twisted away among the trunks. Coming to the edge of the wood, I paused at a small, stone bridge over the stream tumbling out of a narrow gully higher up, before spreading out to come chuckling down over the scattered rocks and stones towards the last of the trees. A short distance upstream, a small white dot was visible, moving up and down, and through binoculars it resolved itself into the white bib of a dipper. Standing on a flat stone at the edge of the water, every so often it would bend its legs in a sudden curtsey like an over-anxious ballet dancer. Eventually, as though finally making up its mind, it walked into the water and began to peck at the sides of the stones or, with its head underwater, turn over small pebbles looking for caddis nymphs and other insects. Sometimes it submerged completely, popping up to the surface again a short distance away like a cork, and finally returning to its stone by the side of the stream. Another dipper flew upstream with a musical clinking call, and was followed by the first bird, both of them disappearing round a bend in the rocks towards the top of the gully.

I crossed the bridge and started to climb the slope opposite, crushing the clumps of wiry moor grass and the twisted rosettes of rushes underfoot

A dipper, on a flat stone at the edge of the water . . . it would bend its legs in a sudden curtsey like an over-anxious ballet dancer (C.H. Gomersall, RSPB).

and brushing past the patches of golden brown bracken which marked the areas of deeper soil. The presence of these plants, so common on the British uplands, is usually a sign of overgrazing. The sheep consume the more nutritious bents and fescues leaving the coarse, indigestible plants, which, unchecked by grazing, spread at the expense of the finer grasses and herbs. Eventually, great lawns of mat grass and heath rush are created, providing the poorest of poor grazing, a monument to man's stupidity and over-exploitation down the centuries.

At the top of the slope, I stopped for a breather and looked back over the water, girdled by woodland, which clothed the valley sides and spread up to the blacker crown of heather on the tops.

Turning onto the moor, the sheep path led through the heather, patchworked by fire, where the keepers had burnt strips and squares to provide fresh young heather shoots for the grouse, whose droppings could be seen among the young plants. A skilled job this; if the fire gets out of control a whole hillside can be burnt: if too hot and slow, the heather plants and seeds are

Left *I passed the grouse themselves, flying with whirring wings and throaty chuckles onto the short heather* (John Marchington, RSPB).

Right *A short-eared owl rose like a ghost . . .* (Robin Williams, RSPB).

also killed and regeneration takes a long time with competition from quicker growing grasses. Sometimes, when burning before a strong breeze, the fire is too quick, leaving the mineral soil covered with old leaves and stems through which the tiny seeds cannot root. Not only grouse benefit from proper moorland management, birds like golden plover also feed on these open areas in spring and summer. Before long, I passed the grouse themselves, flying with whirring wings and throaty chuckles onto the short heather, and running among the shoots as they landed.

The only other birds to be seen were meadow pipits, perching on the stems of the tall heather plants or flying up onto the dark, sandy-coloured boulders with thin, repetitive calls. The path passed along the ridge and then led down into wetter ground where large ankle-twisting tussocks of purple moor grass made difficult walking, their deciduous leaves lying in drifts between the clumps. At the edge of the bog, a startled short-eared owl rose like a ghost out of the cotton grass and flew to a heather hummock a short distance away. Its body facing away into the wind, it turned its head to stare over its shoulder through yellow-rimmed eyes, indignant at being disturbed. Soon, it took off again like a giant moth, so small and light did the body seem

between the large ochre-coloured wings, and drifted out of sight behind the hills. Going across to the roost, I found a hollow in the grass and two grey pellets, indigestible remains coughed up after its last meal. Teasing them apart, I found fur and small bones, including the skull of a vole.

Moving down the hill, I followed an ancient grass-grown track which wound through a patch of rushy field where a few sheep were grazing. The fields were separated by old turf-covered stone banks on which grew a scattering of hawthorn and rowan, now all that remained of a long forgotten hedge. Hard-by were the ruins of a small farmstead, now just a memory of stones over which the dead nettle stems swayed mournfully in the wind, and to one side, the cow byre, used more recently but now abandoned, its roofless walls still providing some shelter to the sheep when winter storms sweep down off the moor. But in the morning sunlight, the old farm looked cheerful and busy with the calls of birds. A flock of starlings moved industriously through the grass, thrusting their black, daggerlike beaks into the short turf and opening them slightly to prise apart the mat of leaves and roots in search of leatherjackets. Between thrusts, each bird took a few steps, sometimes pausing to swallow a grub, before enthusiastically digging into a fresh spot,

196

like small jaunty pirates looking for hidden treasure. In the old hedge a group of redwings was feeding on rowan berries, edging out along the dipping, laden branches to grab a prize and stepping back to swallow this before reaching out for another. Under the rowan a blackbird too was eating berries, finding it easier and quicker to scavenge the food dropped by the redwings. A mistle thrush perched on a nearby ash appeared to be watching its winter food supply diminish under this onslaught from its Scandinavian cousins.

As I turned a bend, a large slate-backed bird came towards me, flying fast and low to the ground and taking advantage of the cover provided by the low bank. Suddenly, it jinked and flew swiftly through a gap between two thorns and between the rushes towards the starling flock. A harsh rattle from the watching mistle thrush high up in the ash gave the alarm, and the starlings, rising in panic, fled to the safety of a thick thorn bush where they were joined by the redwings. Baffled, the cock merlin turned, and flying past the old byre, turned and sped away to look for prey along the edge of a small plantation of larch. From the hawthorn, a chorus of catcalls and whistles from the starlings reminded me of a group of small boys taunting the school bully

from a safe distance. Back at the car, I drove alongside the water to a point where the conifers ended and a small birchwood swept down to the edge. There I stopped to eat lunch.

On the water, three goldeneyes had similar thoughts and were diving for food, two females and a male, the latter with smart bottle green head and white cheeks. At each dive they seemed to leap almost clear of the water before vanishing with characteristic rounded tails under the surface. A cormorant too was feeding, sitting low in the water between dives. A pair of mergansers flew past, their white wing patches showing clearly against the dark hillside, heading for the shallower water at the head of the valley. In the birches a small party of siskins was feeding, stripping the tiny seeds from the disintegrating catkins and cascading a shower of debris to the woodland floor below. It was time to move on.

The road took me up over the Snake Pass to Glossop and on into Cheshire, and then by way of the motorway past the Mersey. Ringed by towns and factories and sitting alongside a massive petro-chemical works and the ship canal, the estuary survives the pollution and disturbance, and still supports huge numbers of duck and waders each year. Now threatened by a barrage, the age-old feeding grounds still support pintail and teal, dunlin and knot. Even as I passed, small clouds of duck could be seen in the sky, and on the flat arable lands beside the carriageway, golden plovers and lapwings were feeding, oblivious to the roar of the passing traffic. On past the ancient town of Chester, and the huge sheds of the steelworks at Shotton, I came at last to the Dee. Around the coast a vista of houses and gardens suddenly gives way to the flat expanse of the estuary, a huge wilderness of marsh and sea, where water meets land in a barely perceptible line far out on the muddy foreshore. At mean high water, the slow moving tides drop their burden of sandy silt to form embryo mudbanks; as these grow, saltmarsh vegetation begins, at first sparse and precarious on the shifting, treacherous muds. Gradually, the hardy plants tighten their grip and grow in confidence, establishing a dense community of salt-tolerant specialists. Plants with names redolent of their strange sea-washed world: sea purslane and sea plantain, mauve flowering

Left *View over the Dee Estuary* (M.W. Richards, RSPB).

Right *A male hen harrier, first of the winter, flies across the saltings* (Robin Williams, RSPB).

Below *Two sanderling and a dunlin explore the tideline for sandhoppers and other small creatures* (Dr John Woodward, RSPB).

lavender and heady smelling sea wormwood. Another plant, cord grass, is well established on the estuary, forming vast stretches of new saltmarsh as it traps, and then grows up through successive layers of water-borne silt. Arising from a natural cross between a native and North American species, this new hybrid plant has all the vigour and dynamism to be expected of a colonist, and has spread over many acres of old saltings on our southern and western estuaries.

Here, at the estuary mouth of the Dee, is a spit of shingle, constantly changing in shape with the vagaries of wind and tide, but at this moment providing secure haven for flocks of wading birds driven off their feeding grounds by the advancing tides. At the water's edge, below the bank, a few dunlin probe the sandy mud, intermixed with ringed plover, moving like automated toys as they pick small insects off the strand line. Further round, where the mud of the estuary gives way to sandy beach, the lighter coloured sanderling, on flying feet, chase sandhoppers. Higher up on the shingle, a huge flock of knot, with bar-tailed godwits and redshanks, rest or preen, while above, on the most exposed part of the shingle, the hardy oystercatchers are seeing out the tide, a black backdrop to the browns and greys of the smaller waders.

Behind the shingle bar, curlews are sleeping with bill under wing or stalking majestically through the saltmarsh pools. From time to time, a small group of waders detach from the main flock and, flying a short distance, drop back onto the shingle higher up, a sure sign that the tide is making. Out on the water, a few mallard are resting, while in the distance a small outcrop of rock thrusting up through the thick layers of estuarine sands, stands out above the choppy waters. This is Hilbre Island, another roost, where Eric Hosking took some of his finest photographs of massed waders on the rocky terraces.

A small group of black-headed gulls, some feeding, others preening on a nearby saltmarsh runnel, suddenly rise with harsh cries and, settling into a loose flock, move away down the marsh. Seconds later the waders too are up, in larger numbers than I had suspected, as dense masses of birds erupt from the hidden hollows and furrows in the shingle. Wheeling in tight formation in the sky, the flock of knot is like a

single synchronized sky wraith, guided by a single brain, now as a light round ball, now drawn out into a thin line, and again reforming. Shortly, the waders settle again, first the larger godwits and knot, then the smaller dunlin and plovers, all except a large group of oystercatchers which fly off up the estuary, sensing that the tide has turned, and that the mussel beds will soon be uncovered. The cause of all this alarm is not difficult to seek: a male hen harrier, the first of the winter here, flies across the saltings. Immaculate in grey mantle and black-tipped wings, the harrier flies slowly and steadily up the marsh towards a patch of scrub at the field edge where finches and sparrows, already filling the roost in the late afternoon, are both numerous and catchable. As the tide starts to go down, the waders begin to leave the roost and in ones and twos or small flocks, they slip away towards the distant mud flats to begin again the cycle of feeding and roosting, their lives ruled by the pattern of the tides. Dusk is falling as I start the car and continue round the coast to the stuccoed gentility of Llandudno, ready for the final stage of the journey.

The next morning, under a cloudless sky, I climbed the rolling curves of the Great Orme, each curve blanketed by a covering of short, wiry grasses, interrupted here and there by patches of black heather. In places the white limestone broke through the surface in water-smoothed terraces, dotted with sheep-scarred and wind-twisted blackthorn emerging boldly from the cracks and crevices in the natural pavement, but flattening out and crouching over the surface to avoid the salt laden winds. The heather grows in patches of deeper soil, where the rains had washed out the limestone base, to leave a crust of acid soil over the alkaline bedrock. At first few birds were to be seen, apart from a gathering of crows and jackdaws quarrelling over the carcass of a dead sheep: they moved away with cries of frustration as a solitary raven dropped down in their midst, scattering them like burnt paper from a fire. Then I noticed small loose flocks of other birds flying in from the sea, not stopping, but heading purposefully inland as though anxious to reach some distant destination. Chaffinches, linnets and goldfinches, unusually silent, went flitting past, although why they had left the mild

winter of Eire and adventured the Irish Sea to reach the colder climes of a winter in North Wales was a mystery to me.

Out to sea, ships moved over the flat surface like disembodied steel skeletons, only their upperparts, the gantries and masts, visible: in the distance the lines of unmoving cranes in the Liverpool docks broke the dark low coast of Merseyside on the horizon.

Looking through a telescope, the unmoving sea sprang to life. Parties of auks, guillemots and razorbills, whirred through the circle of the lens, like uneven beads on a string. Everywhere, small flocks were flying past, all heading south away from the northern winter. At one point a scattering of gulls was wheeling and circling, the individuals like moths round a candle, slowly moving away across the sea surface as they followed the school of small fish brought to the surface by chasing mackerel. Among the gulls, larger birds, wicked-beaked and black-tipped wings; a party of gannets came together to dive with folded wings like arrowheads into the shoal of deeper swimming mackerel, a predator of predators.

Immediately below me, the cliffs echoed to the cries of wandering gulls, and occasionally a kittiwake flew past, often young birds with black zig-zag wing patterns, their dainty flight quite unlike the solid, determined wingbeats of the larger gulls. Below the kittiwakes, there was a constant passage of commuting cormorants, flying with rapid wingbeats just clear of the water, flying between their fishing grounds and the flat rocks at the base of the cliff, where their fellows sat gorged with food, and drying their outstretched wings in the weak heat of the sun. Eventually, tiring of the search for migrating shearwaters, for I had hoped to see these from the headland, I turned and started back. A little way up, where the path ran alongside a stone wall, the rocks encrusted with fossils, a small tortoiseshell butterfly came fluttering past to alight briefly on a late-flowering daisy before flitting over the wall and across the pasture beyond.

Climbing to the summit, the Conway estuary could be seen stretched out in front and guarded by the castle, one of the finest in Wales, built by Edward I between 1283 and 1287 to subdue the Welsh in their mountain fastnesses. From up here the castle looked small and insignificant against the foothills of Tàl y Fan, and the rearing crest of Carnedd Llewelyn behind, masking the peak of Snowdon itself. Driving through Conway later that morning though, under the castle walls, the huge gaunt structure, with its many turrets and towers, dominated the valley and the town below.

Further round, I crossed the Britannia Bridge to Anglesey, driving past the statue of the Marquess of Anglesey on his high column and on to the island. Where the road crosses the flat pasturelands of Maltraeth, flocks of lapwings were wheeling against a clear blue sky. Showing alternate black and white whole flocks turned as one before drifting down like leaves onto the grass. With the lapwings feeding on the sheep-grazed short turf, were gulls, common and black-headed, curlews and oystercatchers, and where the field was wet, a few redshanks probed the soft earth.

Passing the narrows, I headed towards the mountain, the highest hill on the island, although only 270 feet (240 m) high, and parked by the heather-studded maritime heath above South

Main picture *Anglesey, with South Stack Lighthouse in the distance. The RSPB manages a reserve on the island and the information centre at Ellin's Tower provides panoramic views of seabirds (M.W. Richards, RSPB).*

Below inset *Purple sandpipers are wintering waders that love to feed on coastal rocks (R.T. Smith, RSPB).*

Right inset *Occasionally fulmars glided past with fixed wings (L. H. Ware, RSPB).*

Far right inset *I saw the unmistakably powerful form and pointed wings of a peregrine . . . (John Wightman, RSPB).*

Stack cliffs. From above and behind, shrill jackdaw-like calls announced the presence of a party of choughs, flying down onto a grass field where they began to feed, probing the tussocks with their sickle-shaped vermilion bills. One bird, a little apart from the others, had found a cow pat and, digging its beak in, it flicked its head from side to side sending a shower of debris flying in all directions. Its industry was soon rewarded as it found and swallowed one grub, then another, until having demolished the cow pat to its complete satisfaction, it flew up onto a wall to wipe its beak on a patch of moss before rejoining its fellows. Walking to the cliffs, I could see the rock ledges, thronged with breeding auks in summer, but now deserted high above the waves breaking in yeasty foam far below. Occasionally, fulmars glided past with fixed wings, taking advantage of the up-welling air, and on the far side a flock of rock doves fed busily on a grassy buttress.

On past the lighthouse, and looking up, I saw the unmistakably powerful form and pointed wings of a peregrine, circling high up in the sky, and gradually moving away until lost to sight behind the mountain. Nearby, a stonechat appeared on the topmost spray of a gorse bush, leaving me wondering, not for the first time, how they manage to find safe footing among the mass of thorns. Particularly vulnerable to hard weather, stonechat populations can crash during harsh winters, but they usually recover again quickly since they can rear up to three broods in a single season.

The cliffs were lower here and gave way to bladderwrack covered rocks, washed by the sea, their seaweed skirts moving in slow symphony to the movement of the waters. A small wader was feeding down there, running back and forth across the rock, picking food off the weed at the tide edge. Every time a wave swept in to wash across the lower rock terraces, the tiny bird seemed to be in imminent danger of being swept away, but each time, miraculously, it danced away out of the reach of the water, and then followed the retreating green swell back down onto the rock. A purple sandpiper was playing catch as catch can with the waves. Breeding in the high Arctic, these hardy little birds migrate to our coasts, returning to the same area each year and spending the whole winter on one short stretch of shore. As I neared the auk cliffs once again, the rock doves left with a noisy clattering of wings, and flew out over the sea heading for the short sea turf by the lighthouse where a flock of jackdaws was already busy. I idly followed them through the glasses, when a large scythe-winged bird came plunging through their midst and sweeping up, hit the last bird in the flock in a burst of feathers; the peregrine had returned. The remaining doves scattered, some towards the lighthouse, and three back to the cliffs. Meanwhile, the peregrine, clutching her unfortunate prey, flew heavily back to the headland, and disappeared behind the cliffs, no doubt making for a favourite feeding ledge.

As I made my way back to the car, past the choughs still feeding in the field, it seemed a fitting end to my journey. Starting in the flat, intensively farmed fenlands of East Anglia, I had made my way across England and Wales to the wild, unspoilt cliffs of Anglesey. No particularly rare birds had crossed my path, nor had the number of species been great, but it seems to me that there can be few places outside Britain where one can enjoy such a variety of species in such contrasting habitats and scenery within just three short days of winter travel. In each location I had seen different types of bird too, and even a bird of prey in each. I was content with my good fortune.

DECEMBER

VOYAGE SOUTH TO SUMMER

KEITH SHACKLETON

Rockhoppers hop around me on New Island, Falklands. Such tameness in animals begins here . . . the greatest compliment that man could be paid (Jean Bartlett).

KEITH SHACKLETON was born in England in 1923, spent part of his childhood in Australia, and was educated at Oundle. He served five years in the RAF and after the war joined the family aviation business, before devoting himself full-time to painting. His painting has been influenced by a wide variety of subjects and places, but he remains principally a marine painter, perhaps best known for exciting interpretations of sea and seabirds.

There is a welcome law of nature that smooths the paths of 'ornithologists' like me. It may also have played a significant part in shaping my passion for high latitudes north and south in general and in particular, the wildlife that belongs there.

The law, roughly outlined, proclaims that the further one gets from the Equator, the fewer the species, and therefore for such as me, the lower the confusion factor when it comes to identification. It is very simple.

By species I mean everything, birds, mammals, reptiles, insects, plants — everything that lives. Someone once told me there were near enough a quarter of a million different insects and spiders in the Amazon Basin alone, of which less than one third have been scientifically described. There are 100,000 plants, 2,000 known fishes and 1,700 birds — one fifth of the check list for this whole planet. It is small wonder that I plied around this area in my working days there in a state of permanent mental seize-up. To be blinded by colours and markings is all excitement; it is the confusion that saddens.

But move away from the tropics with its intricate, arcane and often minute ecosystems that flourish in the damp heat and things begin to change. By the 40s and 50s of latitude north and south, the picture is beginning to look a lot less daunting. (Ability to recognize every British breeding species is no uncommon feat for the average birdwatcher, though some of the vagrants can still be perplexing.) Get into the 60s and finally the 70s and the exercise begins to freewheel gently downhill. Though populations may run into millions of individuals, their actual species can be totted up on fingers.

These are the hardened, perfected, indomitable forms that have filtered through the evolutionary process. They are the ones designed to live and move and have their being in the harshest environments of all, and they look the part.

Frigate birds hanging on the wind over the harbour at Rio and jewel-like, scissor-tailed hummingbirds taking midges on the hover over dockside shrubs are the last reminders of the

'Oakum boys' and adults. The king penguin rookery at Bay of Isles on South Georgia where upwards of 10,000 pairs breed (Jacqueline Shackleton).

tropics. With the gentle lift of the seas on a southerly course and the last of the flying fish skipping away from the bow-wave, there is soon the feel of the South Atlantic.

It is early December.

Great shearwaters are around, completing their yearly ocean circuit. These are birds that have passed off Britain, moved on through the North Atlantic, spent the late summer days skimming the Davis Strait. They will have seen the massive Greenland icebergs in Melville Bay and the pack ice off Baffin Island. They have sped like little shadows in and out of the fog veils over the Grand Banks, passed off Hatteras into the Gulf Stream, and on southward. Now in the late Austral spring, they are on their way to Tristan da Cunha to breed and a few to the Falkland Islands.

The Falklands, to a south-bound birder, is the last place that looks a bit like home. Here are a handful of real 'LBJs', (little brown jobs!) the occasional storm-driven landbird from continental South America, a collection of vagrants that more than double the breeding total of some sixty species. The land has the look of the Hebrides: racing clouds on a boisterous wind, sharp showers and idyllic sparkling clearances over an ochre landscape. Grey rock buttresses thrust through the generous sweeping lines of weather-moulded uplands. Everywhere the sea; rafts of kelp and pristine beaches. There is no view on the Falklands without its counterpart somewhere in the Northern or the Western Isles or across in Connemara.

The weather too is warm, or at least what is euphemistically called 'parka warm'. Sir Ernest Shackleton's comment that he had never been so cold in all his life as he was in the guest room at Government House, Port Stanley, has to be taken in the spirit of the moment. The stabilizing effect of the southern ocean keeps winter averages surprisingly close to the mean temperatures of summer. To be sure, it can be cold, but there are many shirt-sleeve days. One I shall always remember was spent watching Des and Jen Bartlett film a peregrine eyrie. We sat on the clifftop rocks, shirtless in blazing sunshine. The sea below was wrinkled by a balmy breeze and blue as the Mediterranean. Little rusty butterflies — the endemic Falkland fritillaries — jigged along close to the turf, as if fearful that a change in the weather could blow them away from their islands forever.

Above *Alpine oxalis is among the 250 different plant species that flourish in the islands* (Keith Shackleton).

Left *Gorse in bloom on West Point Island, Falklands* (Keith Shackleton).

Right *Black-browed albatross and rockhopper penguins on Beauchene Island in the Falklands* (Keith Shackleton).

The Falklands are a paradise for botanists too. The same natural law applies — luxuriant growth but fewer species. Moreover another law manifests itself here. The nearer one gets to the Poles, the closer to sea level can be found what we think of in milder latitudes as traditional Alpine plants. On Mount Kenya, for instance, one would need to climb nearly to the snow line to find the type of vegetation which in the Falklands thrives just a few feet above the maritime splash zone. The springy upland turf and hill bog that inspired the word 'yomping' into our language is as lovely a surface to walk over as exists on earth, the word itself a constant reminder of the professionalism and fortitude of that march from San Carlos to Stanley to liberate the islands in 1982.

Over 250 plants flourish here, of which 163 are native species. Many are familiar old friends with essentially English connotations — buttercups and clover, daisies and dandelions, and all growing — just as they do in Tierra del Fuego — larger, taller and sweeter scented than they do at home. Sickening, is it not?

Gorse is a prime example. Brought in by settlers from Scotland for hedging and windbreaks, it flowers so densely in November and December that some bushes are literally all flowers and scarcely a green prickle can be seen. But when the flowers go, they go without trace. The old Scots saying 'when you can find no flower upon the gorse, love is out of season' would indeed cast a dreary shadow for a good ten months of the year if applied to the Falklands.

The most striking difference lies with the wildlife. September sees the elephant-seals hauled out and the ponderous, vociferous rut beginning. Big bulls are shaping up to rivals all along the beach. Arched up like giant maggots, inflated noses wobbling, vying with one another for the few extra inches of height which proclaim supremacy.

Fur seals and southern sea lions are ashore too and the penguins are coming in. By Christmas, penguin rookeries are in full swing. Hardy, seemingly indestructible little rockhoppers are bouncing in from the sea, tumbling over the rocks, assembling miraculously for a moment only for the slate to be swept clean by another thunderous wave. Then back they come and

keep on coming until finally they make it. Hopping double-footed in bouncing ranks, they mount the cliffs, 200 feet (60 m) or more, to nest beside the lordly, black-browed albatrosses: the masters of soaring flight and the flightless within bill-touching distance of one another and in perfect harmony.

Family parties of steamer ducks, kelp geese and crested ducks swim offshore with their rapidly growing young, coaxing little fluffy flotillas through fronds of weed. The opportunists are about too. Brown skuas and 'Johnny rooks' — the striated caracara — have their eyes on the main seasonal chance — unguarded eggs, lost chicks and storm injured adults. Johnny rook is the joke bird of the islands. Stories both true and apocryphal abound and all concern its fascination for assorted human artefacts and its reactions to them.

In appearance it is somewhere between a crow and a mini-vulture, smartly striped as the name implies and with the hoppity truculent gait of an investigating magpie. Nothing could give it more delight than coming upon an unattended rucksack — especially one with zip pockets.

Left *Kelp geese at West Point Island, Falklands. The gander is white; the goose is dark-coloured to camouflage her while she is incubating eggs* (Keith Shackleton).

Right *Magellan penguins on New Island, Falklands are one of the five penguin species that inhabit the islands, filling a similar ecological niche to the auks of the nothern hemisphere* (Keith Shackleton).

Below left *The striated caracara — better known as 'Johnny rook' — is inquisitive and opportunist* (Keith Shackleton).

Johnny rook will unzip and zip up each pocket in turn, seeming to savour the rasping sound so close to its ear. But should it find goodies inside the pocket, there is no end to the possibilities. Films, a bar of chocolate, string, gloves, hip flask, penknife, compass. All will be taken out, examined, turned over, picked up, dropped and even kicked. Once I watched powerless as a Johnny rook removed a pair of binoculars — one of the much publicized green ones with a red spot on — examined them critically, dragged them a short distance over the rocks by the strap, before it took off and with an air of decision, dropped them into the sea!

This tameness in animals begins here and carries right through to the Antarctic — the tameness of unfamiliarity with man and the greatest compliment that man could be paid. It is something more than a simple tolerance of close approach, rather an impulse to make the play, to come and meet you, either out of curiosity, the hope of gain perhaps, or some indefinable urge for companionship. The tussock bird will come to a stranger's hand for crumbs of bread. The nesting albatross will lean over as if to check the progress of a sketch, responding with interest to the sound of pencil tip on paper. The young elephant seal will writhe in ecstasy when scratched, and fat little Commerson's dolphins swim between sea-booted legs, escort the boat, all but run themselves aground in their impulse to communicate and join the party. The more the applause, the more they love it, and with their unique communication system, they seem to send for their friends to come and join in.

Every major group of birds on the British list is represented in the Falklands except for the gamebirds and the alcids, whose niche in the islands is filled by five species of penguin and two diving petrels. To press on south from Port Stanley is to leave the last of this essential Britishness in the bird field — and others as well. By the time South Georgia is reached, a voyage of 750 miles, an altogether different picture is waiting, with the demure little local pipit the last indigenous landbird, the last true LBJ before the Great White South.

South Georgia, though a good deal further east, lies only 2° south of the Falklands. One could be excused therefore, for expecting a

Above *Black-crowned night herons on Carcass Island, Falklands* (Keith Shackleton).

Left *Rockhoppers coming ashore on West Point Island, Falklands. They bounce in from the sea, tumbling over the rocks* (Keith Shackleton).

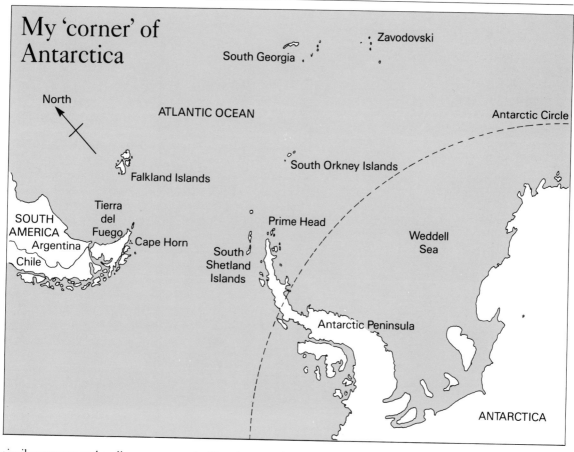

My 'corner' of Antarctica

Zavodovski

South Georgia

North

ATLANTIC OCEAN

Antarctic Circle

Falkland Islands

South Orkney Islands

Tierra del Fuego

SOUTH AMERICA

Argentina

Chile

Cape Horn

Prime Head

South Shetland Islands

Weddell Sea

Antarctic Peninsula

ANTARCTICA

similar aspect and a climate to match. But the truth is very different.

The rounded, peaty, Western Isles look exists only in very isolated and restricted places and at lower levels: the flavour of the island as a whole is pure Antarctica. Peaks 9,000 feet (2,743 m) high thrust into the clouds and snow fields, great glaciers and rock faces are the backbone of a beautifully forbidding island some 90 miles (144 km) long, lying like a monstrous frozen crescent across the west wind drift in the 50s of south latitude. Height is not the only reason for the snowy aspect and the harsh climate: much has to do with the Antarctic Convergence.

Cold north-going waters that surround the continent of Antarctica meet a point at which they sink below the warmer layers of surrounding ocean. At this point, heading south, the water temperature drops several degrees in a few miles. Sedimental nutrients from warmer seas well up and nourish the surface phytoplankton. The seas are enriched and team with life, a glimpse of the very beginning of a short but virile and finely balanced food chain, which with only a few links connects single-celled drifting plants to the largest animals that ever inhabited the earth.

The circumpolar position of the Convergence is surprisingly constant and is marked on most charts. It passes to the south of the Falklands but sweeps north of South Georgia. In true geographic terms, the Convergence is the actual threshhold of Antarctica, and by such reasoning, South Georgia, lying within its cold embrace, is properly an Antarctic island. And yet here a pipit still sings, though it sings alone.

More human feet have trod this island than any other in the sub-Antarctic. It began when Captain James Cook's party from *Resolution* fired a 'discharge of small arms' to mark its formal possession in the name of King George on 17 January 1775. In the early 1800s, sealers of many nations plundered here, and soon the fur seal population was all but gone. Whalers followed. The beginning of this century saw the first of the big land-based whaling stations. They were industrial townships, some with churches, even

First Ice — Drake Passage (Keith Shackleton).

cinemas. There were six of them in all, employing caretaker trades all the year round with an influx of thousands in the southern summer. When whaling was at its peak 32 catchers operated out of South Georgia and over 7,000 whales might be killed in a single summer season.

Then in the early '60s it all came to an end, more it has to be said through considerations of economics than conscience. Today the stations are in ruins, hovering in that limbo area that to some are unsightly litter, to others industrial archaeology. Elephant seals and fur seals doze indolent on the slipways and flensing plan. Machinery and buildings lie rusted and silent, here and there vandalized — most by trawler crews from the Soviet Bloc and in Grytviken, bullet-riddled from the last of the Falklands' conflict.

Throughout the island's 200 years of human history, exploration ships have visited, re-fuelled, taken on stores and rested in what Shackleton termed 'the gateway to Antarctica'. Bellingshausen

was here in the *Vostok* and *Mirny* during his survey of the South Sandwich Islands, Weddell, Bransfield and Biscoe. Nordenskjöld was here in the *Antarctic*: Scott in the *Discovery* and *Terra Nova*. Shackleton came in the *Endurance*, and finally the *Quest*, to die in Grytviken harbour and to be buried in the whalers' cemetery. Hardly a ship of note bound for the peninsular side of Antarctica failed to visit this island, which is probably quieter now than it has been for a century.

Not the same, however, can be said for the wildlife, and of these the most sensational comeback has been staged by the Kerguelan fur seal. During the summer rut they are ashore in numbers that must have compared with the spectacle that greeted Cook when he first sailed into Possession Bay. In their breeding free-for-all, albatross colonies — grey-headed in particular —

Above right *The skeletal hull of the last of the whale catchers at Grytviken, South Georgia* (Keith Shackleton).

Right *Kerguelan fur seals on South Georgia were once hunted to near extinction but the species has made a spectacular comeback* (Keith Shackleton).

Left *Elephant seal among the oil drums in the South Orkney Islands. This, the largest of the seal family (bulls can measure up to 20 feet (6½ metres) in length) was once hunted extensively for its oil, but the population is now recovering* (Keith Shackleton).

Below left *Humpback whale sounding. The seas are enriched and team with life but only a few links in the food chain connect single-celled plants to the largest animals that ever inhabited the earth* (Keith Shackleton).

are driven to higher ground, their favourite tussock areas flattened by the raucous mob of pinnepeds.

A handful of reindeer introduced by Norwegian whalers before the First World War have been a constant food source ever since and now stand at about 2,000 in three distinct herds — again looking bigger and better than their relations back in Norway. Elephant seals, once hunted hard for oil, are on the ascendant too and provide a note of timeless repose, stretched out on the beaches and among the tussocks in somnolent contrast to the active, aggressive and surprisingly athletic fur seals. Sadly it is only the whales that have not returned. They are still a rare sight, even the

smaller species, where but a few decades ago, fin and blue whales were shot by the score in Cumberland Bay itself.

One legacy of the whaling days lingers on in the empty buildings in the shape of rats and as might be expected, they are bigger and fitter. Rats the size of young rabbits thump about on the rotting floorboards of the hayloft in Grytviken, as if they were wearing climbing boots, their heavy tails rasping over the woodwork. Imported rats spell disaster to any island — with the small underground nesting petrels the first at risk. But birds of all kinds suffer, and while rats seem to stay mostly around the shelter of the ruins, it is little wonder that no pipits are to be found anywhere near, and only survive in strength on offshore islands where no rat has made a footing.

In South Georgia, our law of the higher the latitude, the lower the species count, clicks up a further notch. We now have only 29 breeding bird species with about the same score of

Ice in the Gerlache Strait, Antarctica (Keith Shackleton).

Above *Immature wandering albatross at Bay of Isles, South Georgia. The slow-growing chick is nourished at the price of far-flung ocean sorties* (Jacqueline Shackleton).

Left *The wingspan of the wandering albatross of 11 feet (3½ metres) makes this one of the giants of the bird world* (Keith Shackleton).

Right *Light-mantled sooty albatross at Husvik on South Georgia. No bird I know exhibits such an air of serene composure as the albatross* (Keith Shackleton).

recorded vagrants. This time, all but the Antarctic pipit, the endemic South Georgia pintail and the yellow-billed teal, are birds of the sea and without any question the most spectacular is *Apenodytes patagonicus* the king penguin. Although not quite the size of the truly Antarctic emperor, it is over a yard (1 m) high and makes up the shortfall in sheer displacement by its elegance, its poise, the long-flippered dignity of its walk.

Though larger rookeries exist on Crozet and Kerguelan in the Indian Ocean and Macquarie in the Pacific sector of the southern ocean, the South Georgia population is impressive. The main concentrations are to the east in Royal Bay and St Andrew's Bay, with a third close to the Grace Glacier in the Bay of Isles to the northwest, and all carry upwards of 10,000 breeding pairs. Many smaller rookeries are dotted about here and there so that there are few beaches which lack the classic spectacle of parties of kings, immensely self-important, standing about chatting like delegates at some great Austral synod. Among them will be all-but-fledged young, the 'oakum boys' as early sailors

knew them. Oakum was stock in trade to a shipwright carpenter for caulking the seams of ships' boats, and the young penguins resembled nothing so much as a wad of familiar caulking fibre — in colour as much as texture. Indeed, the density of the young coat puts a good few inches on a penguin's diameter, making the adults look positively undernourished beside their offspring. King penguins have a breeding cycle which is unusual to say the least, resulting in a normal pair producing two 'oakum boys' in a three-year period.

Across the bay a similar cycle is acted out with the great wandering albatross — resulting in a single young bird every alternate year. At the risk of appearing over-imaginative, I believe that the albatross lifestyle is clearly written in its eye. No bird I know exhibits such an air of serene composure, of timeless content. Even a mild protest is conducted with gentility. A look of would-be disapproval comes across with scarcely a shred of concern, let alone dislike. Even in the passion of courtship composure prevails. Whilst tossing the head, clacking the bill, extending a magnificent 11 feet (3½ m) of wingspread and

prancing about in unashamed self-advertisement, there is no significant change in the eye beyond perhaps a hint of amusement. Then the bird will utter its triumphal fanfare (likened by Niall Rankin to 'a man with a cleft palate endeavouring to reason with a restive horse') while the eye persists with its reflection of a deep inner peace.

The single egg is laid around Christmas time but will not hatch until late in March. A slow-growing chick, nourished at the price of far-flung ocean sorties will not be fully fledged until the middle of the following summer. It will sit there, wearing its inherited composure like a warm eiderdown through blizzards of winter that pile driven snow against its weather side, making the colony look like garden ornaments in a hard white Christmas. The following December it will be ready, with white head and patchy liver-brown plumage to waddle splay-footed up to some point of vantage and from there lift off into the wind alone. Three hundred days on the nest have been crowned with success.

Just under 300 nautical miles east-south-east of South Georgia lies the northernmost island of the South Sandwich group — Zavodovoski. The

Russian name, bestowed by Bellingshausen in 1819 during his survey, supersedes the group's collective title from James Cook's original discovery in 1775. His name was for Lord Sandwich, current First Lord of the Admiralty, a man ironically destined to achieve more lasting fame as the inventor of the original stopgap meal, the butt of a thousand jokes against railway catering for generations to follow.

The island of Zavodovoski is unique — almost certainly the 'uniquest' of an already unique archipelago. Here is a fully active volcano, belching great cauliflowers of malodorous smoke and steam from its conical summit, 1,800 feet (550 m) above sea level. Indeed, the aptly-named Mount Asphyxia, is itself the island, the names are inseparable. The steeply sloping upper levels are shifting, sliding banks of ash that deny any permanent footing. On the west side are

King penguins with gentoo penguins in the background. Standing over three feet (one metre) tall, the king penguin is second in size only to the emperor penguin, which breeds even further south (Keith Shackleton).

Crab-eater seals with a population of about 30 million, are the world's most numerous large carnivore (Keith Shackleton).

precipitous cliffs, but down on the north and east-facing areas there are gentler slopes that end at sea level with low rocky buttresses and cinder beaches, and this part is entirely given over to penguins. To all practical purposes, Zavodovoski is wall-to-wall penguins: chinstraps mostly and a few macaronis, carpeting the slopes like pepper and salt. An estimated 21 million nest here!

Lying to leeward the air is filled with the sulphurous fumes of the mountain itself, but blended with the overtones of volcanically-toasted penguin guano and vomit on an industrial scale. The ears are battered with the kind of clamour more akin to an aural affliction than an identifiable sound. And there is surely no other ornithological spectacle to match it — anywhere. Only 6°20' further south, but 29°40' further west lies Prime Head, the extreme northern tip of the continent of Antarctica itself.

The peninsula of Graham Land, now called the Antarctic Peninsula in deference to the treaty,

reaches like a long, crooked finger northwards, as if flicking the assorted islands of the South Shetlands group in the general direction of Cape Horn. It is by far the nearest point of the continent to the rest of the world, its tip reaches as far north as a little over 63° south, and not for nothing is it referred to as the 'banana belt' of the Antarctic. One can be much colder in Cambridge in January than on a summer's day here, but it is wise to remember that this fearsome and beautiful land always has another meteorological shot in its locker.

I will forbear to mention yet again all those fascinating statistics with the '-est' suffix of the superlative — the coldest, the highest, the windiest, the loneliest, etc. Antarctica is indeed all these things and many more, but most important I feel, is that it is the last remaining true wilderness and its beauty that of intrinsic natural perfection.

I began with the law of declining species against increasing latitude. We are now down to 17 breeding birds, either on or in sight of Antarctica itself. There are so few they can easily be listed now: four penguins, seven petrels and

The blue-eyed shag on the Antarctic Peninsula is the lovelist of all cormorants (Keith Shackleton).

storm petrels, one cormorant, two skuas, one gull, one tern and the inimitable and lovably ridiculous sheathbill — Antarctica's only answer to the Falkland's Johnny rook, and the only bird here without a webbed foot.

Though a fair crop of mosses, lichens and algae abounds, there are but two vascular plants — *Deschampsia* and *Colobanthus* — both as diminutive and humble as a vascular plant can be. All other life on the land comes in the microscope bracket.

But life exists in the sea in enormous abundance, nourishing the penguin hordes, the few remaining great whales and six species of seal. Equating species against biomass is very striking when it comes to the ocean. The commonest seal for instance is the crab-eater — curiously named because there are no crabs for it to eat — which has an estimated population of about 30 million. There are actually more crab-eaters than the rest of the world's seals put together. It is the most numerous large carnivore on earth.

So the goal is reached. There is no end to look

at but none of it needs a field guide to name. Perhaps one of the greatest joys, especially for those who like to draw birds, is the opportunity to see species in bulk and thereby glean a wealth of attitude studies at every sitting. The backdrop has a beauty and grandeur that is devastating. There are no problems of approach, the subjects are both willing and infinitely drawable. Some are exceptional — Antarctica's blue-eyed shag has to be the loveliest of all cormorants, but the one great star in the firmament for me will always be the snow petrel. Sat tight on her egg in a crevice, the whitest of plumage against lichen-encrusted rock, the clear jet-black boot button of an eye; the perfection of aerodynamic shape over the endless ice floes. This is the bird.

Even more than a penguin, the snow petrel is the spirit of the white continent itself, the one that sticks pleasurably in the memory through northern summers and the siren that brings one irresistibly back.

Footnote

In 1991 the Antarctic Treaty, agreed by sixteen nations, comes up for review. It grew from the goodwill of the International Geophysical Year, 1957 to 1958, came into being in 1959, and in essence is a blueprint for political and scientific harmony that could be a lesson for the world.

It covers Antarctica south of the sixtieth parallel but sadly omits the ocean. From it has grown a wealth of valuable concepts. The Scientific Committee on Antarctic research (SCAR) co-ordinates the scientific and logistical effects of the signatory nations ensuring that data is shared and plans for future research made known to all members. It is hard to imagine a higher degree of international co-operation, and geared to the conservation of a very international heritage.

The year 1991 will be critical. The fervent optimist will always hope that a vote of no change, an endorsement of present policies but extended to protect the ocean environment, would be the outcome. By the same token the realist cannot help noticing signs of national chauvinism penetrating the scientific accords.

One of the cornerstone articles of the treaty agrees to the shelving of prior territorial claims, yet these are still driven home by certain nations, kept alive and even developed. Another article forbids military activity except for the logistical support of scientists in the field — but barrack blocks are in places more noticeable than laboratories. Moreover they tend to be used as a cynical means of proving 'settlement' and thereby a device for bolstering a claim of sovereignty.

Anyone who truly loves this place recognizes 'ownership' as preposterous. It is very much a world asset, a place of immeasurable value in its own right — provided the rapists can be held at bay.

Anyone who has studied the history of exploration knows the sacrifice, dedication and courage enshrined in Antarctica, and can take pride in their own country's enormous contribution. But that was the past and the future begins today. All that can be done now is to urge every kind of diligence to ensure that this last inviolate land stays that way: exerting its age-old influence on the weather patterns of our planet and serving as a perpetual source of inspiration to the human spirit.

The Royal Society for the Protection of Birds is *the* charity that takes action for wild birds and the environment.

The largest voluntary wildlife conservation organization in Europe, it has a membership of over half a million. Members receive a free quarterly colour magazine, *Birds*, which keeps them in touch with conservation matters and developments at reserves – currently 113, owned or leased, and covering over 178,000 acres (72,032 ha). They are also entitled to visit over seventy reserves free of charge.

Unashamedly looking for new supporters, the Society offers a free nestbox or birdtable to new members. To claim the free gift, send your name and address, together with your first annual subscription of £12.00 to RSPB, Dept. 1880, The Lodge, Sandy, Bedfordshire, SG19 2DL, not forgetting to indicate your choice of free gift!